Theatre in Education in Britain

Theatre in Education in Britain

Origins, Development and Influence

ROGER WOOSTER

Bloomsbury Academic
An imprint of Bloomsbury Publishing Plc

B L O O M S B U R Y
LONDON · OXFORD · NEW YORK · NEW DELHI · SYDNEY

Bloomsbury Methuen Drama
An imprint ofBloomsbury Publishing Plc

Imprint previously known as Methuen Drama

50 Bedford Square	1385 Broadway
London	New York
WC1B 3DP	NY 10018
UK	USA

www.bloomsbury.com

**BLOOMSBURY, METHUEN DRAMA and the Diana logo are trademarks of
Bloomsbury Publishing Plc**

First published 2016

British Library Cataloguing-in-Publication Data
A catalogue record for this book is available from the British Library.

ISBN: HB: 978-1-4725-9148-7
PB: 978-1-4725-9147-0
ePDF: 978-1-4725-9150-0
ePub: 978-1-4725-9149-4

Library of Congress Cataloging-in-Publication Data
Wooster, Roger.
Theatre in education in Britain : origins, development and influence /
Roger Wooster ; foreword by Philip Taylor.
pages cm
Includes bibliographical references and index.
ISBN 978-1-4725-9148-7 (hardback) – ISBN 978-1-4725-9147-0 (paperback)
1. Drama in education–Great Britain. I. Title.
PN3171.W666 2016
792.071'041–dc23
2015020583

Typeset by Integra Software Services Pvt. Ltd.
Printed and bound in India

To colleagues and students who taught me
And for Stuart Bennett (1937–2015)

Online resources to accompany this book are available at
http://www.bloomsbury.com/theatre-in-education-in-britain-9781472591470.
Please type the URL into your web browser and follow the instructions
to access the Companion Website. If you experience any problems,
please contact Bloomsbury at: academicwebsite@bloomsbury.com

CONTENTS

LIST OF ILLUSTRATIONS

FOREWORD

In the 1970s, I first heard about the phenomenon of Theatre in Education, otherwise known as TIE, while I was studying drama in a four-year teacher education degree in Australia. I learned about the inspiring work of the Coventry team in Britain, and discovered that a few of the graduates from my School had been hired by TIE companies, most notably by the *Woolly Jumpers*, a troupe based in what was then a lower socio-economic area on the outskirts of Melbourne. Interestingly, the Australian actress, Rachel Griffiths, proudly lists her work with the *Woolly Jumpers* as one of her early career jobs.

At college, it was expected that drama majors would be creating and evaluating TIE programmes and taking them out into various school and community settings. One of the first projects I worked on was dealing with adolescent angst and it was pitched at 13–16 year olds.

The basic plan was that a group of *actor-teachers* (as the TIE facilitators were known) would devise scenes focussed on a teenager whose life was spiralling out of control. The audience, being the school students, would be invited to take on various roles, like a guidance counsellor or concerned family member, and then asked to help the teenager cope with the situations that were presented. There were other projects I can recall we devised on such themes as family violence and race relations, as well as various social/cultural issues that were the concern of the day.

When I was hired as a schoolteacher, I had an opportunity to engage teams like *Woolly Jumpers* to present their participatory work, and I witnessed first-hand as an employed full-time educator how important these programmes could be in elevating the critical thinking and communication skills of my students, all through the power of the aesthetic medium. I also experienced the helpful educational resources guides that the TIE companies were producing.

These curriculum materials would enable teachers to illuminate for their students the themes of the projects, the background that informed the creation of them and they valuably suggested drama and other activities that could be implemented to enhance school groups' encounters with TIE.

After six years of full-time school teaching, I registered for graduate school, and it was there that I learned that not everyone was a fan of TIE. The detractors would focus on the political imperatives of some teams, the didactic nature of projects and most famously the lack of artistic imagination.

The latter involved an especially juicy feud between a married couple, Lowell and Nancy Swortzell, who co-founded New York University's Program in Educational Theatre, where I now teach. Nancy taught courses in TIE, was a pioneer really in bringing this groundbreaking effort to the United States, and she was instrumental in helping the Creative Arts Team, the largest US TIE company, get its start in life. Indeed, CAT's initiators had studied TIE through a summer school partnership Nancy had developed at Bretton Hall in Yorkshire with John Hodgson, John being a very influential figure in the evolution of the Educational Theatre movement.

Lowell Swortzell, a theatre historian, lover of musical theatre and a playwright, felt that many TIE companies focussed too much on content, not form; and were fairly predictable in their political views; and that often they lacked an artistic edge. Swortzell (1993) famously wrote a controversial article, 'Trying to Like T.I.E' for an edited volume over twenty years ago that ruffled more than a few feathers.

You can imagine how tricky it was for me, on an NYU teaching fellowship then, being caught in the middle of the couple and the debate. But as I was to discover, the feuds and rivalries were not delimited to TIE. Drama in Education, or DIE, had its opponents too, as did Theatre of the Oppressed (TO), and even now we see a growing body of critical analysis in the applied theatre movement.

Sadly, both Lowell and Nancy have gone now but their legacy lives on through their students, publications, outreach and a generous multimillion-dollar gift to NYU, known as the Nancy and Lowell Swortzell Permanent Fund in Educational Theatre. Such a gift will enable artist educators across the world to continue to practice and investigate the contributions of collaborative and participatory forms like TIE and to sit comfortably in the dissonances and disputes when they emerge.

In this respect, I am very grateful to Roger Wooster for building on the formative work of the Swortzells, and other pioneers. Wooster has presented such a rich insight into the field's history and examined the ways in which TIE approaches and techniques have been developed and adapted by other genres of educational and therapeutic theatre. He has explored the major programmes and international trends and presented revealing discussion on why, and how, TIE makes a difference to the educational lifespan of the young.

In my view, this book is an invaluable addition to our libraries. *Theatre in Education in Britain* should be required reading in all programmes with a vested interest in educational theatre and related disciplines. We will be certainly listing this fine book at NYU.

Philip Taylor
New York University

Reference

Swortzell, L. (1993), 'Trying to Like TIE: An American Hopes TIE Can Be Saved' in Jackson, T. (ed.), *Learning through Theatre: New Perspectives on Theatre in Education*, 2nd Edition (pp. 239–250), London, Routledge.

ACKNOWLEDGEMENTS

Firstly I must thank Persephone Sextou of Newham University. The original idea for this book came about through prolonged discussions with her that clarified my own thoughts and determined the shape of the argument I have tried to make.

Thanks also to the many early TIE practitioners who have helped me recall events that I was in danger of overlooking and who have been most supportive of this project. These include Adam Bethlenfalvy, Brian Bishop, Edward Bond, Tony Coult, Steve Davis, Colin Hicks, Tag McEntegart, David Pammenter, John Prior, Paul Swift and Ian Yeoman. Thanks especially to Tim Prentki for his guidance and to Warwick Dobson, Chris Vine and Anthony Jackson for providing insights, corrections and thoughtful advice along with their Afterwords.

Tessa Gearing and Louise Osborn (formerly of Theatr Powys) provided me with resources otherwise unavailable as have Matt Hinks and Dan Brown (Big Brum), Deborah Pakkar-Hull (Theatre Company Blah Blah Blah), Claire Simpson (Belgrade), Paul Swift (Leeds TIE) and Steve Davis (Spectacle). Examples of the international legacy of TIE have come from Gábor Takács (Káva), Atilla Farkas (Round Table), Wendy Lement (Espresso) and Helen Wheelock. I am particularly indebted to Shkëlzen Berisha for his hospitality when visiting Qendra e Hulumtimit Progresiv in Tirana. Many thanks to John O'Toole who apprised me of work going on in Australia, New Zealand and South East Asia. As a result, I received help from Stephen Dallow (Applied Theatre Consultants) and Estella Wong (Hong Kong Academy of Performing Arts). Thanks also to the Herbert Museum in Coventry (Robert Witts), to Lucy Bevan and Powys County Council Archives, to Morgan Conlon and to Don Adamson for their work on the video resources and to Geraint Cunnick who formatted the photographs. Additionally, thanks are due to the many academics that assisted by giving information about current TIE modules and particularly to Annie McKean for her information and insights into Prison Theatre. Finally, I would like to thank Philip Taylor for providing the Foreword.

LIST OF ABBREVIATIONS

AATE	American Alliance for Theatre and Education
AC	Arts Council
ACE	Arts Council England
ACGB	Arts Council of Great Britain
ACW	Arts Council Wales
A Level	Advanced Level (of examinations)
ASSITEJ	l'Association Internationale du Théâtre de l'Enfance et la Jeunesse
CAT	Creative Arts Team (New York)
CBI	Confederation of British Industry
CPD	Continuing Professional Development
DES	Department of Education and Science/Department of Education and Skills
DIE	Drama in Education
ERA	Education Reform Act
ERM	Exchange Rate Mechanism (system for regulating European exchange rates)
GCE	General Certificate of Education
GCSE	General Certificate of Secondary Education
GDR	German Democratic Republic (1949 until reunification of Germany 1990)

GYPT	Greenwich Young People's Theatre
IATA	International Amateur Theatre Association
ICTIE	International Centre for TIE
IDEA	International Drama/Theatre and Education Association
ILEA	Inner London Education Authority
ILP	Independent Labour Party
IMF	International Monetary Fund
ITI	International Theatre Institute
KS	Key Stage (of the National Curriculum)
LA	Local Authority
LEA	Local Education Authority
LMS	Local Management of Schools
LO	Learning Objectives (of the National Curriculum)
NATD	National Association for the Teaching of Drama
ND	National Drama
NGO	Non-governmental Organization
NHS	National Health Service
NPO	National Portfolio Organization (Arts Council list of supported companies)
Ofsted	Office for Standards in Education (formerly HMI)
O Level	Ordinary Level (of examinations)
PSHE	Personal, Social and Health Education
PSHCE	Personal, Social, Health and Citizenship Education
SATs	Standard Assessment Tests
SCYPT	Standing Conference of Young People's Theatre
TiHE	Theatre in Health Education
TfD	Theatre for Development

TUC	Trade Union Congress
WAC	Welsh Arts Council (later Arts Council Wales)
WTM	Workers Theatre Movement
YPT	Young People's Theatre
YT	Youth Theatre
ZPD	Zone of Proximal Development (from Vygotsky)

Introduction

The 1988 Education Reform Act (ERA) and the National Curriculum for schools that it ushered in brought about the most significant changes to education since the end of the Second World War, more important even than the Tripartite System introduced by the 1944 Education Act or the move to Comprehensive Education in the 1970s. Created by Kenneth Baker as Education Minister in Thatcher's final government, ERA was hugely controversial, uniting teachers, academics and opposition parties against it. Twenty-five years on and the substance of ERA is now the hegemonic approach to education in Britain. Scotland and (following Devolution) Wales also have their own National Curricula. No mainstream political party is suggesting that the National Curriculum should be abandoned nor that funding of schools should be returned to Local Education Authorities (LEAs). An analysis of ERA and its effect on education and Theatre in Education (TIE) in particular is to be found in Chapter Four. The rise and decline of TIE hinges around ERA.

This volume has been divided into three sections: 'Roots', 'Fruits' and, with less assuredness, 'Shoots?'. The first section deals with the origins and development of TIE prior to ERA in 1988. I look first, in Chapter One, at the post-War period that was characterized by the aspirations of the British people for a fairer society, free of want and with the possibility of advancement. This determination for change can actually be traced back to the Great War (1914–18) and could no longer be ignored in the wake of the Second World War. The mechanics for change in society had education at its centre and, though the 1944 Education Act tended to entrench rather than challenge social structures, it was accompanied by some progressive ideas that filtered into the system from educational theorists and child psychologists. Key amongst these ideas was the notion of the importance of 'play' and I argue that the fusion of child play and theatrical play create the unique pedagogic tool that came to be known as Theatre in Education. These progressive educational ideas were especially interpreted into schemes of education by drama practitioners and I have tried to give a sense of how such approaches started to unify ideas of psychology, education and drama. This opening chapter also looks at the theatrical DNA coming to TIE from alternative and agitprop theatre and, of course, the dialectical struggle with ideas posited to audiences by Epic Theatre. These roots became creatively entwined to produce the first examples of what we can call Theatre in Education at the Coventry Belgrade Theatre in 1965.

The next phase of the development of TIE takes us into the industrially and economically troubled times of the 1960s and 1970s. The nature and content of TIE is closely bound up with the nation's public investment and educational policies and so Chapter Two begins with an overview of the political situation and the developing war of attrition between trade unions and both Conservative and Labour governments. Key to the period of Labour government were programmes of social liberalization and the initiation of a reform of the Tripartite System into a Comprehensive System. During this time TIE continued to expand, becoming more profound and proficient in its techniques and reflecting both the reformist agenda and the political uncertainty of the times. Increasingly TIE programmes moved away from myth and legend and grappled more assertively with social issues. The return to power of the Conservatives in 1970 largely ended the period of liberal reform but also initiated a crisis in already poor industrial relations culminating in a Miners' Strike (1974) which effectively brought down Heath's government. TIE was feeling mature and confident enough to start to deal with these issues often using historical contexts. The chapter concludes by pointing out that, despite the development of TIE theory and the ideas permeating from Drama in Education (DIE), there was still a general lack of pedagogical analysis being employed which was preventing the ability of TIE to take its place at the centre of pedagogic processes.

Chapter Three is a study of theoretical pedagogies that, retrospectively, can be seen to be present in the more sophisticated TIE work. The ideas of Freire, Boal, Vygotsky and Bruner can be seen in the shadows of the work that TIE companies were starting to produce though, paradoxically, it seems that only a limited number of company members (usually the directors) might be aware of these influences. TIE seemed to be embodying the pedagogical approaches of these political philosophers and social scientists almost by a process of osmosis. Non-immersive forms of participation, often involving older children, are also discussed in this context. The use of role and 'frame' is explored as a means of encouraging participation where once again a debt is owed to drama practitioners. We also see the influence of Brecht and *gestus* in these techniques as well as a heavy reliance on the ideas of Boal and especially his most famous theatrical structure, Forum Theatre. The usefulness to TIE of these approaches is clear. Brecht's theatrical premise is that theatre could and should seek to facilitate change. He requires a careful spectatorship in his audience so that they leave the theatre thinking that 'something must be done'. Perhaps this is even more strongly seen in the work of Boal where, in Forum Theatre, situations are offered up for analysis by the audience. TIE was sympathetic to both these dramatists in wanting to question the status quo. This being the case, these non-immersive participatory forms inherently contain the same political dangers. Many in education are extremely nervous when young people are given the licence to question. What good does it do them to ask why things are the way they are when, 'of course', there is no way to change them? All it does is lead to dissatisfaction and probably disaffection. So the argument goes.

By 1988 TIE had become an innovative and flourishing aspect of school education. Increasingly companies were set up as outreach organizations by traditional theatres, by Education Authorities and by independent groups of (usually) young actors and teachers drawing appreciation and support from their Arts Councils. Systems of 'matched' funding emerged where two or more of these financial support streams were mutually accessed, awarding the companies the kudos and legitimacy that gave access to schools. These were times when 'progressive education' had not yet become a government term of abuse and schools had the flexibility to massage timetables and internal curricula to accommodate TIE companies (usually at no direct cost to themselves).

Between 1965 and the coming of ERA of 1988 a rather strange and elegant creature had emerged in education: a creature with its ancestry in play, drama and theatre. TIE had become a central part of the pedagogical strategy of many forward-looking LEAs. At its best, it provided a free service to schools offering tightly considered programmes of learning developed in liaison with teachers. In most cases there was an amalgam of carefully framed learning within high quality theatrical performance. The work itself was rooted in an insightful understanding of the ideas of the key educationalists and drama practitioners of the day.

I argue that TIE was a serendipitous creation forged in a unique cauldron of social, philosophical and economic conditions. At the core of the debate will be the nature and purpose of education. Today we find ourselves in a hegemony of utilitarianism where it is almost universally accepted that education is about 'preparing children for the real world', by which is meant preparing them to slip into their predestined niche in the world of commerce, service or production. The twentieth-century expansion of education in Britain, which is usually lauded as evidence of enlightened liberalism, can also be seen as a result of a hard fought struggle against establishment fears that education leads to discontent and rebellion. Knowledge is a dangerous thing. However, the economic growth of the nineteenth and twentieth centuries required a better-informed workforce who could access ideas and follow written instructions. Once the genie is out of the bottle, not only can you not put him back but neither can he be relied upon to give you your wishes. Education is access to ideas and through them to hopes and aspirations.

The fact that elite schools in the private sector as well as supposedly elite 'academies' in the public sector are exempted from many of the strictures of the National Curriculum should alert us to the fact that something else may be going on here and that what we are seeing is a demarcation between those children being raised to lead, those being raised to serve the leaders and those being raised to serve the economic needs of the first two groups. The politics behind the education of the masses is one of the themes taken up by Dobson in his Afterword to this section. He considers the way that TIE and the Standing Conference of Young People's Theatre represented an alternative approach, a 'curriculum for living'.

The second section of this volume is entitled 'Fruits' where I seek to identify some of the most valuable achievements of TIE prior to the carcinogenic influence of ERA and the new educational landscape. In Chapters Five and Six, I take two TIE programmes – one participatory and one performance/workshop based – as paradigms of good practice at the height of TIE's strength, contextualizing the techniques and theoretical bases outlined in previous chapters. In an analysis of Theatr Powys' *Careless Talk* (1986), I consider the mechanisms by which the educational processes take place in a fully participatory piece of TIE. The second programme, *When Sleeping Dogs Awake* (Belgrade TIE: 1988), was devised by the company and then written by Geoff Gillham, one of the most significant thinkers in the TIE movement. *When Sleeping Dogs Awake* employs a highly theatrical metaphor of stray dogs in order to explore issues of racism and prejudice. This piece also used a workshop technique that eschewed the need for verbalization, with the young people invited to deconstruct the themes of the play through the practical means of creating an exhibition.

I cannot claim these to be the 'best' work that emerged before ERA but they are good pieces of work, with which I am familiar and which will help concretize the pedagogic theory I have so freely banded about in earlier chapters. Chris Vine, in his Afterword following this section, challenges some of the techniques employed in these projects, offering further consideration of the tension between didacticism and constructivism in the pedagogy.

Chapter Seven seeks to confront the prejudice that stereotypes TIE as being, of its nature, less professional and less sophisticated in its aesthetics. Here I consider not only performance quality but also argue that the integration of art and education was both highly complex and a natural melding of 'play' as performance and play as a tool of human development within the theories that underpinned the work. TIE is a largely hidden art form, though thousands of children engage in it each year. It is hardly ever seen by parents, by non-drama teachers, by head teachers, the media, politicians and rarely even by significant officers in funding organizations. This has allowed the prejudices to emerge that TIE is a lesser art form with lower artistic values and concerned only with communicating a message with little regard for performance and production quality. If there were any validity to the accusation of aesthetic paucity, it is certainly not applicable to some of the fine work that was emerging in the 1970s and 1980s as the genre matured. However, a lack of artistic value (and concomitantly) educational value remains a threat when the work is undertaken by those without theatrical skill, experience and pedagogic insight.

Chapter Eight considers the basic working and contractual processes that were the nursery for this new theatre-education hybrid. Most companies from the 1960s through to the early 1990s sought to develop working practices that were collaborative and democratic. Here I consider the political and emotional struggles that this involved including the artistic decisions around moulding devised work and/or the employment of a writer, as well as issues of training, finance, internal and external governance and employment contracts. Despite the heavy burden that cooperative working practices represented, they too were a 'fruit' of the TIE movement, offering a catalytic cauldron of artistic and educational precepts and ways of working from which we may still learn.

The final gathering of 'fruits' that I offer is the influence of the TIE movement internationally. The genesis of l'Association Internationale du Théâtre de l'Enfance et la Jeunesse (ASSITEJ) parallels that of TIE closely. It is hard to offer any evidence that TIE had a hand in this development, but both at the conception and again by the end of the 1990s we find that those involved in TIE also took an interest in this children's theatre organization. Both ASSITEJ and TIE reflect that post-War belief in the importance of theatre to children in order to preserve and nurture humanness.

This chapter also considers TIE's involvement with the International Drama/Theatre and Education Association (IDEA). Here there is a clearer concurrence of purpose, with individual and company members of the Standing Conference of Young People's Theatre (SCYPT) in the vanguard of the creation of this organization in 1992 (just as TIE in the UK was feeling the pressure from ERA). This was not to last, however, and I show how this international vision of educating children through drama and TIE fell foul of suspected financial mismanagement, accusations of homophobia and geopolitical ambitions. I document the dispute that led to the withdrawal of many British TIE companies and the National Association for the Teaching of Drama (NATD) from IDEA at the turn of the century as well as considering the alternative international vision that was offered through the setting up of the SCYPT Co-operative and the International Centre for TIE (ICTIE). Chris Vine, in his Afterword, identifies further theoretical influences on TIE, highlighting DIE and pre-SCYPT political thinkers such as Pammenter, Baskerville and, once again, Bennett.

The final section of this volume, I have with a little trepidation, entitled 'Shoots?'. Against the decline of what is often now referred to as 'classic' TIE, I offer some examples of where the DNA of TIE survives. Chapter Ten considers the context of Thatcher's Britain and the market reforms that she introduced into industry and the wider economy including education. The Thatcher governments from 1979 to 1990, and the further Tory governments of John Major until 1997, represented a period of the most radically rightist agenda since the Second World War. TIE had always been left-leaning and such sensibilities were to put it on a collision course with the new policies both explicitly and implicitly. This chapter charts the way in which TIE was either completely undermined and marginalized by the combined effects of changes to curriculum and funding, or mistrusted because of its political opposition to the education reforms. The avoidance of political content (whatever that means) led to companies turning their attention to 'safe' social and health issues. TIE, as it had been developing, was being gently eradicated and to survive it would have to mutate.

As previous models of TIE declined in the 1990s, a wide range of related uses of theatre emerged. These new shoots included Theatre in Health Education, Prison Theatre, Theatre for Development and Museum Theatre which all expanded alongside the well-established uses of drama methodologies in therapy. Chapter Eleven seeks to extract from this plethora of social and personal applications of theatre the legacy that can be discerned from previous TIE. I maintain, however, that the content and approaches of these new shoots of TIE praxis, emerging from the decimation of previous practice, often fall short of the educational aims of classic TIE and frequently run the danger of socializing rather than conscientizing. This tendency is considered alongside developing government arts policy and the changing nature of training opportunities that seek to respond to the career opportunities offered by these new socially orientated genres.

The international TIE diaspora has been well-examined by others, but in Chapter Twelve I first undertake a brief consideration of projects that are responding to similar political and social pressures. The range of work mentioned is not intended to be comprehensive but, I hope, allows a sense of how TIE praxis is being transplanted and evolved elsewhere in the world. I then describe in some detail a selection of international projects where a memetic connection to classic TIE can be observed. This is most clearly present in the work of companies in Hungary and Albania where fully participatory programmes are to be found working under similar drama and educational influences as informed early British TIE. The direct support of practitioners such as Chris Cooper and Ian Yeoman has been key to this.

By this stage I have found it necessary increasingly to use the term 'classic' TIE in order to differentiate the work from the multitudinous forms and approaches of educational theatres (described in Chapter Eleven). The final chapter seeks to identify some examples of 'classic' TIE work still being forged in the UK. The companies cited are not the only ones worthy of mention and there will be companies, or individual programmes equally worthy. My choice is based on a desire to example, with contemporary evidence, the presence of classic methodologies in their work. This is not to say that their work will 'look' like the TIE of the 1970s and 1980s, but rather that it demonstrates the same intentions, socially and educationally. It has the same belief in young people and their right to be respected and their dreams empowered. The companies endorse the child's right to seek to make a better world and not just to fit into the one they have inherited. Companies mentioned are the long-running Leeds TIE (1970) and Big Brum (1982), as well as Theatre Company Blah Blah Blah (1985). Even these companies are forced to be constantly vigilant against misrepresentation of their work and are vulnerable to the frequently adjusting arts and education policies. Had the company not been cut in 2011, the groundbreaking work of Theatr Powys, led by Ian Yeoman, would have played a major part of this chapter. Powys' work was out of political favour and, as with so many companies in the 1990s, funding was lost for ideological reasons masquerading as financial imperative. One remains in constant fear for the survival, in the UK at least, of the unique pedagogical hybrid of theatre and education that has been so influential in the lives of young people.

Perhaps there is no call for such pessimism as appears in my Conclusion. The world has never needed a creative and authentic teaching approach more than it does today. It is perhaps time to revisit the ideas of 'progressive education' of the 1950s and 1960s that offered a holistic approach to giving the tools for living. Paradoxically, humans have limitless power to develop but only limited time in which to do it. It is possible that this will be realized in time, but for now the periodic attacks on teachers are getting more virulent as a gap widens between what children need and what governments expect of them. As a result, educational approaches are driven further to the right. At a time when creativity and inspired thinking are required, solutions that stifle creativity, offer old solutions and suppress inspiration are offered. Gradgrind is back in favour and absorption of facts is offered as the key to educational success and employment.

Many of my observations are personal and there are other interpretations of events to be had. The writers of the Afterwords have been invited to freely augment or challenge my analysis. Anthony Jackson, in the Afterword to the final section is certainly less pessimistic about the survival of TIE praxis. Our views do not always completely coincide but where there are differences, I invite the reader to take the opportunity to rigorously question the argument that I have set forth. Perhaps such a debate will help future TIE shoots to blossom.

PART ONE
Roots

CHAPTER ONE

Society, Theatre, Education and the First TIE Experiments 1965–6

Social conditions and expectations between the Wars

The end of the Second World War is immediately identifiable as a watershed in British social life. Returning soldiers and their war-weary families voted for a radical shift in the governance of their lives. But, as Selina Todd points out in her study of the working class in the twentieth century, *The People* (2014), the First World War had similarly changed class relationships. Against the backdrop of the Russian Revolution and the sacrifice of mainly working-class young men, resentment grew towards the intractability of the establishment. Though women had 'manned' the factories through the War, until 1918 only *men* could vote. In 1918 suffrage was extended to property-owning women over 30 years of age – a small reward for the middle-class suffragettes but a rather sour insult for working-class women who, far from owning property, struggled to feed their children. There remained resistance to ideas of education for the masses. The middle classes feared loss of privilege – and the loss of servants. The allies had won the war at huge cost to the working classes but in the aftermath they were rewarded with high levels of unemployment and stubborn expectation by the middle class that things would now get back to 'normal'.

The deteriorating economic situation led, in 1926, to a General Strike, broken in a few days by troops and a middle class happy to play at driving lorries and buses (Todd: 2014: 52–3). Working-class resentment grew and, in the eyes of the establishment, the trade union movement threatened to emulate the Russian Revolution and overwhelm society. The Wall Street Crash three years later exacerbated the plight of the poor and increased the feeling of 'us' and 'them'. By the mid-thirties recorded unemployment was over 20 per cent with the real figure much higher. Such social benefits as existed were subject to harsh means testing and kept those claiming state aid in poverty: 'poverty was a common experience of working class life, and … it was caused by government policy' (Todd: 2014: 62). Traditionally, unemployment affected the young and unskilled, but now even skilled workers of the depressed iron and steel industries were in the dole queues. Far more people were descending the social ladder than were managing to climb up it (Todd: 2014: 73).

With another European war on the horizon and the concomitant investment in arms, unemployment dropped to around 14 per cent for both men and women by 1938 and we see the beginnings of consumerism and the modern techniques of the assembly line. Would this be enough to placate an impoverished working class? Living in the same household as the children working to support their unemployed parents were perhaps the grandparents who had lost siblings and husbands in the Great War: a war that rewarded them with hardship, little social reform and no expectation of social mobility. The concession, in 1928, giving all women over twenty-one the vote, only compounded the issue, for here was tacit recognition that working-class women were indeed 'equal' to anybody else. Expectations would be ignored at the risk of social disruption.

Additionally, in 1939 there were hundreds of thousands of 'teenagers' who, by 1945, would have fought in a war, reached maturity and come home able to vote. These same children, during the 1930s, had seen their parents cope with desperate privations:

They were the generation that gained the vote in 1945, and who, with one eye on the 1930s, gave Labour its first majority government. (Todd: 2014: 74)

Those who voted Labour in 1924 or, with the wider suffrage, in 1929, had been promised reforms in nutrition, health care and maternity services, none of which had materialized, due to the vigorous opposition of a Tory party who felt that such needs were best met by the charitable sector. Perhaps sensing the mood (and the possible repercussions if concessions were not offered) some reforms emerged in the late 1930s including, in 1936, education reform that raised the school leaving age to 15 (and was immediately postponed for three years). At this time parents had to pay to educate their children beyond elementary stage and though Local Authority scholarships were available (for about 25 per cent of pupils), very few takers were from the working class as their earning power was required to ensure the survival of their families.

After the outbreak of war in 1939, those who *had* been in well-paid work now found themselves enlisted and surviving on a soldier's wage. Todd argues that following the disastrous start to the war and the humiliation of the Dunkirk withdrawal, there was a real danger that the British working class lacked the will to fight and it was only the hope of brighter days to come that sustained the war effort:

> During the war the government struck a contract with the people: work hard in return for a guaranteed job, a living wage and care in times of need. (Todd: 2014: 120)

The War itself enhanced working-class solidarity and created a determination to resist pre-war class complacency. It did not go unnoticed that the rich middle class could afford to 'up sticks' and relocate to less bomb-prone areas whilst the masses huddled together for warmth and security in makeshift shelters. There was resentment too that middle-class women avoided conscription by often tokenistic volunteering and were assisted in maintaining their lifestyle by having their servants exempted from National Service. How must the munitions workers have felt when, returning home to a rationed meal, they passed restaurants serving unrationed food to the middle and upper classes? But it seemed to be dawning on the ruling classes that they were dependent upon these soldiers at the front and their wives in the factories: they were more than just uppity strikers and dole claimants. Even whilst the War progressed, plans were underway to offer a level of reform that would prevent serious social unrest. The door to egalitarianism was being prised open and would be hard to close after the War.

Post-War expectations and education policy

The Beveridge Report (1942) produced its vision of a 'cradle to the grave' welfare system, setting clear ambitions for a new order eradicating want, disease, ignorance, squalor and providing full employment. In a move that probably cost them the post-War election, Churchill's Tories refused to accept 'unaffordable luxuries' such as universal welfare provision. When the War ended the people voted for a National Health Service (NHS), full employment and social security despite Churchill's accusation that the Labour proposals were akin to the ideas of the Gestapo. Labour received 48 per cent of the vote and a majority of 146.

In the next five years, despite huge war debts and the beginning of the Cold War, the working class undoubtedly found their lives improved. Promises were kept as regards full employment, social security and the NHS. Wages rose and the differential in incomes between the middle and working classes narrowed. Todd identifies a negative aspect to this however, noting that the Labour government's decision to accept the United States' Marshall Plan to assist in reconstruction, also tied the UK into US-style free-market consumerism from which it was never able to escape (Todd: 2014: 157). The 'social contract', set up in 1945, was forced to mutate from its social intervention approach to one based on supply and demand. In this decision can be seen the seeds that led, over the next thirty years, to an increasingly hegemonic approach to social, economic and education policy. Labour's ambiguous relationship with socialism was to lead to an eventual distancing of the party from social radicalism. Increasingly over the next sixty years, despite being the party of the trade unions, left-wing policies became marginalized and the unbending logic of market forces accepted. Because of dependence upon the United States, the best intentions of post-War Labour were undermined. The steel, coal and railways industries were remarkably similar after nationalization to how they were before the War with the same bosses and workers. Housing shortages also clouded the post-War record of the Labour government and expectations remained high and unsatisfied. Loan repayments to the United States and the developing nuclear arms race meant that finance for reforms was running out by the end of the decade. The government wanted more women to work but failed to provide nurseries. Women who did work earned about half of what men earned. Young people (of both sexes) with few financial ties and a determination to live better lives than those of their parents, took otherwise unfilled jobs thus creating a new youth culture market.

Though much had been achieved, for many it was not enough and, in 1950, the Labour majority shrank to thirteen. Sue Bruley (1999: 117) notes that the high expectations of the post-War years were being replaced by a mood of disappointment. Women's faith in Labour had been undermined by the restitution of male dominance in the workplace and the negative attitudes they faced if, though having children, they chose to work (Bruley: 1999: 118). With the electorate weary of austerity, when the government collapsed a year later, Churchill was once again called upon even though, in one of those quirks of the British electoral system, Labour received more votes in 1951 than in 1945. An electorate hungry for faster and deeper change voted in the party that was, by definition, steeped in traditional values.

Before the War there was education provision for those up to the age of 14 but little advanced education except for those who could pay. The content of the curriculum was classical with an emphasis on the 'Three Rs'.[1] The 1944 Education Act, piloted into law by the Tory Rab Butler, established compulsory (and free) secondary education for all children aged 11–15 in a Tripartite System that offered an academic route (via the Grammar Schools), a vocational route (via Technical Schools) and 'Secondary Modern Schools' which were to cater for the 'less able'. Selection to these schools was via the '11+' exam that, at age 11, deemed children to be academic, artisan or ... or not! Technical Schools never really gained a foothold in the system and the main 'choice' was between 'Grammars' and 'Secondary Mods'. Although apparently a meritocratic approach, these schools reflected and entrenched social disparity. The middle classes, having steered their children through the 11+ examinations, could now get access to an academic education at no personal cost.

The examination itself tested the traditional subjects of literacy and numeracy along with the new-fangled (but culturally biased) IQ tests.

The selective approach of the Tripartite System reflected the needs of employers, channelling working-class children into the new low-skill factories. This Education Act was unashamedly based on a cross-party acceptance that 15 per cent of children would attend Grammars, 15 per cent Technical Schools and the remainder would be sent to Secondary Moderns which promised a 'revaluing [of] the dignity of labour' (Jones: 2003: 25). The message for working-class children was clear: you are destined to a life of menial work no matter what your potential. These attitudes were endemic, with Secondary Moderns housed in sub-standard buildings, serviced by less qualified and poorly paid staff and offering no qualifications. Such inadequacies did not create the backlash that one might expect. Lack of ambition was internalized by many, content to be free of the pressures of exams. Some working-class families feared the loss of their children to class ascendancy and some doubted the usefulness of educating their daughters to the age of 15 (Todd: 2014: 220). Jones (2003: 27) points out, however, that the freedom from curriculum and examinations often facilitated experimentation in dialogic learning and progressive education.

The Tripartite System was attacked by both right and left but remained the consensus of the political centre. As the Newsom Report was to point out in 1963, 'some schools have everything and some have nothing' (Ministry of Education: 1963: 250). Whilst the system seemed to contain the possibility of social mobility, in reality class equality remained stubbornly impervious to change. Notions of equality had in fact been subordinated to those of 'social inclusion', implying that even though 'you're not the same we will make a space for you'. If working-class children managed to claw their way through the Grammar school system (itself designed to fit the needs of boys rather than girls) they would still find barriers to entering university or the more prestigious professions. For example, whilst public schools[2] educated 5 per cent of children in the 1950s, they took up half of the places at Oxford and Cambridge. This disparity remains an obstinate one. Just as the new NHS had had to concede continuation of a private medical sector, so public schools were left untouched by the Tripartite System and '... a universal system of state schools was thus compromised from the first' (Jones: 2003: 16). Ability to pay was the gateway to preferential advancement. Preferential advancement meant more highly paid employment and the ability to pay for preferential advancement. The cycle continues.

It has become accepted wisdom that these post-War years were a hotbed of progressive pedagogic approaches and this view needs to be tempered. There was a real desire for the young to have a better life accessed through education but new educational approaches were not uniform and most children remained seated in serried ranks. What the Tripartite System reflects is the strong sense of 'function' in British traditions of education. There are those who we are going to train to think, those who will design and craft what the thinkers have thought of, and there are those who will toil at making the things that others have thought of and designed. Lazarus (2012) sees the same tendency emerge in the United States' school reforms of the early twentieth century when schools 'were literally re-formed to prepare factory workers for the emerging Industrial Revolution' (Lazarus: 2012: 28). She goes on:

> Students were taught to follow directions, repeat tasks, and be responsible citizens. Now, in the twenty-first century, many schools still use that same model when in fact the world has need of creative thinkers and independent, problem solvers. (Lazarus: 2012: 28)

This approach to education is structured around the immediate needs of a consumerist society and is less concerned with the possibility of educating the whole human being to their fullest potential.

The roots of progressive education

We do not have to go very far back into history to find a time when universal education seemed a ludicrous concept. Since the invention of the printing press and access to ideas, there has been a deep fear of exposing the lower echelons to knowledge that might lead to social upheaval. And the working classes themselves have not always embraced the need for education. Across classes and cultures, the education of women has been seen as less necessary or of a distinctive nature (see, for example, Rousseau's outrageous comments on this subject in Book V of *Emile*). It was only the development of industrialization that made it *necessary* to educate the working class and clearly this was done only insofar as specific tasks demanded. But even basic education can be the Prometheus that brings knowledge to mankind and once people can read, they will seek out ideas that might improve their lives. The response of the establishment to this is to stratify education; to give the masses what is required for their designated roles, whilst reserving access to holistic education to themselves. A decision had to be made, in Lawton's words, as to 'whether the purpose of education was to develop individuals or to socialize children to fit in to the existing social structures' (Lawton: 1980: 2).

Rousseau famously set out his ideas for education in *Emile* (1762). Here, and in *The Social Contract*, he envisages an education that recognizes the essential good in human beings that enables them to be free of those influences that corrupt our nature. We are naturally good, argues Rousseau and 'we are born sensitive' (Rousseau: 1762: trans. Foxley: 1977: 7). The child should be allowed to play and develop in his or her own time. Our impulse to act comes from mental curiosity and we learn from direct experience. 'Life is the trade I would teach him!' he declares (Rousseau: 1762: 9). We can see perhaps John Locke's ideas behind his own, and certainly we can identify a legacy that was to be passed down to the 'progressive educationalists' over the next two hundred years:

> Put the problems before him and let him solve them himself. Let him know nothing because you have told him, but because he has learnt it for himself. (Rousseau: 1762: 131)

These ideas reappear with Pestalozzi and then Froebel. Pestalozzi (1746–1827) in his *How Gertrude Teaches Her Children* (1801) tries to systematize into a programme of work the idea that children may learn to think and draw conclusions by pursuing their own interests. In the manner developed by Vygotsky, the emphasis is on spontaneity and holistic learning, discovering the known from the unknown, moving from the simple to the complex and from the actual to the theoretical. Froebel (1782–1852) saw education as a means to attain the divine within oneself through a system of play and activity.[3]

Maria Montessori developed a related approach. Her influential system outlined in *The Montessori Method* (1916) called for an education of the senses that would lead to education of the intellect. Emphasis is laid upon discovery and self-determination, seeking to engage a child's whole personality, interest and curiosity. The teacher is the observer of the process, aiding from the outside. John Dewey, the great American educationalist, died in the same year as Montessori. It is perhaps to these two philosophers of pedagogy that we can attribute the most direct influence on the progressive teaching that emerged in the 1950s and 1960s. Dewey maintained that education must draw on and thus expand experience, essentially through reflection. For Dewey, progressive education was not just a matter of rejecting formalist education of the past but rather to return to questions of why we educate and how we learn in order to see 'a new mode of practice' (Dewey: 1938: 5) which forged an 'organic connection between experience and education' (Dewey: 1938: 25). He rejected ideas of education that merely served up the knowledge and patterns of the past expecting young people to fit in with traditional expectations. This he saw as:

> To a large extent the cultural product of societies that assumed the future would be much like the past, and yet it is used as educational food in a society where change is the rule, not the exception. (Dewey: 1938: 19)

These are the pedagogic roots of the drama theorists who were in turn to inform the development of TIE. Amongst these are Harriet Finlay-Johnson (1871–1956) and Caldwell Cook (1886–1939). Clearly walking in the footsteps of Rousseau, Finlay-Johnson argues in *The Dramatic Method of Teaching* (1911) that 'childhood should be a time for absorbing big stores of sunshine for possible future dark times' (Finlay-Johnson: 1911: 27). Prescient words in 1911. Her book describes her work with children using play, including dramatic play, as a means of self-development quite distinct from the perceptions of any adult who might be looking on. The aesthetics inherent in the child's play were themselves the learning experience – an approach that pre-echoes Slade's 'Child Drama'. To the twenty-first century drama teacher her ideas will seem predominantly 'theatre' orientated, but Finlay-Johnson proposed that through the period of preparation a child's personal experience could be drawn upon and enhanced by means of a group process that would express the pupil's vision rather than the teacher's. Her aim was to arouse curiosity in her pupils and to allow them to learn at their own pace.

The title of Caldwell Cook's publication, *The Play Way* (1917), and his self-designation as the children's 'playmaster' might raise a quizzical eyebrow today, but once again, in ways reminiscent of Rousseau, Froebel and Pestalozzi, he aimed to place the child nearer to the centre of their learning with an extensive use of play:

> It is the core of my faith that the only work worth doing is really play. (Cook: 1917: 4)

Again there is a bias towards oracy (the 'Littleman Lectures') and theatre (especially Shakespeare). In addition there are somewhat 'twee' experiments with the creation of stories around invented 'Ilonds', and the physical creation of a model village in the schoolyard called 'Playtown'. The essential drive here is towards an all-encompassing drama-based approach to curriculum delivery similar to that developed later by Heathcote in 'the Mantle of the Expert'.[4] His dream is of a school 'of which it would be true to say, "here we learn", instead of, "here they teach"' (Cook: 1917: 13).

Some of these ideas for using drama, and the philosophy behind the ideas, did find occasional traction. In 1921 a Ministry of Education report detailed how drama could be used in the improvement of verbal skills (cited by Bolton: 1998). As with the work of Cook and Finlay-Johnson, the report has a strong theatrical orientation, suggesting performances to an audience and visits to the theatre. Post-War optimism revived these tentative experiments with drama and official publications offered occasional encouraging signs of the recognition of the value of drama in schools. E. M. Langdon was commissioned to write a report entitled *Dramatic Work with Children* (1948) that recognized that drama has a place to play in a child's development and called for a systematic approach for its use. Then, in 1949 the Ministry of Education published a pamphlet entitled *The Story of a School*. This document noted that 'expression in the arts gives not only a natural approach to academic subjects but also a more confident basis for tackling the difficulties of social relationships' (Ministry of Education: 1949: 36). This was a reflection of the age; the most important thing was that children should be allowed to be children during their education.

What is surprising today is that such educational approaches caused little controversy. The government's focus was on the economy and the *appearance* of better times. When Macmillan, Tory prime minister, boasted in 1957 that 'you've never had it so good' many had actually 'never had it' at all. The divide between rich and poor, was again growing and there was a sense that, fifteen years after the War, there were many who still 'never wanted it so badly'. As Todd succinctly puts it:

> In the 1950s, many found it hard to keep their families in the style that prosperity seemed to demand. (Todd: 2014: 208)

For others:

> There was great disillusionment – particularly amongst that first generation to be educated out of the working class – with the tokenism of Labour governments in nationalising industry and setting up the welfare state. (Itzin: 1980: 6)

An NHS with private hospital beds, nationalization with the same bosses as before and an education system that entrenched class divisions had become accepted. The socialist utopian dream had been betrayed to the gods of consumerism and consumption in the 1940s and not even the Labour Party had the will to try and construct a new social reality. Instead, a capitalist system (accepted by all the major parties) was tinkered with in order to mitigate the worst abuses and offer limited social reforms but with no real shift in power or ownership. In education, whatever progressivism was going on in the primary sector, the stratified secondary system would ensure that the 'cream' rose to the top. The influential Newsom Report (1963), *Half Our Future*, addressed issues of inequality in the education system. Whilst not primarily about drama, it did make some important points about the purpose of education:

> We need to train children to look critically and discriminate between what is good and bad in what they see. They must learn to realize that many makers of films and television programmes present false or distorted views of people, relationships and experience in general …. (Newsom: 1963: 156)

Rather too much paternalism for modern tastes, but clearly an indication was being given that children should be taught to think and not merely instructed. The report goes on to affirm that 'drama ... is a creative art embracing much more than English'. It is also a means by which children 'can work out their own personal problems' and thus 'come to terms with themselves more surely than by any other route' (Newsom: 1963: 157). Again, the tone is patronizing and, for Newsom, drama was clearly a way of learning to cope with the world rather than a mechanism for change. Such ideas, though, were encouraging the use of drama in the classroom.

In some ways, another significant report, in 1967, set back this understanding. *The Plowden Report* seems to rather miss the point argued for by Newsom when it calls for drama in schools to be more geared towards verbal skills (106) and the study of plays. Improvisation should be used, but also shaped, to develop clarity of ideas and theatrical form (Newsom: 1963: 107). Importantly the Report noted that, 'the growing interest in the profession of TIE is of the greatest significance'. The committee suggested though that this 'enthusiasm must be tempered with policy'.

Play and child psychology

The common strand running through all the approaches of the educational philosophers mentioned, and now seeping into government policy, was that children should be allowed to be children in their learning. Central to this is 'play':

> The young of animals play, as it were, by instinct and ... the form of their play is a rehearsal for life. (Lowenfold: 1935: 207)

All manner of mammalian young can be seen to be fighting, stalking and pouncing, learning the skills to feed and protect themselves in adulthood. It is instinctive and essential behaviour. The baby human is the most sophisticated of all, with a long period of childhood in which play is crucial in preparing them for maturity. The baby will play with sound, with motor skills and physicality in space, in order to grow and thrive:

> Play in childhood is an exceedingly complex phenomenon. It is an activity which combines into a single whole very diverse strands of thought and experience. (Lowenfold: 1935: 16)

I argue that these skills of play stay with us as adults and protect us, with degrees of competence and satisfaction, into roles we 'play' in our social and working lives. Cook expressed it thus:

> It would not be wise to send a child innocent into the big world … [But] it is possible to hold rehearsals …. And that is Play. (Cook: 1917: 1)

Further, unlike other animals, we are aware of 'tomorrow' and of death. With that awareness comes a desire to make tomorrow better than today, to learn from errors and to change our world. Other animals live in and arguably adapt their world; only humans can seek to radically change it. Bruner (1992: 113) would add that another quintessential human characteristic is that we learn. Because we learn and we play we have the potential to envisage change; that burden and blessing is part of the human condition. This is the future battleground for education and TIE: is education to socialize or promote change?

In Western culture the word 'play', in many languages, has developed two related meanings. The first is that which we primarily associate with childhood. The second is the art form of theatre where, usually, adults 'play' at being someone else for our amusement and, perhaps, erudition. This is not behaviour we see in other animals. The human use of 'play' has become so sophisticated that not only do we learn by playing, but we can learn from *others* playing (acting). We have created an art form that involves playing with alternative personas, pasts and futures. As a player on the stage we have learned to be our-self and an-other at the same time. The argument here is that play is a most fundamental gateway to learning that stays with us throughout our lives and is part of our humanness. I concur with O'Toole when he maintains 'that drama, and all the arts may usefully be viewed as playful activities' (O'Toole: 1992: 21). As we will see in later chapters this bestows on TIE, *combining* the child's play with the theatrical play, a most astounding learning potential.

It was not until the twentieth century however that the developing science of child psychology was able to help frame and codify these notions of learning and bring them in from the 'romantic' wasteland. Chief amongst these was Piaget who, from the 1920s, offered an increasingly profound schema of a child's cognitive development. The central concern of his work is developmental rather than educational, but his ideas remain very influential amongst teachers as a means of devising approaches that enhance and humanize the learning experience. These ideas encompass the use of age-appropriate play and intellectual stimulation to assist children in understanding the world around them. As Beard explains:

> When children are introduced too soon to any kind of activity the probability is that they will become confused and develop a distaste for learning of this kind. (Beard: 1969: 73)

As we will see, this danger was addressed by Vygotsky's development of Piaget's approaches. Particular influence on progressive education can be perceived in Piaget's ideas of the uniqueness of the child and the active relationship that exists between them and their environment. In the years between the wars there was an increasing use of the term 'personal development' by psychologists as a way of differentiating factual knowledge from human intellectual growth. Piaget is a key driver behind this understanding.

Alternative theatre

Before we consider the key proponents of classroom drama in the sixties we will first turn to the theatrical context which was to provide the other major taproot of Theatre in Education. For most of the twentieth century traditional audiences would go to traditional theatre buildings to be entertained by traditional 'well-made plays'. Middle class audiences sought an undemanding experience in a safe setting. This is not to insinuate that this theatre is apolitical. All theatre will either support or challenge social reality. As Samuel, MacColl and Cosgrove point out (1985), since the late nineteenth century there has been a strand of theatre allied to working-class movements that sought to challenge society, ethically and politically. TIE is in some respects part of this tradition. Early left-wing theatre was 'socially conscious rather than politically engaged' (Samuel *et al.*: 1985: xviii–xix) and shared much of the ethical sensibility being shown by the new wave of theatre from the likes of Ibsen, Chekhov, Shaw and even Galsworthy, all of whom can be seen to have brought ethical dilemmas to the stage.

Before the First World War and between the Wars we see increasing use of theatrical techniques in order to propagandize socialist ideas and mobilize the working class. In order to reach their audience, as with TIE fifty year later, it was necessary to move out of theatres and to the places where their audience could be found. For the agitprop theatres this meant the workingmen's clubs (where the audience would generally be self-selecting and existing converts) and street corners. These plays were often 'social problem' dramas (for example, Brighouse's *The Price of Coal* 1917) but others, such as Lyttleton's *Warp and Woof* (1904) were used to unionize workers. The Independent Labour Party was especially keen to use culture in the service of the 'cause' and, during the 1920s a large number of sketches were produced to broadcast the message of socialism within a dramaturgically sound format. Many of these plays were ethically based, dealing with the 'balance of humanity and necessity, the idealist and the materialist, liberation and violence ...' (Samuel *et al.*: 1985: 28). A schism was soon to emerge between Labour and more radical leftist ideas over the primacy of aesthetics. Labour groups tended to emphasize the elevating and inspirational potential of access to the arts, whilst others emphasized the need to radicalize. As we will see, related arguments were to emerge as TIE developed. The aesthetics of TIE would be important because, for many children, it would be their only exposure to theatre arts. Then there would be the question of whether TIE should be restricted to consideration of moral issues or should attempt to offer political analysis. The different approaches of the ILP and the Workers' Theatre Movement would certainly rival any ideological antagonisms that SCYPT was later to produce. The WTM was much more focussed on the revolutionary struggle and created a range of work in response to contemporary industrial flashpoints. For them 'all art was propaganda and the theatre itself a splendid weapon of struggle' (Samuel *et al.*: 1985: 46).

They regarded groups allied to the ILP and the Co-operative movement as pandering to capitalist art, their productions showing the situations of workers without offering the revolutionary solution. Innes sees the WTM as coming out of a desire to eschew the usual working-class stock comic characters and, influenced by the theatre of the Russian Revolution, offer an analysis of the dark social times of the 1920s (Innes: 1992: 70). These theatrical pieces were often little more than sketches with political songs and with basic production values. According to Innes there was a deliberate avoidance of Naturalism, since this offered a validating, photographic but superficial view of reality. Rather they sought a 'dialectical realism' (Innes: 1992: 72) to bring to view that which was hidden, in the manner that the new 'X-Rays' exposed the internal workings of the body. The WTM believed their theatre expressed the workers' struggle and was a weapon of it, exposing capitalism and inspiring workers to fight back using proletarian, not bourgeois, theatre. Further, the WTM insisted on a 'positive message' (Samuel *et al.*: 1985: 54) and this confidence in the imminence of the revolution tends to disappoint, as MacColl recalls (Innes: 1992: 213–14), and some of the more radical TIE companies were to discover.

MacColl started his own group in 1931 and, in 1934, he was joined by Joan Littlewood in the *Theatre of Action*. Under their influence political theatre took on a tighter structure and used more stage effects with a continuing Russian influence from Vakhtangov and Meyerhold. The nature of their style can be gauged from their first show, *John Bullion*, adapted from a US agitprop show, which Littlewood described as 'a constructional ballet with words' (Innes: 1992: 73). The *Theatre of Action* became *Theatre Union* in 1935 and was under constant suspicion by the authorities. With Hitler's rise to power the ideological differences of the left became subsumed in the 'Popular Front' against fascism. This and the increasing involvement of the intellectual middle classes in left-wing parties made the WTM an embarrassment to the left and it foundered in 1936. Workers' theatre was becoming part of the mainstream in terms of the actors, the writers and the production values.

During and after the War, MI6 monitored MacColl and Littlewood due to their communist sympathies. Their company, now called *Theatre Workshop*, took over the Theatre Royal Stratford East after an unsuccessful experience in touring and settled to a more conventional existence, though their productions of Brecht and, famously, *Oh! What a Lovely War*, allow us to acknowledge Littlewood's influence on what was to become TIE. Many companies share the legacy of the Workers' Theatre Movement (Belt and

Braces, Red Ladder, Monstrous Regiment, in the UK and Bread and Puppet Theatre and the San Francisco Mime Troupe in the US) but these were spawned after the emergence of TIE. Even McGrath's *7:84* only emerged in 1966, a year after the Coventry Belgrade TIE team had started to tour its work.

Superficially there are many overlaps between the revolutionary theatre movements of the first half of the twentieth century and the work of TIE in the second half, not least the taking of the theatre of ideas outside bourgeois buildings. But the starting point of the theatre of both the soft and hard left was ideology: using the medium to agitate and proselytize. For TIE the generator was heuristic education, albeit from a left-wing perspective, and the nature of the social construction of reality; through education comes empowerment for change. For the ILP and WTM the aim was to convey a message and, at its best, TIE eschews such an outcome, seeking rather to facilitate forensic understanding. Revolutionary theatre will seek to cram in as much of the ideological message as the form can bear, whereas the TIE programme will allow access to ideas of change via a theatrically tangential examination of the personal. As we will see, accusations of dogmatism have often been levelled at TIE though the most effective programmes offered no 'message' but only the ability to reflect and understand. It is with the rise of Theatre in Health Education in the 1990s that the ideas of 'telling' and 'giving a message', sully the TIE form.

Brecht's work was a much later influence in Britain, performed there for the first time in the mid-1950s. The political attitudes, the dialectics, the performance and production tropes (which offered performance styles using minimal resources) would all find a home in the emergent TIE movement. The *Lehrstücke* were even less familiar to British actors than the Epic Theatre productions but, as Nicholson points out, TIE takes Brecht's theatrical project to its next stage:

> As in the *Lehrstücke*, the methodology of TIE was inseparable from its social and educational function, and the participatory performance of TIE marked a significant development of Brecht's unfinished cultural project. (Nicholson: 2007: 32–3)

We see here an explication of TIE's theatrical roots, for TIE actors were more likely to be aware of him than of educationalists, making

TIE 'a true inheritor of Brecht's political aesthetics' (Coult in Craig: 1980: 76). But, as Nicholson indicates:

Arts have that special ability to integrate children's thoughts and feelings with their actions – a process that, in Dewey's terms, brings together the child's internal subjectivity and the external world of objects. (Nicholson: 2007: 15).

The awareness of Dewey, Montessori *et al.*, and an exposure to the ideas of Piaget and child psychology, would have come from the teachers involved in TIE rather than the performers.

A further source of inspiration was, naturally enough, Children's Theatre. Redington's research (1983) cites the German Companies, *Grips Theatre* and *Rote Grutze Children's Theatre* as developing radical approaches to theatre for children offering shows with humour that also encouraged analysis and thought (Redington: 1983: 8). In the UK, a name now synonymous with DIE comes to prominence. Brian Way, whilst working with the Old Vic Company, developed ideas for a children's theatre, forming his *West of England Children's Theatre Company* in 1944. His theatre contained moments when the children would participate, albeit as a seated audience. He also paid attention to audience size and to the age profile of the children rather than producing generic 'shows for kids'. Separately, experiments in using teachers to put on productions in schools were being attempted in Aberdeen and in Essex (Redington: 1983: 34). Such experiments potentially received a boost from the 1944 ERA that empowered Local Authorities to subsidize extra-curricular activities – an example of how a 'quality of life' agenda was receiving cross-party support as the War drew to a close. Needless to say such munificence was aimed at inculcating culture and a love of theatre arts rather than introducing the Trojan horse of dialectical thinking into the curriculum, but for the moment it was accepted that theatre, along with progressive ideas of learning, was a way forward to a better future. Touring children's theatre has remained a strong genre since this time, often being confused with TIE. In later years children's theatre was to become either 'plays for children' with a primary motive of entertainment or 'educational theatre' where a message was to be transmitted to a selected age group. Whilst the latter can share an umbral overlap with TIE, the argument here is that TIE works in a very specific way related to its progressive educational and theatrical roots.

Peter Slade, Brian Way and Dorothy Heathcote

Brian Way, Peter Slade and, a little later, Dorothy Heathcote share a particularly honourable mention in relation to emergence of TIE. As we have seen, Way had developed a children's theatre that encouraged creative participation in the performance process. In addition he had a vision of the value of non-performance drama and of its centrality to the personal and creative development of the child. *Development Through Drama* (1967) is based on a philosophy that remains pertinent. He wanted a drama in school that would offer 'genuine emotional training' (Way: 1967: 237) and pointed out that 'through drama it is possible to try out "what happens if ...?"' (Way: 1967: 178). Such ideas were to be the bedrock of the new TIE form. In Way's theatre, and in his classroom, the children willingly suspended their disbelief to address this intriguing question.

Way's contemporary and friend, Peter Slade, equally championed the power of drama to transform lives. He developed a way of working with young people that he saw as a 'high Art Form in its own right: Child Drama' (Slade: 1954: 68). His book details exactly how children learn through dramatic expression at different ages and he chronicles the way in which emotional maturity can be nurtured. He is less interested in performance and would only occasionally permit his 'Child Dramatists' to show work to adults. The work was for the young people themselves – its value in the process. It was not to be judged on the basis of adult critical expectations. Rather:

> The Drama is often used for playing out situations in which the individual has to make decisions about morals. By making situations conscious, the child is able to look at life as an observer and make slow inward decisions. (Slade: 1954: 73)

It is most unlikely that Slade was aware of the theatrical approaches of Brecht that only reached London (in German) in 1955 but these notions of reflection and objective understanding of one's self have resonance both with Epic Theatre and the TIE that was to come. Interestingly Slade is one of the first theorists to posit the notion of the 'actor/teacher':

> By this I mean persons who are primarily teachers ... and know how to take work with Children. They come to school with the freshness of outsiders and may be dressed up. They come for acting. They are trained actors. Actor-teachers, a new profession. (Slade: 1954: 272)

Like Slade, Dorothy Heathcote had an antipathy for audience and gave primacy to the *journey* rather than the destination. There is not space here to do justice to her enormous contribution to drama as a learning medium that lasted from the mid-1950s until her death in 2011. Her influence on TIE though can be seen in her maxim that children must be enabled to discover 'what they know but don't yet know that they know' (Wagner: 1979: 13) and to work in a 'no-penalty zone'. Her developing techniques have offered constant inspiration for the TIE movement, as we will see in later chapters.[5] Through her perception many companies were to find direction and coherence in their praxis.

In discussing these key drama practitioners, we have arrived at the mid-1960s where there is a 'brief collision of national affluence and educational idealism' (Coult in Craig: 1980: 76). Many young teachers, subject to this idealism and optimism, and often with a leftist analysis of the world, took up the progressive ideas, whilst outside, middle-class assumptions about theatre were being challenged. Teachers would have been exposed to ideas of Piaget but not yet Freire, Vygotsky or Bruner. Even the reassessment of education demanded by Holt (1964) and the de-schooling movement of Illich (1973) and Postman and Weingartner (1969) were still waiting in the future to give coherence to these instincts: children must be at the centre of their learning; they should learn through play; and what they learn should include an ambitious desire to shape their world. Whilst we must acknowledge the legacy from Rousseau, Froebel *et al.*, we must also accept that quite possibly many of these names remained unknown to the new teachers who wanted only to build a 'better' education for the children in their charge. It is unlikely that the actors taking work into schools were familiar with these educationalists. Their agenda was formed by the new ideas coming from Brecht and, at home in the UK, from Wesker, Pinter, Osborne, Bond, and others. Turning from the safe plays that were still the mainstay of the London West End, they responded to the questioning socialist perspective of the new playwrights. Itzin (1980) correctly detects the influence of alternative political theatre in Britain from Russian revolutionary theatre (5), but whilst there were some who undoubtedly had studied and considered these sources and theoretical perspectives, most actor/teachers were responding to post-War *zeitgeist* rather than following a theoretical imperative. For a brief period in the decades following the Second World War, there was a general mood circulating in theatre and in education that capitalism was destructive of society – and that this could be challenged (Itzin: 1980: x). TIE, she argues, developed in 'the wake of widespread politicization and the raising of political consciousness' (Itzin: 1980: xii). It was in Coventry in the geographical heart of England that this theatrical movement was first to emerge.

Coventry and its TIE experiment

As a major centre of the car industry in Britain, Coventry soon became a thriving and prosperous part of the post-War consumerist economy. It was the first city to build a civic theatre after the War and it took the visionary step of making provision for young people part of the theatre's brief through workshops in drama, improvisation and writing (Redington: 1983: 43). There was a touring schools' project and a 'Young Stagers' Club' aimed at increasing audiences for main house productions. This role was to receive a major boost when, in 1962, the Liaison Officer, Gordon Vallins, with the cooperation of the artistic director Anthony Richardson developed this outreach into improvisation sessions in schools, led by one of the main house actors, Paul Harman.

Redington describes (Redington: 1983: 44ff) how Richardson and Vallins put together a project to present to the city authorities that aimed to be a forum for the city's issues. They called this idea 'Theatre in Education' which would make 'theatre an integral part of education, and by this means ... make the pupils more aware of the world around them' (44). Despite the difficulty of explaining exactly what was envisaged, £15,000 was allotted for a year's trial. In an astute move the TIE team was created as a separate body answerable to the City Council with a budget held by the Education Department, not the theatre. Such arrangements can be critical (as later funding crises were to demonstrate) since it meant that the money was effectively 'ring-fenced' and could not be subsumed into the main theatre's general budget.

At this time (1964) the Labour Party regained power with a slim majority of four that they enhanced to ninety-six when they called a second general election in 1966. In the interim, Winston Churchill had died and the effusive state funeral may be seen as a psychological watershed, allowing the country at last to look forward towards liberal change. The teenagers of the 1950s were now married, working in out-of-date factories and aspiring to cars and consumerism. Despite overt prosperity, working-class militancy grew within what Gramsci would have identified as the bourgeois cultural hegemony underlying social systems that refused to adapt to the new reality. Genuine socialist change was not on the agenda for more than a few. This undersurge of desire for more reform manifested itself in an extensive range of liberal changes including changes in education. The mood was still that the world could be changed for the better, albeit within a capitalist system.

Although TIE did not emerge fully fledged, there are many aspects of the early Belgrade projects that would become the tropes of similar companies over the next fifteen years. The Coventry service was free to schools and the team would spend a whole day with the target group. There was extensive preparation involving staff, and support materials were provided for following up the work after the visit. The team made an effort to build a rapport with a limited number of local schools rather than follow the usual Children's Theatre model of a 'hit and run' tour. The distinct approaches of 'actors' and 'teachers' reflected the hybridity of the emerging genre, with drama workshops forming the first part of projects followed by a performance. As confidence with the medium grew and the possibilities became apparent, this 'workshop into performance into discussion' model was overtaken by more sophisticated participation by the class within both workshop and performance elements.

Belgrade's first theatre in education project

The Balloon Man and the Runaway Balloons

The first project was typical of early approaches and shows clear influence from the children's theatre work of Brian Way. *The Balloon Man and the Runaway Balloons* was an infant programme that involved the children listening to a story and adding sound effects and movement ideas. Then the story was performed, with the children playing the part of the train, the horses, the children at the seaside, and so on. The balloons escape whilst the balloon man sleeps and the children participate in a rescue. What takes this work in a new direction is the responsibility laid upon the children to come up with a plan to solve a problem; their ideas form the structure of what actually occurs in the narrative.[6]

The first Secondary school work showed more influence from agitprop and Brecht. Based on the theme of 'responsibility', and adapted from a radio play about the building and later destruction of the first River Tay bridge, the story was told using sound effects, props and folk songs of the era. After the performance the pupils took place in a drama workshop in which they had to devise a situation in which someone's carelessness caused an accident. The teachers were provided with material to develop the theme in class. A further secondary project focussed on the problem of 'noise', extending this theme of 'responsibility'. The programme ended with a 'march on the Town Hall' to complain about noise and the ultimate teaching objective seems to have been one of encouraging maturity and respect for others. Such themes are not curriculum based, and, though social issues are being addressed, there is little encroachment into dangerous 'political' territory. The logical consequence of dialectical thinking has yet to emerge. Stylistically too, the actors seem to be at the 'role-playing' end of the performance spectrum. Thematically and aesthetically, TIE was yet to find its feet.

Relationships with schools were a little uneasy initially. Theatre and education seemed somewhat strange bedfellows with neither discipline quite understanding or trusting the other (Redington: 1983: 39). The title 'actor' and the novelty their appearance in a school presented led to professional jealousy, which the fact that many 'actor/teachers' were trained educationalists did little to dispel. Many teachers envied these touring troupes, travelling from school to school, causing excitement and wonder and then passing on, leaving them holding the follow-up pack. As we will see, companies worked hard over the next fifteen years to win pedagogic respect for their work and in most cases succeeded in doing so.

The year's experiment in Coventry was a great success and the TIE programme was extended indefinitely under a new Head of Department, Rosemary Birbeck. Vallins understandably resigned when he failed to get this more permanent position, but he had created a legacy of approach, governance and indeed personnel that was passed on to companies across Britain that were set up in Belgrade's wake. In 1967 a great number sprang up, usually with main house theatre and/or civic support. These included companies in Bolton, Bristol, Canterbury, Chesterfield, Dundee, Exeter, Farnham, Glasgow, Ipswich, Lincoln, Liverpool, Salisbury and Watford. By 1973, over half of regional repertory theatres were offering Young People's Theatre (YPT) projects (Redington: 1983: 89). Theatre in Education had arrived.

Notes

1 Reading, Writing and Arithmetic.
2 It remains a historical quirk of British schools that in this instance 'public' means privately paid for and outside the state education system.
3 See *On the Education of Man* 1826.
4 Mantle of the Expert is a system of drama in the classroom created and developed by Dorothy Heathcote and that encourages cross-curricula approaches.
5 Readers who are less familiar with her work are pointed towards O'Neill (ed.) *Dorothy Heathcote on Education and Drama: Essential Writings* and the commemorative collection of articles published by the National Association for the Teaching of Drama (NATD: 2012) as a starting point for further study.
6 I am indebted to Redington (1983) for these descriptions of the early Belgrade work.

CHAPTER TWO

The Development of the Theatre in Education Movement 1966–76

Political context

Expectations built up over half a century had not been satisfied, but paradoxically people were becoming accustomed to comparative affluence. Consumerism had framed economic development and many people's aspirations had turned from wider political hopes to narrower domestic concerns. Car and white goods ownership were expanding and for many wages improved though personal debt also increased. Britain was coming to the end of its role as 'workshop to the world', but it hadn't really noticed this yet and was failing to invest in research, engineering and development. Ironically, Britain was suffering from the comparative integrity of its industrial infrastructure after the War as compared to the devastated European countries that had no choice but to invest anew.

During the 1950s, however, Britain still held the post-War advantage and her industrial strength (whatever the underlying dangers) was matched by demands for improved conditions from trade union leaders who continued to follow a socialist agenda, albeit limited to seeking improvements within the capitalist structure. The Cold War and the stories of life behind the Iron

Curtain did little to stoke fires of revolution. There was a mismatch between revolutionary aspirations and those of the British working class who seemed willingly to follow the union lead whilst actually being primarily concerned with workplace solidarity and domestic consumerism. Few now voiced the desire for wider and more fundamental nationalization; it was accepted that the only way to improve one's lot was through a *de facto* industrial war of attrition. The fact of capitalism was largely accepted. There was however, growing disillusionment with the education system and during this period (1964–73) we see growing calls for reform of the Tripartite System.

This desire for a new start was based in a new liberalism rather than revolution. Whether a response to this could come from the Tory party, and whether they or Labour could best 'keep the unions in check' seemed uncertain. The post-War consensus was generally holding firm and no party was offering alternatives to a consumerist-capitalist manifesto that kept most of the people mostly happy most of the time. This ambiguity can be seen in the general election result of 1964 that returned Labour to power with a majority of just four seats, even though whilst out of office their policies had moved further from the left-wing tendencies of its founders. Consumerism was accepted with all the trappings of the United States' influence, from music and fashion to foreign and fiscal policy. The repeated election of Tory governments through the 1950s had demonstrated that the electorate were happy to accept superficial comforts. The radical left were becoming increasingly marginalized, accused of bolshevist sympathies and being un-British. Such revolutionary thinkers who spoke out did so at fringe meetings, on university campuses and in trade union conferences where their words seemed to confirm their alienation from the new reality. At the ballot box, though the working class was remaining faithful to Labour, middle-class support was seeping back to the Tories. They had benefitted most from the 1950s and were less inclined to take risks with whatever a Labour government (and their trade union sponsors) might attempt. Harold Wilson, the new prime minister, had promised revitalization of both the drive towards reform and industrial modernization. After 1966 (with a majority of ninety-six), a period followed epitomized by investment and the speeding up of a consumerism fuelled by personal and public debt. Trade union power was, in the opinion of politicians across the spectrum, increasingly a problem. In a time of affluence workers had strong bargaining power and demanded their share of the wealth they were creating (without demanding ownership however). Barbara Castle, the Secretary of State for Employment and Productivity, offered a new relationship with the unions with her plan in 1969 entitled *In Place of Strife*. It sought to instigate reduced union power to strike and would also have set up a Commission of Industrial Relations. The Trade union Congress (TUC) regarded this as treachery by their own party and major strikes and demonstrations followed which resulted in the legislation being replaced by a less formal arrangement. The schism that had been apparent in the left in Britain throughout the century, between Labour and more radical socialists, was never more wide. This was to be artfully exploited by the right and the shift began that was to lead, in 1979, to the adoption of Thatcher's brand of Conservatism and the formal ending of the post-War consensus. The right to strike was to be seen as a threat to social democracy rather than a democratic quintessence. A contradiction was apparent between worker's rights and the rights of the community not to have their lives disrupted. Worker's militancy was viewed by many as a threat to the nation's economic security that was accepted to be the priority.

The reform agenda

The election of Labour in 1966 did not precipitate a socialist agenda, but it did initiate a liberal one and this period saw far-reaching social reforms that changed the outlook of the UK. In 1965 the death penalty was abolished and racial discrimination outlawed. Poverty was addressed by the setting up of the Child Poverty Action Group in 1966. The Equal Pay Act was introduced in 1970, largely as a result of the successful campaign by the female Ford workers in 1968. Also in 1968 theatre censorship was abolished. In the sphere of personal relationships male homosexuality was decriminalized in 1967 and the first Abortion Act introduced. In 1969 'no blame divorce' was made possible. In 1964 the first Brook Clinic, offering family planning advice, was set up (the pill had been available in the UK since 1961). A little further ahead was the Sex Discrimination Act of 1975. The late 1960s and early 1970s was a period of change undreamt of by most citizens of the 1940s, marking a new age of liberality from which there could be no turning back. This was the age of the 'swinging sixties' and the pre-eminence of youth culture (fashion, music and lifestyle), which had begun in the 1950s. No political party had the inclination to rock the entrepreneurial boat that floated on this liberal tide. The opiate of consumerism took minds off the grim realities of the Cold War (which reached a new low temperature with the Russian invasion of Czechoslovakia in 1968) and distracted voters from the revolutionary uprisings in Paris in 1968, which echoed to a lesser extent on the streets of London. In the United States the 'whole world was watching' as police brutalized Vietnam War protesters at the Democratic Convention. Also in 1968 Martin Luther King and Robert Kennedy were assassinated and Nixon elected. On the other side of the world, Mao's Cultural Revolution was at its height. In the UK, racial tensions grew following Conservative politician Enoch Powell's warning of 'rivers of blood' whilst the Labour Government, to their credit, agreed to accept Asians who were being driven from their Ugandan homes by the dictator Idi Amin. University buildings all over the UK were occupied by students demanding changes in their education. Greer published *The Female Eunuch* and Millett, *Sexual Politics*. The Wooton Report on cannabis recommended legalization. All this in 1968 – 'an era of agitational fervour' (Billington: 2007: 166).

In education new ideas were also afloat. In the Primary and Junior Schools there was, in many areas, a continuing flirtation with progressive teaching. 'Child-centred learning', 'group work', 'personal development' and 'project work' were the buzz-phrases of the day, though many schools, it must be acknowledged, still had their children learning much of their curriculum by rote. The content of the curricula was largely determined by teachers and head teachers under the watchful eye of their Local Education Authorities. In the secondary sector (in each strand of the Tripartite System), traditional teaching methods predominated and it would be almost impossible to find a classroom where the teacher was not dictating notes from the front of the seated class. There was still great freedom about what to teach and at what point, constrained only by the content of the examination syllabi. For the Grammar Schools (and to an extent the Technical Schools), this meant preparation for 'O' Level[1] exams. For the Secondary Modern Schools, there was no examination structure until 1965 when Certificates of Secondary Education (CSEs) were introduced.

The entrenched inequities of the education system remained and were becoming out of step with British liberal society, the needs of the economy and the aspirations of working-class parents. It simply was not acceptable that children should be categorized at age 11 by a culturally class-biased examination that would eternally determine their prospects. Further, as Billington points out, citing the Robbins Report on Higher Education of 1963, 'the root cause of the economic malaise lay in the failure to promote advanced learning for anyone other than a small, public school elite' (Billington: 2007: 124). The cabinet in fact contained more Old Etonians than women in 1963, a situation which is little changed fifty years later.

Thus in 1965, Tony Crosland, Minister of Education, circulated a request (not an 'instruction') for Local Authorities to offer plans for a more comprehensive education structure which would widen opportunity for the gaining of qualifications and to help young people fulfil their social and creative potential (DES: 1965: 10/65). As a result of this change, by 1970 a third of children were attending 'Comprehensive Schools'. Many 'Comprehensives' continued (and continue) to 'stream' students by supposed ability and so, whilst it became slightly more possible to claw your way to success within the same institution, for many the system remained Tripartite on a single campus. Holt (1964), Illich (1973), Postman and Weingartner (1969) and others have demonstrated the power of expectation as a determinant of academic success; to be placed in a lower stream was to be condemned to poor qualifications and career expectations. Children tend to live up to our lack of expectations. It was not until ten years after Crosland's initiative that Comprehensive Education became the norm. (Even today there are bastions of reaction in the UK who refuse to adopt the system and there is a constant clamour from the right to 'bring back the Grammars'.) Meanwhile the public schools remained virtually inaccessible to all but the very rich or well-connected, restricting access to the most prestigious universities and thus to the highest levels of economic and political power.

The expansion of TIE

Against this volatile backdrop, TIE continued to expand. Amongst the intellectual left and the baby-boomers of the 1940s now entering university, there was still a spirit of radicalism and it should be of no surprise that these ideas – however unformed – would be present in the young actors and teachers entering the new profession of TIE. As Itzin points out, '[1968] marked the coming to consciousness of the war baby generation' and they had an awareness of how much of Western prosperity was built upon the exploitation of the Third World, and the planet. This, she argues, led to 'disillusionment, despair, pessimism and anger' (Itzin: 1980: 3). Those attracted to work in TIE were almost exclusively of the left. As has been asserted in Chapter One, this leftism was often unspecific and lacked underpinning study, but TIE workers were driven by a belief in the power of education, and specifically TIE, to create social awareness in children. As Nicholson puts it:

> Many early TIE practitioners were motivated by Marxist politics, and they saw theatre as integral to the class struggle. (Nicholson: 2009: 20)

John Prior, an early member of Belgrade TIE, maintains that there was a general leftist ideology in the company but no adherence to a particular political 'line'. It was assumed that one had a generally socialist outlook to be part of the company (Prior: interview: 27 May 2014). Ian Yeoman and Tag McEntegart agree that the grasp of educational theory amongst actor/teachers was sketchy until, in the mid-to-late 1970s the influence of SCYPT orientated the TIE movement *away* from showcasing its work to external bodies and individuals and *towards* the organization of regular internal professional development opportunities for itself and its members (Yeoman: interview: 28 May 2014, McEntegart: interview: 23 June 2014). This 'generalized leftism' can be seen in the programmes being devised by Belgrade and others in the late 1960s. Perhaps the preponderance and strength of TIE in the industrial heartlands of the UK is related to a more left-wing perspective of the local governments in those areas; there was a political meeting of minds even if the actual praxis was opaque to funders. In schools, much of the early mistrust of TIE was overcome through a process of liaison, teachers' courses, induction before, and debrief after, the TIE programmes (Redington: 1983: 57).

With a company of eight actor/teachers, a system developed at Belgrade that was allowing them to run programmes in both Primary and Secondary Schools, creating twelve projects per year.

Despite this challenging workload, actor/teachers tended to stay with the company for an average of two and a half years – much longer than with most acting contracts (Redington: 1983: 58). The large number of projects allowed the work to mutate quickly making early workshop/performance projects such as *The Balloon Man* (outlined above) appear pedagogically weak and little more than educational entertainments. In the late 1960s, the company became more adventurous, creating projects for the Junior sector (6–10 years old) based on historical themes that required much greater involvement by the children. In turn the experience gained from these projects fed back into the work generated for infants.

Most of the work thus far cited can be seen as fairly 'safe'. Myths, legends, and historically distanced events are likely to be uncontroversial but could be used to create moments of contention. Many early projects contain potentially challenging material for the young people to address, but as yet the companies were pedagogically unable to plumb this profundity. This was possibly due to a lack of theory, a lack of dialectical understanding or a lack of confidence to take up the big challenges offered by the way they were starting to work. This began to change in 1969 with a programme for infants about Romanis ('gypsies' in the parlance of the day).

The Mysterious Wanderers[2]

This programme had the aim to introduce children to ideas of cultural difference and to stimulate research into the Romani way of life by the class before and after the TIE visit. The structure of what follows sets us clearly on a trajectory to participatory TIE. After an initial session in the classroom children are gently moved into role as 'gypsies', take up the reins of their imaginary caravans and 'travel' for a while before making camp – a straightforward session using imaginative drama during which incidental learning is taking place about the culture of the Romani. What follows introduces an element of dramatic conflict, in role, and this is a new departure. Half of the group are expelled from the camp by the local farmer. They go back to the classroom (in their caravans) where they learn about the working lives of the Romani. The remaining group also get evicted (for poaching) and retreat to the playground where they learn about Romani dancing. The first group return to the camp to find it deserted and the farmer still angry, but the children placate her by telling her fortune and she gives them work in her orchard. The second group then return and are also given work, are paid, and go to the Horse Fair where they dance and listen to a story told by the teacher in role as a traveller. She is able to continue with this role back in the classroom using materials provided by the company.

This programme contains in-role participation by the children, occupational mime, a range of performance elements and, crucially, elements of conflict that have to be resolved by or with the children. There will be much further to go with this approach in TIE, but here we see an early example of children being faced with a dilemma *which they have been equipped to resolve*. These children are not 'acting'. They are not solely themselves. And they are not confused! As in any creative dramatic play they undertake, *they are being themselves whilst wearing someone else's shoes*. They are using play to rehearse their lives and hone the decision processes they need to master. They are empowered, in a small way, to come to terms with the world in a totally secure environment where one could not be 'wrong' and where there were adults, also 'playing', upon whom they could rely to structure events. Additionally we can see that TIE was on a journey from fantasy to social realism.

From 1967 Belgrade's work can be seen to have a social and often local relevance, created with the support of teachers. Even a history-based project would be located locally as, for example, with *If it was not for the Weaver* and *The Lunt Fort at Baginton*.

The Lunt Fort at Baginton

This project was based around the coming of the Romans to Coventry. We see a move beyond 'mere' history, for the programme allowed children to interpret their own lives through a fictive clash of cultures portrayed in the programme. The structure of the piece is straightforward. The teacher prepares for the TIE visit by teaching about the events of the Roman invasion. During the TIE programme itself one class of children are inducted as Romans and learn about their military and cultural life. A second class learns about Celtic culture, including taking part in a Celtic funeral. The two cultures later meet face to face with the Romans expecting to be paid taxes and the Celts feeling oppressed. The two sides negotiate the situation. In a mixture of drama and theatre each side prepares 'scenes' to explain themselves to the other. When the Romans are distracted by rebellion 'elsewhere' the Celts attack in a stylized and controlled drama but are forced to withdraw. The Romans discuss what they should do about the Celts: the Celts discuss whether to flee or return to their farms. Spokespersons from each side then report back to a general meeting in the hall.

Such projects as this raise interesting dilemmas. The truth of such an encounter would have been bloody and prolonged battle, exacerbated by lack of any means of communication. Clearly that is not helpful in an educational context. However, what the company were seeking to do with this project was to get underneath the 'facts' of history to the underlying cultural issues that pertained both then, and now in their own lives. Through a mixture of occupational mime, role-play and theatre the children were both 'inside' and 'outside' the events at the same time. They knew they were 'playing' but the play was being structured to allow them to examine feelings of oppression, dominance, anger, justice, cultural confusion and personal loss within a safe context. Whether the Celts or Romans would get the upper hand was not in doubt; outside the drama they knew the history. The value lay in what they could learn from that history of relevance to their own lives.

Approaching the socio-political

Stuart Bennett joined the Belgrade team in 1967 and in 1970 became Head of Department. It is under his stewardship we see a more direct approach to contemporary material. Whilst projects about Coventry weavers or Celts and Romans can undoubtedly be relevant to young people, they also offer the distance of time to remove any political sting. During the 1970s we can detect a braver approach. We have already indicated that this period was one of industrial unrest, even militancy, and this was nowhere more true than in the car-making industries of the Coventry area. The company had already dipped its toe into this water with a workshop about The Great Strike of 1860. This workshop was carried out with teachers who then took the work back to their schools to develop projects with their children about Coventry's transition from a centre of weaving to a centre of engineering. It was a theme to which the company was to return with *The Carmakers* (1971) (Figure 2.1). The current company publication *Theatre in Education at the Belgrade: Building on Our Heritage*, describes the programme as being created for 'English, History and Social Studies Students … exploring historical fact, lived experience and social impact'. This description is perhaps a little disingenuous and what is overlooked here is that Coventry in the 1970s was at the heart of the struggle between the trade unions and industrial bosses – the fact of which the young people of Coventry would have been very well aware. The undoubted political analysis inherent in this programme is now discreetly veiled beneath the more delicate description of 'social studies'.

FIGURE 2.1 The Carmakers *(Belgrade TIE: 1971)*. Workers confront the bosses. Photo: Tony Baker *(www.artmedia-associates.com)*.

In some ways during this period, the company seemed to be struggling to maintain its initial momentum and this may be due to the lack of a theoretical underpinning of TIE precepts. There were plenty of pedagogic theories that might have helped fertilize these roots, but even trained teachers amongst actor/teachers were generally not privy to them. The company had certainly begun an important analysis of education. It clearly spent time considering what worked best with different age-groups, how to use participation, the interface between acting and teaching and how to help children's personal development. Further the company was aware of the progressive educational ideas and the importance of learning by discovery. It was to be a few years, however, before questions of *how* children learned and *what* was important for them to learn would be addressed. Perhaps as a result of this lack of relevant ideology Belgrade TIE, as well as breaking new ground in the classroom, was still umbilically attached to Children's Theatre and flirted with a perceived responsibility to produce work to support examination texts and/or the work of the main house theatre. In secondary schools the company was discovering that teachers found it almost impossible to loosen the timetable and the demands of examination curricula to facilitate the work. For the primary sector, however, the company was creating a pattern of work that was being replicated across the UK.

The political shift

It is necessary for a moment to return to the political background, for as TIE was beginning to flourish as a coherent approach to teaching, there was a shift that resulted in a victory for Heath's Conservatives (1970) spelling the end of the process of liberal reform. The narrowness of the victory (a majority of thirty) Todd puts down to 'voter's uncertainty about who could best satisfy their desires for greater control over their working and domestic lives' (Todd: 2014: 299). In the election – and following it – the Tories made much of blaming the militancy of a greedy working class for the industrial troubles that were infecting Britain. Todd argues that this view of history has been successfully woven into the fabric of folk memory and certainly the 'bogey man' of 1960s and 1970s socialist 'chaos' is frequently dangled before voters even today, and even by the Labour Party.

Todd sees it somewhat differently, pointing out that this same period was one of surveillance of trade unionists, heavy-handed policing at picket lines and finally 'a dramatic and catastrophic intervention in British domestic policy by a group of international financiers' (Todd: 2014: 299). Heath's response to the 'chaos' was the Industrial Relations Act that severely curtailed workers' rights and made working-class industrial solidarity illegal. Heath was determined to reign-in the influence of the trade unions. Relationships between the government and the working classes became progressively worse and in the four years of his government Heath declared five different states of emergency and implicitly accused workers of being enemies of the state (Todd: 2014: 301). In 1973 miners went on strike in protest at Heath's new wage controls. This lead to fuel shortages that impelled the government to impose a three-day week. For older voters the shortages and power cuts 'recalled the worst privations of wartime' (Billington: 2007: 206). Heath called a snap election under the slogan 'who governs Britain?' – and discovered that it was not to be him. It was a defeat that the Tories remembered well into the eighties and the scars remain today.

Given the make-up of TIE companies, this period of political uncertainty and social disillusionment led to a more provocative approach to the material contained within programmes. It was a time to stand up and be counted. Indeed, this can be seen not only in TIE work but also in mainstream theatre, with the plays of Wesker, Arden, Hare, Edgar and Bond being amongst the clearest examples. Heightened political awareness was bound to affect the work of the socially motivated workers in TIE and impact the choices made about what was felt to be important to set before young people. At this time, for example, Belgrade bravely chose to reflect, albeit at a distance, some key political debates of the day.

The Price of Coal

This piece was produced (1973) under the directorship of Dave Pammenter, who had taken over from Stuart Bennett in 1972, and was clearly an attempt to get young people to think more analytically about the issues and to respond 'to the media misrepresentation of the miners' strike' (Pammenter in Jackson &

Vine (eds): 2013: 87). It was aimed at 9–11 year olds and placed them in role as miners in the 1840s. The progression of the narrative depended upon decisions that the children had to make based on research that they carried out. In Part Two of the programme one of the characters is killed and the children take part in a 'Royal Commission of Inquiry' to determine responsibility. Pammenter describes what followed as 'complete ownership by the children' (Jackson & Vine (eds): 2013: 88). The actors took a back seat as the children took over the character roles, writing, playing out and analysing what occurred in 1840 – except, of course, that they were working against the given backdrop of their own lives: the Miners' Strike of 1972. The work itself was not overtly political, but the intrinsic contemporary political dilemmas resonated strongly.

We have noted that the experiments at Coventry were quickly emulated in a variety of forms all over Britain, especially industrial Britain. The tendency for companies to form in regions of population density has several causes the most obvious being the economies of scale: it is more economical to work in a small geographic area with many schools than to have to spend large amounts of resources visiting small rural schools. For many working in the profession, urban levels of facilities and opportunities were also important. A further reason for this urbanization of TIE was the fact that most companies were spawned by local repertory theatres. Often these main house theatres had merely spied an opportunity to market their main productions to schools and to build empires. Indeed, this had been the intention at the Belgrade but the determination of a series of visionary directors ensured at least a partial independence. John Prior, for example, who had worked at Belgrade on *The Carmakers* amongst other programmes, notes that 'many reps [repertory theatres] had jumped on TIE and Children's Theatre just to get their hands on the money' (Prior: interview: 27 May 2014). Fortunately many TIE workers, having 'apprenticed' at the Belgrade, went on to set up companies elsewhere and they took the developing philosophy and political analysis with them. Examples would include Watford, Bolton, Edinburgh, Leeds and, in London, Greenwich and Cockpit – all setup between 1968 and 1971. Neither funders nor main house establishments knew quite what to expect from setting up a TIE company, but there seemed to be money for it and there was kudos to be gained. The issue for actor/teachers and TIE directors was managing erroneous expectations. Indeed much of the work that initially came out of this expansion of young people's theatre based in main houses was clearly Children's Theatre. Some created work based on local stories and others, trying to demonstrate their educational credentials, would tour scenes from examination texts, especially Shakespeare. The 'theatre education' in these projects usually centred on rehearsal methods, acting and production techniques and this view of 'theatre in education' was to find its way into the first National Curriculum of 1990. What many in theatre, including those calling their work 'TIE', were finding difficult, was to make the leap from theatre as a staged art form to theatre as a springboard for understanding and change, theatre that gives us space to reflect upon the reality of being human. Redington (1983) argues that all forms, from Children's Theatre to drama projects in schools, can fall within the title 'Theatre in Education'. My personal definition is much narrower and I seek to draw a distinction between DIE, educational theatre and TIE that, amongst these approaches, fuses theatre and learning in a uniquely empowering way.

Developing the Belgrade legacy

Leaving aside the companies that had been drawn into the Children's Theatre and Educational Theatre sphere, I will turn to some of the work where there was a clear borrowing of ideas from the Belgrade 'parent', using similar structures and adapting them to local events and traditions. For example, the Edinburgh team produced a programme (1969) about mediaeval life in Edinburgh that clearly reflected early Coventry projects and dealt with resolving conflict. Both followed a three-part structure with classroom sessions about the period followed by a participatory event and finishing with a rehearsed theatrical event. The best of the new companies had learned from the experience at Coventry and ensured they had LEA and teacher support. In many TIE companies there was a remarkably slow turnover of staff. There is a great deal to commend in this, though some might argue that actors need to be environed in new situations, new working practices and with alternative stimuli to avoid getting stale and/or complacent. On the positive side is the relationships that can be built up with schools, pupils, funders and, most importantly, fellow workers; together it is possible to develop economic ways of working and a pedagogic/ artistic coherence and shorthand. So it was at Leeds, where the trust grew to such an extent that the company was soon allowed to decide on its own priorities and material.

For other companies the battle to get established was much tougher. What TIE is and how it can work is often barely understood, even by teachers and conventional actors. Local Authorities and teachers hear the words 'theatre in education' but understood this to mean 'plays in schools'. For many in the teaching profession what was happening mystified and disturbed them. Mark Woolgar, for example, writes in 1971, 'theatre people are theatre people, not educationalists'. He concedes that TIE might be a useful innovation as long as the groups worked closely with drama teachers (Woolgar in Dodd & Hickson: 1971: 91–2). This is just what TIE companies were trying to do, but the mistrust in Woolgar's comments is clear:

> The teacher should be trusted to choose the right children to be used [in TIE programmes]. (Dodd & Hickson: 1971: 110)

In the same essay there is a report of a conference for teachers on 'Drama and Theatre in Education' held at Bristol in 1969 (Dodd & Hickson: 1971: 110–11). There was a general view expressed that 'it was unsatisfactory for professional theatre groups to go into schools to give drama lessons'. The level of misunderstanding of the purpose, nature and potential of TIE can be seen in the summary of conference outcomes: it was agreed that TIE might be of some use to liberal studies and to encourage lively lessons, but the conference questioned how such lessons could be geared to the examination system.

This was the level of conceptual alienation from TIE that many teachers displayed during these early years. The demands being made by actor/teachers that teachers should attend previews, follow-up the work and for 'audiences' to be limited to thirty children must have seemed indulgent if not absurd. Actor/teachers though felt that 'TIE teams have a responsibility to the education system but a greater responsibility to the children' (Pammenter in Jackson: 1993: 63).

Greenwich Theatre, in southeast London, opened in 1969. The TIE team (two actors and a director) also had responsibilities to take part in main house productions. The grant from the Inner London Education Authority (ILEA) was insufficient to support the company so, whilst work mounted for ILEA was provided free, the company also offered their product outside the area for a fee. Understandably schools wished to minimize these costs by maximizing audiences; although there might be a workshop for a class of children in the morning, the performance to two hundred in the afternoon would hardly fit any definition of TIE. The situation for Greenwich only changed when they allied themselves with the well-established Youth Theatre and distanced themselves from the main house theatre. Again, it is interesting to note that the traditional theatre establishment was unable to conceive of what was happening; it could only see this new upstart as a way of getting children interested in their theatre. It did this of course, but much more. Chris Vine describes the work of Greenwich Young People's Theatre (GYPT) thus:

> The GYPT Company had a long tradition of innovatory participation work: from the early 1970s it had given particular prominence to the development of complex forms involving the audience working alongside the actors in a theatrical context, often framed within elaborate theatrical environments. (Vine in Jackson & Vine (eds): 2013: 63)

Also in London, Cockpit TIE was set up under another Coventry-trained director (Alec Davison). They took a different approach that is worthy of note. Rather than visit schools, classes of pupils were brought to their studio theatre. Like GYPT it was funded by ILEA but worked exclusively with pupils over 14 years old. This in itself was quite radical as drama-related work was (and still is) considered by many to be more appropriate with younger children. Bringing the children out of school and to the studio avoided many of the timetabling and institutional problems, though at the expense of a certain level of teacher liaison. Because of the location within an equipped theatre the company was able to offer more complex production standards for the performance elements of the work.

The participatory work that Vine described above was to become the defining quiddity of TIE over the next ten years and the most powerful, provocative and effective way of offering an authentic educational experience to young people. Regretfully, however, its very nature has made it hard to preserve and archive. In this early period of the development of TIE filming of projects was prohibitively expensive and little has survived. In later years, when the use of participation techniques was flourishing, video became available but was intrusive and technologically limited. By the time video became compact and discreet, fears about abuse made schools and parents disinclined to allow recording of children, and it could also be contractually problematic for the actors. Further, as so much of a participatory piece is engendered by the children, with only 'set pieces' being tightly scripted, the publication of scripts is often not reflective of the actual experience for the children on the day. Published TIE scripts tend to be of performance-based programmes. Let us note though, that the idea of children taking part, in role, with the actors, is an identifiable trait from the earliest programmes at Belgrade.

The writer David Holman was very much influenced by the participatory work he observed at Coventry and Bolton. In his chapter in Bennett's *Theatre for Children and Young People* (2005: 115) he reports his fascination with the work the children undertook as part of the TIE programme *The Emergent African Game*. Here the children were brought into the drama to deal with the political and social decisions and priorities that newly liberated countries were having to make. He also cites *Poverty Knocks*, which explored the history of Chartism[3] and, as such, was closer to normal school curriculum fare. As we have seen with other projects, the children had been prepared 'factually' by the teachers, but in the programme were faced with costumed characters and placed in role as citizens of the period. As the narrative unfolded the 'workers' are faced with dilemmas and complex decisions. Holman went on to work on the TIE project entitled *The Carmakers* previously mentioned.

These ideas about working *alongside* children rather than performing *to* them had identifiable genesis within the companies and it is important that many actor/teachers were teacher-trained rather than acting-trained. These young educators would become practised in the art of structured learning through drama, slipping in and out of role, whilst the children 'lived through' an experience in a manner that was becoming the hallmark of Heathcote's practice in the late 1960s and early 1970s. However, in considering these early experiments in participation one is left with the impression that companies were following their instincts rather than developing a coherent and cogent theatrical pedagogy. Few actor/teachers or TIE directors were yet familiar with her work, but consider what the drama practitioner, John Hodgson, was saying about Heathcote's work in 1972:

> Playing out of situations challenges the child's social attitudes, his verbal control and language ability, his unselfishness, his physical energies and his imagination as he 'lives through' the situation of interest to him. (Hodgson: 1972: 159)

Like Stanislavski-trained actors, the children are asking 'what if?'. The symbiotic forces of Heathcote's DIE and the actor's power to 'be' and 'not be', (to be and to observe ourselves being) are drifting towards each other and will meet in TIE praxis as the 1970s turn into the 1980s. In her chapter in *Drama and Theatre in Education* (1971), Heathcote asserts that a teacher is 'one who creates learning situations for others' (Dodd & Hickson: 1971: 42). She continues 'I want my classes to learn to make decisions, and to understand the problems and rewards of the decisions' (Dodd & Hickson: 1971: 48). TIE companies were inventing a similar wheel, but for the moment the companies were in the strange situation where they were experimenting with practice and, at the same time, needing to inspire teachers to use the work and funders to fund it. They had to convince them that they knew what they were doing! They were on a journey without a map and they needed one. The practice was running ahead of the theory, and it was to be during the next fifteen years that the influence of Freire, Vygotsky and Bruner was to enter the consciousness of companies and then for the work to be theorized and expounded in publicized forums. For the present many directors, and most actor/teachers, continued to run on a mixture of socio-enthusiasm, experience and a general belief in the importance of young people's education. All of this was rooted in a belief that creativity and education offered hope for a future by offering visions of change.

During the period in question, the Department of Education and Science published a report on drama in schools (1967). The schools' inspectors made some observations about isolated examples they had seen of TIE. They note with interest 'what may well prove to be one of the most far-reaching projects, that of sending a small group of actors into the schools to work with the teachers and their pupils' (92). The same report acknowledges the term 'programme' to describe the work (rather than 'performance') and describes several projects that have been observed (1967: 92ff). It is a reflection of the ignorance of theories of knowledge acquisition, that many TIE companies regarded participation as just one weapon in their arsenal without perhaps realizing its power and significance. The DES report cited above, whilst being comparatively generous in its support for actors working in schools, does end by noting that:

> Bluntly, there is a grave danger of this kind of work getting out of hand .... Between twenty and thirty repertory theatres are planning to form 'demonstration' groups to work in schools. It is doubtful whether they are all quite clear what it is they are to demonstrate, or why. Not all the work that is done by the theatre for children is contributing much to their education or their artistic appreciation. (1967: 94)

One can almost hear the clipped tones of this confused committee member faced with ideas and approaches that did not fit into his/her concept of what 'real' theatre and 'proper' education should be. The comments are fixed in a world where the only purpose of taking performance into schools must be to demonstrate 'real theatre'. But let us take the criticism squarely on the chin; there was a lack of pedagogy at the beginning, but that was to change as the 1970s got into their stride.

Notes

1 'Ordinary Level' generally taken at age 16, as opposed to the 'A' (Advanced) Level, taken at eighteen and which remain a key qualification for entry to university.
2 Again I am indebted to Redington for her description of this project.
3 Chartism was a movement for political reform – specifically enfranchisement and democratization – amongst the working classes of the 1830s and 1840s.

CHAPTER THREE

Pedagogical Maturity 1976–90

Performance-based TIE

Because terms such as 'theatre in education', 'educational theatre', 'drama in education' (and also 'theatre in health education', 'theatre for development'[1]) do not always translate well across cultures and education systems, it is probably the right moment to offer my definition: TIE is using the techniques of theatre arts to educate. That is pretty straightforward, but it does beg the question of what we mean by 'education'. This chapter explores the development of TIE into the 1980s and we will see examples of both participatory and performance TIE with an increasingly sophisticated underpinning of programmes by theory. It needs to be made clear (perhaps) that TIE is *not* putting on a play in school. Further, it is *not* about teaching theatre skills nor about building mainstream theatre audiences – though both of these may be incidental outcomes.

Thus far, I have focussed on the development of participatory programmes that were becoming a peculiar strength of TIE and were largely rooted in the drama teacher/actor combination. This work matured with sophistication in the next two decades, but we can also acknowledge the value of performance-based programmes. As companies became more secure financially, more confident in their way of working and more concerned to communicate ideas, projects initiated by performance became more common. In this approach we can occasionally see a return to the ideas of the Workers' Theatre Movement and its documentary style and the desire of actors to present a body of aesthetically cogent ideas. The classic three-part TIE programme *Rare Earth* (Belgrade TIE: 1973) contains the performance piece *Drink the Mercury!* which, in its use of non-western theatre forms, can be seen to be experimenting very much as Littlewood had done with *John Bullion* (1934). The other two parts of *Rare Earth* involve participation and simulation and the programme as a whole offered both theatrical and pedagogic opportunities.[2]

Companies have often found that when working with secondary school pupils, it becomes increasingly problematic to expect them to work in role – to 'play' overtly. This, plus the intractability of secondary schools' timetables previously mentioned, encouraged the use of short, curriculum-related and performance-orientated programmes. If the schools were sufficiently motivated, problems were not insurmountable and, in 1976 and 1977, there was a flurry of TIE performance-based projects dealing with fascism. It can be easier look at our own world through the safety of historical distance and the popularity of these programmes 'about' Hitler were essentially a way of coming to understand the immediate dangers of racism in contemporary Britain. Three such programmes were Cockpit's *Marches*, Belgrade's *The Rise of Hitler* and M6's *'No Parasan' They Shall Not Pass*.[3]

Three Programmes About Fascism

Cockpit's programme used a documentary style performance (at their studio theatre) that was followed by a workshop giving pupils the chance to 'hotseat' the characters. The actor/teachers then followed-up with a school visit that included discussion of contemporary parallels. The aim of the project was to examine the ways in which personal prejudice can be exploited by political groups. *The Rise of Hitler* had some similar aims in exposing how sections of the community are scapegoated by racists to avoid dealing with complex economic issues. In addition the company sought to bring out the ways in which business colluded with Nazism, how state apparatus was used to oppress and terrorize and how propaganda was used to mislead the ignorant. The programme used a documentary style performance at its core, followed by a discussion workshop around the issues arising. Pammenter reports that discussions centred on the use of propaganda, control of the media, trade unions and big business. He notes that 'when the discussions worked well they moved from the problems of Hitler's Germany to the problems of today' (Pammenter in *SCYPT No. 1*: 10). This was TIE that secondary schools could welcome and the tour was highly successful, for it dealt with history from the syllabus and it offered opportunities for objective discussion of contemporary issues. The third piece, from M6, was unashamedly performance based, presenting ideas but leaving the audience with them. The narrative of the first section concerns the career of a young German Jewish boxer (whose success is thwarted by the rise of Hitler) and also considers the events of the 1936 Berlin Olympics. Part Two looks at the activities of the British Union of Fascists in London and explores the class solidarity that should exist between workers and the oppressed Jewish refugees from Germany. Finally the play moves to the Nuremberg trials and we learn that the Jewish hero from the first two sections was killed in the concentration camps. The writer of the piece, David Holman, notes that 'the ending is very low key and emotional and we had no wish to force a quick reaction from the audience' (Holman in *SCYPT No. 1*: 14).

These three pieces rely heavily on theatre performance conventions, especially those of the Workers' Theatre Movement, documentary theatre and, of course, Brecht. To a lesser extent two of the programmes employ discursive workshops, but it is noteworthy that audiences were not only prepared to accept the conventions of theatre acting but also happily continued to suspend their disbelief into the notion of interrogating the actors in role as the characters. This 'passive participation' is an approach perhaps more appropriate to young adults whose use of 'play' still exists but has become more self-conscious.

Using role with secondary school pupils

Further ways of working with this age group, displacing them from their comfort zone and demanding engagement, were also developed.

Key amongst these was the notion of using a 'frame' or group role. Rather than spectating a performance as themselves, the young people would be given a frame through which to view, interpret and comment upon the events. A class might be given the collective role of being 'journalists', 'a board of enquiry', a team of scientists or detectives. This frame would offer a secure filter through which to participate at a distance. The individual pupil can engage with the role to the extent they feel comfortable (and this may develop during the programme). They are not 'acting' and, by virtue of the frame, they are not themselves either. However, they are provided with a perspective, an attitude, through which to respond to events. Responses will be theirs, or created by their assumptions of the role, or a mixture of the two. They are using 'play' to investigate the content of the presentation. A character can talk to them and they can respond from the standpoint of their frame-role. If they wish to say nothing, the actor can pass the interaction to another without breaking the conventions of the game. Geoff Gillham, in conversation with Heathcote (*SCYPT Journal No. 13*: 13–23) about Action PIE's project *The Crossing* (1984) examines the notion of a group role. The programme deals with the nature of censorship of the arts by looking at the death of the German artist George Grosz. The young people, it is explained, were placed in role as 'friends of Mrs Grosz' but, as Heathcote points out, this is not a role that will lead to the analysis of the artist's work or his mysterious death. To give the role of 'policemen' would have skewed the programme since the authorities were clearly implicated in censoring his work and possibly in causing his death.

When I observed the project, the frame that had been chosen was that of journalists. This allowed for high levels of investigative analysis and gave context for interactions with the characters, as well as a standpoint from which to critique his art, politics and the notion of censorship. McEntegart (interview: 23 June 2014) reports that Geoff Gillham in his artistic leadership and his writing led the move away from didactically inclined 'what to think' projects (powerful and relevant though many were), consciously seeking out ways of developing 'how to think' methodologies in both performance and participatory elements of TIE programmes. 'Frame', as developed by companies such as Action Projects in Education (Action PIE), worked with adolescents as full participation does with younger children by protecting them into engagement with the performance on the terms required by the TIE programme. As O'Toole puts it:

> Even if there is no theatre building, if the drama takes place in a classroom, this **context of the medium** is present: there has to be an agreement to use the … space for the fiction; the group has to be united in agreeing to have a drama. (O'Toole: 1992: 49)

Given that by 1977 there were around ninety companies working in some sort of YPT (Redington: 1983: 136), it would be impossible to give a full account of all the ways of working being employed. The 'fascism' examples above offer examples where either the theatre was allowed to speak for itself or the 'participants' were offered a safe way of engaging with the concepts via interaction with the characters. With younger children more immersive techniques were being evolved and the manipulation of them dextrous. Perhaps this maturation of TIE methodology was a matter of evolutionary chance, a process of natural selection? But evolution is driven by a host of environmental determinants and, to extend the metaphor a little further, by selective breeding. The initial impetus clearly seems to have come from Belgrade; directors and actor/teachers who worked there predominated in the genesis of companies set up in the 1960s and early 1970s. There were also educational ideas around (as yet not common currency) that fitted well into companies' egalitarian instincts. By the 1970s, there was an increasingly widening gulf emerging between companies producing Children's Theatre and those with an educational mission.

The Standing Conference of Young People's Theatre

An opportunity for developing these new approaches was offered by the setting up in 1976 of the Standing Conference of Young People's Theatre (SCYPT). SCYPT emerged from a symposium in 1974 of companies, local authorities and other funding agencies that discussed the content, philosophy and funding of the work. The Gulbenkian Foundation agreed to offer seed funding for three years to establish SCYPT which in time became the cauldron for the advancement of TIE theory. Initially the focus was on practical rather than theoretical matters. McEntegart recalls that the major gear-change that enabled this turn towards theory, driven by Stuart Bennett, Geoff Gillham, Colin Hicks and Mike Kay, occurred at the 1978 Conference when a motion was passed to transform SCYPT into a 'professional development organization' (McEntegart: interview: 23 June 2014). Anthony Jackson (interview: 24 June 2014) has a slightly different viewpoint and, whilst accepting the importance of SCYPT in the encouragement of critical thinking about theory and practice, feels that Gillham too often got waylaid by having to adjust ideas to fit with his party line. (Gillham was a member of the Workers' Revolutionary Party.) For Jackson there was never enough focus on 'how children learn'. The publication of the SCYPT journal can be seen as central to the process of professionalization and the development of praxis.

For example, it was through SCYPT that Heathcote's approach to working with children became known, opening up new ways of facilitating workshops using Socratic questioning. The Forum Theatre techniques, now so beloved of drama teachers, were introduced to TIE companies at SCYPT conference. Certainly there was also a 'lions' den' aspect to sharing your work at conference, for this was a time when the social and political context was being thoroughly interrogated and, in addition to pedagogical ideologies, the politics of feminism, race and (at that time to a lesser extent) sexual orientation were at the forefront of TIE workers' sensibilities. The ideological struggles within SCYPT were often passionate, wearing and inconclusive. Frequently the conference agenda was abrogated in order that motions relating to the political events of the day could be debated. On one occasion, the conference was suspended so that delegates could join the picket lines of the Miners' Strike (1984–5). These issues mattered and support had to be shown but some argued that SCYPT companies' strengths lay in the work they produced; it was there that one could make a difference.

Under each other's influence, SCYPT companies were producing some highly experimental work during this period. Explorations of colonialism, nationalism and of significant though less well known historical events were undertaken, as well as programmes dealing with social, class and feminist issues. Leeds TIE was at the forefront of these developments.

Raj

*R*aj (1982) was undertaken by the company partly to challenge the cultural bias within their own work. They had come to realize that, despite the multi-racial identity of the company, they were still producing work culturally embedded in British traditions and middle-class values (Leeds Playhouse Theatre in Education Company: 1984: 5–6). The company forced themselves to confront their own class and educational backgrounds. The play that emerged was less about racism (most of the white characters display a good deal of liberality in this respect) and more about imperialism and paternalism. The exception to this liberality is the trigger happy private who shows no empathy for the plight of the Indians. The complexity of attitudes could have been deconstructed in a workshop that, unfortunately, this piece did not include. The financial restraints of the 1980s were affecting budgets and the participation format was susceptible to this (Jackson & Vine (eds): 2013: 29). The play itself avoids portraying the Indian characters as victims but rather as people who had been brought up in the contradiction of lauded British values and increasingly violent suppression. It has a straightforward narrative that brings these contradictions together in the context of the Second World War and the Indian uprising. For the young Punjabi immigrants to Leeds Schools, it offered a view of their history they had not been previously exposed to, and despite the lack of an investigatory workshop, the piece will have resonated for the 10–12 year olds who were dealing with the tensions of forging friendships across racial lines and in spite of cultural misinformation. Some children intuited universals beyond their own lives too, with one child observing, 'the play reminded me of Ireland and El Salvador' (Sophia Ahmed: Jackson & Vine (eds): 2013: 63). In its content the play shares some of the themes of the 1935 *Meerut*, but *Raj* has none of the direct agit-prop anger and is testament to how TIE offers complication through elucidation as compared to inter-War forms of theatre that often sought merely to enrage to action.

Animated debates would take place at SCYPT around any project that portrayed a woman in a stereotypically domestic situation. Should we not always offer a positive role model for young women in schools? Are we not further embedding the oppression by leaving such images unquestioned? What is the role of historical accuracy? Such debates were engendered by the sharings of work. Though often unresolved (irresolvable?) and leaving one's ego severely bruised, the process of analysis was taken back to the companies and to the next devising processes. Stuart Bennett, very diplomatically, describes SCYPT conferences thus:

> [They were] a forum for companies to demonstrate their work ... and engage in discussion and appraisal of its principles and effectiveness ... There were detailed debates and confrontations on a range of political positions .... (Bennett: 2005: 18)

Ian Yeoman describes the founding of SCYPT as 'a practical recognition of the necessity for a social, national and international struggle for theory' (in *SCYPT No 28*: 46). Where there is theory there will be ideological confrontation (as has been noted in the arguments surrounding agit-prop theatre of the early twentieth century). Yeoman is also very clear (interview: 28 May 2014) that inculcating theoretical awareness, such as bringing forward the ideas of Bruner and others that he was subsequently exposed to, remained an important part of his role as actor and director in the companies he worked with later. He maintains that the requirement to introduce younger practitioners to theories of learning and teaching has increased, in proportion to the decrease in collectives.

There is always a need to understand what we are doing, to question how and why we are doing it. Additionally, at a time that British politics was moving rapidly to the right (culminating in Thatcher's election in 1979), companies working to a more egalitarian agenda needed the solidarity of being part of the TIE 'movement'. In the 1980s, as increasing pressure came from financial cuts and threats of censorship, SCYPT offered a framework for mutual support though this was often fractured by disagreements about the best way to resist the attacks.

The theoretical argument was reflected in the organization's annual journal, initially subsidized by Gulbenkian, containing articles on companies' projects and explorations of TIE as a system. There were far too many contributions to list[4] but they varied from very practical advice about the requirements of being a TIE actor to pedagogic contributions from all the prime movers of the TIE movement. The last journal appeared in 1998 having informed, irritated and inspired a generation of actor/teachers and leaving a valuable legacy of ideas.

In 1992, SCYPT published a manifesto in response to the recently imposed National Curriculum in England and Wales. Though SCYPT was very far from having a united voice, the determination to place the needs of the child at the centre of learning was something to which all affiliated companies could subscribe.

Pedagogical theory

Key educational philosophers have already been mentioned in these pages, though it has been pointed out that often their pedagogic insights seemed to have entered into TIE by a process of simultaneous osmosis. Colin Hicks (interview: 18 June 2014) recalls that companies had much self-belief and were generally oppositional, motivated by the pedagogical needs. Although many company members were left-wing, not all were. Looking back, the company (Perspectives TIE was set up in 1972) were more 'soft liberals', with no revolutionary connections but with a powerful critique of how teaching should be: 'we were pedagogues before we were militants'.

The ideas of Holt and Illich (a compatriot of Freire) were now gaining currency amongst young teachers and TIE workers as a way of explaining the shortcomings of a school system that was to come under so much political scrutiny in the late 1970s and 1980s. Holt's influential *How Children Fail* was published in the UK in 1965. His analysis of contemporary educational techniques resonated with TIE workers. They too were learning that what is required is the kindling of a desire to *find* answers rather than *know* answers. Indeed, answers should be sought even when they don't exist, and this is the power offered by a piece of theatre embedded in an educational context. Like Holt, the TIE movement was seeking to get children to think without penalty and to realize that not knowing does not equal stupidity. There are parallels here with Heathcote's work; she too talks about working in a 'no-penalty zone' and developed a whole system (the Mantle of the Expert) that enables children to trust in their own abilities and shrug off the label of ignorance. As Holt puts it:

We don't have to *make* human beings smart. They are born smart. All we have to do is *stop* doing the things that make them stupid. (Holt: 1964: 161)

Holt, crucially, goes on to remind us that just as we have no idea what the future will demand of us, we have no idea what we need to 'know' (Holt: 1964: 291–2). Many jobs that exist now did not exist in 1965 and the employment offered by the next fifty years will probably bear little resemblance to today's. Bruner addresses the same problem. There is so much 'knowledge' out there and we cannot hope to know it all (1996). Faced with this dilemma we either cram children with as much as we can and hope they find something useful to do with it, we select groups of children to train for certain economic roles or we empower them to learn what they need when they need it. There is a political aspect to this: the entrepreneurial classes will have their own agenda and want to determine exactly what children learn in order to fit into the world of work that they are predisposed to create. But in a fast changing world what is needed is wisdom adaptability, not knowledge intransigence: 'you may easily acquire knowledge and remain bare of wisdom' (Whitehead: 1932: 46).

For most TIE workers this pedagogical knowledge was acquired at second hand, and for some not at all at a cognitive level. If we look at the methodologies of TIE and undertake a comparison with key educational philosophers we will certainly see a congruence of approach but there is little evidence that, before SCYPT, such ideas were being systematically applied. There are, of course, exceptions to this generalization, where prime movers in TIE acquired a rigorous knowledge of political and/or pedagogic philosophy that guided their work. It seems that those who have really cared about educating the young were reaching the same destinations via alternative routes.

Paulo Freire

Freire's *Pedagogy of the Oppressed* was translated into English in 1972 and only slowly entered the consciousness of British educationalists. Indeed, for the TIE movement, the acquaintance with this key figure was gained through the work of Augusto Boal.

It is thus impossible to argue a strong link between Freire's ideas and TIE except in hindsight. (The only SCYPT journals that refer to his work directly were published in 1985 and 1988. One was merely a one-page article offering bullet points of some key aspects of Freire's ideas (*SCYPT*: 1989) though the other had offered a more substantial analysis of Freire's educational philosophy (Baldwin: 1988).) But when Freire states that, 'just as objective social reality exists not by chance, but as a product of human action, so it is not transformed by chance' (Freire: trans. Ramos: 1972a: 27), he is stating a truth that most TIE companies would endorse; they too were trying to empower the young to mould their world, 'to understand it in order to transform it' (Freire: 1972a: 29). The parallels continue with Freire's concept of 'co-intentional education' turning us all into 'permanent re-creators' (Freire: 1972a: 44) and he identifies the fact-based curriculum as anti-dialogical, a 'banking concept of education' (Freire: 1972a: 46), where teaching becomes 'an act of depositing' (Freire: 1972a: 45). In 1972 TIE was already struggling towards similar understandings and by 1992 the authors of the *SCYPT Manifesto* (see above) clearly had a familiarity with Freire's ideas. SCYPT companies, like Freire, recognized the 'historical vocation to be more fully human' (Freire: 1972a: 31) and that the liberation to do this comes through 'reflective participation' (Freire: 1972a: 41). In this utilization of reflection as a learning process we can discern parallels with Heathcote but also with Brecht. In order to strive for the change that TIE practitioners sought it would first be necessary to understand what *is*. Brecht invited his spectators to consider what *is* through the techniques of *Verfremdung*. Through this 'distancing' he wished us to be appalled by the reality and inspire us to seek change. For Freire too, reflection was a necessary preparation for action. Distance must be gained so that abstraction of the oppression can be identified (Freire: 1970). This objectification allows the knowable object (in TIE terms the theatrical event) to become an intermediary in gaining an understanding of the political reality. Both Brecht with *Verfremdung*, and Freire with his notion of codification, seek to offer us a means by which mediation with a socially constructed reality can take place. Freire calls for a codification of the contradictions of existence. He notes that education 'must necessarily represent situations familiar to the individuals whose thematics are being examined [in order to] arrive at a new perception' (Freire: 1972a: 86). This is what TIE seeks to do by employing the tropes of theatre. TIE writers and directors such as Pammenter, Vine, Yeoman, Gillham, Cooper and Bond were of central importance in bringing these ideas to TIE and helping devise programmes that would allow dialogic discourse within the theatre event. The best TIE work increasingly offered a view of the world as 'a reality in process' (Freire: 1972a: 56) that the pupils would be empowered to objectify and question. TIE wants pupils to think. It wants, with Freire, to dispose of the internalized belief that 'to achieve some satisfaction' they must accept the precept 'not to think' (Freire: 1972a: 124).

Augusto Boal

More direct contact with Freire's political analysis came to the TIE movement with the work of Boal, introduced to companies by Chris Vine[5] at SCYPT conference. Interestingly, similar ideas had been experimented with previously, and O'Toole (1992: 129) describes an unsatisfactory attempt in 1973 by Leeds TIE to involve a young audience to explore their own dilemmas in a workshop that seems to anticipate Forum Theatre. (The Forum approach, now too familiar to need much description, involves the presentation of a performance with a problematic theme that is deconstructed by suggestions from, and interventions by, the audience. It is popularly used in drama lessons as well as by TIE companies and later in health and development projects.) In Boal's own descriptions (1979) Forum Theatre was clearly a political tool for the working classes to identify and challenge their oppression, but in Britain it became more associated with personal decision-making (which, paradoxically, was where Boal's own work was to take him by 1995). In his reassessment of the work (Jackson & Vine (eds): 2013: 75), Vine notes the problems of eliciting responses without imposing the ideas of the 'Joker'.

Simultaneously the Joker (sometimes referred to as a 'difficultator' as opposed to a 'facilitator') must be prepared to challenge the audience's perceptions, problematize, and expose the 'inherent contradictions of the real world'. Vine goes on to describe how they sought to overcome these problems by encouraging the audience to reflect in groups, being challenged by each other rather than solely by the Joker. When I have seen this technique used, my concerns

FIGURE 3.1 *Augusto Boal creator of the Theatre of the Oppressed.* *Photo: Hugh Hill.*

have always been about 'who participates?' Whilst theoretically intervention is open to any member of the audience, without a very highly skilled Joker/facilitator most members of the audience can be left as observers of the ideas and talents of the more forthcoming. Even with a competent facilitator not all members of a group will have the chance to participate and there can be a tendency amongst those sidelined to view the work of their peers as egotistic rather than dialogic.

There are dangers even when sessions are run by a competent Joker and the outcomes are often therapeutic rather than transformational leaving 'the oppressed' feeling less, not more, empowered. Forum can be very effective at identifying inequities and oppressions but cannot contain empowerment to change social reality. If a group or individual is made aware of these oppressions they can be accepted, resisted politically or they can be ameliorated. An amelioration may be achieved if the 'oppressor' is brought to an understanding of their actions and that these actions are wrong. This will not usually be the case. In the hands of inexperienced Jokers bland resolutions may be accepted and enacted. 'The boss should give them better wages,' comes the suggestion. This is enacted, various arguments tried out, and the problem 'solved'. Of course, in the real world the oppressor is unlikely to accept this solution, so what is being offered? The oppressed are being offered a catharsis for their frustration but not a formula to negate the oppression. Most oppressors (drug dealer, violent husband, child abuser, multi-national corporation …) are not susceptible to arguments, however reasoned. Thus what can be offered by Forum is a range of tactics but with little attention paid to the strategy for societal change that underpins the oppressive behaviour. Forum can raise issues and identify problems but will rarely offer solutions and, as such, will tend to carry the subtextual message of acceptance tainted by the awareness of inequity. Participants could become resigned to situations rather than liberated from them.

Dorothy Heathcote

This is not the case with Dorothy Heathcote whose ideas (often mediated to us by Gavin Bolton) gave a sound structure to the participatory work of companies in the 1980s. Aspects of her methodology had become increasingly current amongst drama teachers but, through the offices of SCYPT, Geoff Gillham introduced her notions of 'authentic teaching' to the membership. We have already noted her observations on the use of role in TIE programmes and these ideas had been first set out in a highly influential article in *SCYPT Journal No. 9*, 'Signs (and Portents?)'. Here she interrogates the notion of 'signing' that occurs amongst all human beings and is part of the repertoire of the actor's skill. She points out that for the TIE actor there is an additional level of responsibility rooted in the educational purpose. When talking to participants an actor/teacher cannot allow themselves to 'sign' that they already know the answer. The role has to be flexible enough to give space for the children's interventions to be voiced and accepted. Teachers and actors have given permission to be stared at; children have not (Heathcote: 1982: 20), and TIE gives an opportunity to present the spectators with something to spectate; an 'other' (the actor). Here again we see that children are being allowed to not 'act', but to be protected into situations where they are feelingly involved whilst remaining securely objective. They can if they wish disagree.

Role 'establishes their *right* to oppose the teacher's power. No one loses face' (Heathcote: 1982: 23). Wagner (1979) records sessions which demonstrate clearly Heathcote's range of questioning and musing tones that can be used to engage and elicit response without leading, so that the children come to their own understanding of a situation – a Socratic approach in effect.

Another influential aspect of Heathcote's work was her insistence on 'reflection' – something she used extensively in her drama work. There is a natural drive in most theatrical events to move the narrative forward, but Heathcote was resolute in seeking out those spaces where the action could be arrested to give time to consider. This can be achieved in a variety of ways (see Heathcote: 1982: 25–6) but perhaps the most frequently used convention is that of 'depiction' where frozen moments in the drama can be analysed by the children in or out of role. This technique can be seen as a Brechtian moment of *gestus* with the added opportunity to think things through before re-engaging with the narrative. A further examination of this and other Heathcote practices will be offered in the case study of *Careless Talk* in Chapter Five. An aspect of Heathcote's work that will be raised at this point is the ability of drama and TIE to move from the 'particular to the universal'. This is described in Wagner (1979) and is the subject of a fully exampled article in Robinson's *Exploring Theatre and Education* (see Heathcote: 1980a). The basic concept is that in a drama lesson, or a piece of TIE, a particular circumstance is offered by the characters within the story. Through the processes of drama or TIE, the children are facilitated into contextualizing the events, the emotions and the relationships of what is happening in the drama construct at that moment to a more 'universal' observation of the human condition. We have already seen examples of this in the 'fascism' projects cited above, where the historic reality, the 'particular', of fascism and Nazism is 'universalized' to create an understanding of contemporary racism (and by extension any other range of human oppressions). For Heathcote the key to discovering this link is reflection. Byron describes the process thus:

> This dropping of a particular into the universal is the digestion process of the arts, which creates the opportunity for reflection which is what education is all about. (Byron: 1987: 11)

The children are thus starting from what they know (themselves and the role-situation in which they have been placed) and are empowered to build on that knowledge to reach a higher, universal understanding. This relates to Freire's 'dialectical movement of thought' (Freire: 1972a: 77) that uses 'decoding' to move from the 'abstract to the concrete'. The conceptual learning takes place as the learner moves 'from the part to the whole and then returns to the parts'. In this way the learner finds their place within the social construct and is equipped to challenge and 'decode it towards a new reality' (Freire: 1972a: 78).

Lev Vygotsky

Heathcote was aware of the work of Vygotsky and we can see elements of his ideas echoed in hers. Key TIE theorists, such as Gillham, McEntegart, Pammenter, Bennett, Vine, Yeoman and others, accessed his ideas in the 1980s. Vygotsky had inherited some of his thinking from Piaget but was critical of Piaget's concentration on the child's personal development without taking sufficient note of the wider social contexts that influenced it. (See also Bruner: 1972, 1992 and 1996). Where Vygotsky has proved particularly relevant to drama and TIE is with his 'Zone of Proximal Development' (ZPD) and what became referred to as 'scaffolding' of a child's learning. The ZPD is the moment in learning where a child's spontaneous concerns are confronted with adult systematized reasoning to produce a learning environment. A child, at any point, has acquired some knowledge, but there are areas of learning which, at this stage in his or her development, are unobtainable. Between these two, (the ZPD) is a potential area of understanding that they can attain with the help of others who are able to offer scaffolding to their learning – the idea being that once mastered, this scaffolding can be removed:

> For each subject of instruction, there is a period when its influence is most fruitful because the child is most receptive to it. (Vygotsky: 1986: 189)

This dialogic learning requires the 'teacher' to be aware of the child's needs, where they are developmentally and what they might achieve with support. In TIE terms, what Vygotsky is offering is an approach to practice: children have some knowledge and are scaffolded by the theatrical context and the relationship with the characters to heighten their knowledge and build their understanding. Thus, I contend, ZPD offers a systematized framework akin to Heathcote's concept of moving from the 'particular to the universal'. Vygotsky argues that Piaget sees knowledge as a mere product of thought without consideration of 'the practical confrontation with reality' (Vygotsky: 1986: 52). The ability of drama to introduce this element into the classroom is clearly key to the enthusiasm with which later practitioners were to view him. As Harry Daniels pointed out in his article in the *NATD Journal* in 2004, Vygotsky thought that ZPD had the power to transform society by its focus on a child's potential rather than their previously demonstrated achievements (Daniels: 2004: 18). Further, ZPD 'calls on teachers to select items for instruction which are commensurate with active participation in the social world' (Daniels: 2004: 21).

Tag McEntegart has also offered an analysis of how Vygotsky helped codify the use of play in education. She points out (1981: 42) that play is, for the child, a way of accessing experience otherwise not available. The structured 'play' of the TIE programme works in a similar way. The child is allowed an imaginative exploration of the word without being bound by the same rules and dangers that would otherwise pertain. Pam Schweitzer succinctly defines this process thus:

> I hear, I forget; I see, I remember; I do, I understand. (Schweitzer: 1980: 13)

Importantly for the teacher, in play the child finds a desire to achieve and is able to recognize consciously his or her own actions. This distancing is the source of abstract thought (McEntegart: 1981: 46). McEntegart goes on to consider the implications of Vygotsky's ideas for theatre and notes that there is a commonality of purpose with education since theatre also seeks to communicate and uncover meaning and has the potential 'to assist the mental development of its audiences' (McEntegart: 1981: 47). Theatre contains symbols for interpretation and, together with the pedagogic context offered by TIE, they become powerful tools in understanding the personal, social and political worlds of the child. Theatre has the ability to make obvious the relationships between real and imagined situations and it becomes a pivot to trigger insights and understandings. Further, TIE is specifically constructed to enhance those relationships and to enable children to climb within the scaffold without endangering their emotional lives. In most theatre the audience, though physically passive, are actually the 'play-ers', playing with the ideas presented before them and being led to an understanding possibly separate from the actions depicted. When one considers that TIE will often involve children inside the action as participants, *and* outside as audience/play-ers, then the possibility for a profound learning experience becomes clear.

Jerome Bruner

Bruner's *Towards a Theory of Instruction* was first published in 1966 and thus his ideas have been around for almost as long as the precepts of TIE. Again there seems to be a congruence of TIE instincts and the theory that was published later that underpins and validates the work. Bruner argues that growth implies the ability to respond independently to a stimulus in a way that goes beyond mere reaction and to internalize events so that the child is enabled to extrapolate beyond the immediate (Bruner: 1992: 5). This is reminiscent of ZPD and the facilitation of accessing universals via the particular. He goes on:

> *Intellectual development is marked by increasing capacity to deal with several alternatives simultaneously* .... There is a great distance indeed between the one-track mind of the infant and the ten-years-old's ability to deal with an extraordinary complex world. (Bruner: 1992: 6)

This is the territory on which TIE increasingly worked – freeing up children's maturing cognition. This, Bruner notes, occurs not incrementally but more frequently in a series of steps and spurts. The impetus will come from an arousal of curiosity. We have all had those experiences when suddenly a stimulus, perhaps theatrical, will spark an insight. TIE is specifically constructed to offer a framework for that mental growth to take place: 'knowing is a process, not a product' (Bruner: 1992: 72).

Bruner's fundamental enquiry into education has entered the philosophic world of TIE via a few acolytes, and the concerns Bruner raises have been central to the construction of TIE programmes. These fundamental questions include:

What is human about human beings?
How did they get that way?
How can they be made more so? (Bruner: 1992: 74)

Bruner himself stresses the need to get 'children to actively participate in the process of learning – as players rather than spectators' (Bruner: 1992: 95). Of course, in TIE children are empowered to both spectate and participate and to adopt behaviours outside their intrinsic self and thus to explore new ways of being. In Bruner's terms, 'situations have a demand value' which allows for experimentation in, what we might call, participatory 'role'. He is rightly critical (Bruner: 1992: 160) of elements of the progressive education movement that based knowledge acquisition on the domestic banalities of what the children already had experienced. I like to think that he would be highly impressed by the experiences that are offered to children through exposure to high quality TIE. Like Holt, he recognizes that 'facts' can never be enough since we don't know what we need to know. It is a confusion that exists in the National Curriculum, where knowledge of 'theatre' is based on a knowledge of plays and techniques, and the understanding of theatre as a gateway to self-analysis and empathetic learning is neglected (probably because it is harder to assess).

This chapter has attempted to show some ways in which TIE programmes can work through participation and how SCYPT became a conduit for theoretical ideas from drama practitioners and from education philosophers. From the earliest TIE manifestations there has been an attempt to offer 'transformational' rather than 'reproductive' learning though these terms were not then being used. The pedagogic ideas absorbed seemed to have been latent within TIE practice but were shaped and emboldened by overt exposure to theory. What seems clear it that there is a common understanding amongst these educational philosophers and the TIE of the 1970s and 1980s that dialectical thinking is central to authentic education. For TIE, theatre is the catalyst for the emotional engagement that is a pre-requisite to an understanding of the human condition. TIE, through the employment of 'play' as an objective art form as well as a subjective 'felt' event, offers children the dialectic and dialogic framework through which to be scaffolded into a higher level of understanding of the world and themselves within the world. Without this critical theory, Bruner would argue, humanness itself is under threat, for what makes us human is our ability to envisage a future and to engage with the capacity for change. Enquiry becomes a political act and education that questions the hegemony, such as TIE, is seen as a political threat.

Notes

1 A fuller definition of all these terms can be found in Jackson and Vine (2013: 10–14).
2 For description of this project see O'Toole (1992: 79), Jackson and Vine (2013: 88–9).
3 Full descriptions of these three projects can be found in *SCYPT Journal No. 1*: 3–15.
4 A list can be found at http://theatrefutures.org.uk/theatre-for-young-audiences-centre/archive-resources/scypt-journals-database/
5 For a full description of Vine's work at Greenwich Young People's Theatre on Boal, see Jackson and Vine (2013: 66ff).

CHAPTER FOUR

The Education Debate and the Era of ERA

I have argued that TIE was born out of an expectation of social reform, an implicit trust in progressive education ideas and the hope for prosperity after fifty years of thwarted aspirations. In disentangling these roots, we can see that the emergence of TIE in the mid-1960s was extremely fortuitous. It is improbable that such an education/theatre hybrid would have emerged without all three conditions being present. However, the post-War consensus was just consensus, and as memories of deprivation faded and a Gramscian 'cultural hegemony' emerged, those on the orthodox political right felt able to reassert themselves. When the economic situation soured in the mid-1970s it was to be the education system, specifically 'radical' teachers and their 'child-centred' approaches, which was to take most of the blame. TIE companies (who were clearly part of this radicalism) were to be one of the main casualties when ERA 1988 came into force.

Funding

Funding for TIE developed in a variety of ways. The most common source of early funding was via a main theatre to which the companies were attached. This followed an Arts Council report of 1966 that for the first time recommended that theatre for young people (including TIE) should come within the scope of Arts Council support. Theatre for Children (TfC) (which I am differentiating from TIE) had previously relied almost entirely on box office receipts and charitable grants. From this impoverishment would follow poor wages and often a concomitant lack of quality. The assertion of the 'value of theatre work for young people, including TIE, and the paramount need to subsidize it if there were to be any hope of it flourishing, experimenting, developing and gaining the status it deserved' (Jackson & Vine (eds): 2013: 25) was a strong encouragement to theatres and Local Education Authorities to take TIE seriously and not just as an additional revenue stream. With the legitimization of TIE through state support,[1] local government was more inclined to get involved, though often this would be, in the early days, through provision of premises or running costs. Gradually, as the work of TIE companies became more embedded in the arts and education systems, a pattern evolved of 'match funding'. For example, Leeds TIE received a grant from the Local Authority in 1970, of £4,000 rising to £12,500 by 1976. The Arts Council matched this investment with £5,000 rising to nearly £15,000 in the same period (Redington: 1983: 96). This approach was to prove a major strength when companies came under pressure because of economic austerity; if either party withdrew funding the actual loss to the community was doubled. TIE was in a stronger financial situation than many alternative or community touring groups for this reason.

   Once the principle of supporting YPT and TIE had been established the Arts Council of Great Britain (ACGB) reviewed its policy and brought this area of work within the remit of its general Drama Panel after 1971. Where companies were attached to a main house monies were made part of the main house subsidy. The danger that the theatres would absorb the TIE funding into their own work was largely avoided by the ACGB reducing funds if TIE work was omitted from applications. Indeed, the confidence that came with financial security and reputation led some companies to become independent. As non-profit-making charities or limited companies, they could still hope for support from the ACGB and the LEAs but with more control over their work. However, this did not protect them from the inflationary pressures of the late 1970s and many were obliged to seek additional funding from other sources.

One such source was to take advantage of government 'job creation' schemes. Action PIE was one such company, set up in Cardiff by John Prior in 1978. Such state schemes were regarded by the left as designed to massage unemployment figures rather than offer real employment and thus the creation of Action PIE caused some problems for radical members of SCYPT. The company thrived until 1985 by which time Geoff Gillham was director and its politics became less palatable to funders. The situation in Wales, in fact, offers a slightly different context of funding, reflecting the needs of a predominantly rural country. Some companies were attached to a main house but most occupied premises supplied by Local Authorities. More importantly, in the 1970s, the Welsh Arts Council developed a policy of having a TIE company in each of the eight counties of Wales. Each also had a touring community theatre brief and thus fulfilled two objectives.

The implicitly political nature of TIE

Thus arts funders and education authorities saw TIE, from their different but complementary positions, as supportive of their own agendas. For the Arts Councils and theatres, it was a way of engaging young people with performance art forms and creating audiences for the future. For LEAs it fulfilled the need for an arts curriculum whilst engaging children in what seemed to be an attractive way of learning. There were few in either camp that really recognized the educational critique that was becoming the backbone of the work. Few teachers, let alone arts or government bureaucrats, understood the pedagogy at work. Bennett emphasizes that TIE work was not didactic, but it still ran the danger of being perceived as such, even though 'the aim was to empower – not to indoctrinate' (Bennett: 2005: 20). We come once again to the central question of the purpose of education – to develop individuals to the fullest extent of which they are capable? Or to socialize them to fit into the existing requirements of current economic structures? Most TIE companies would have argued that their work involved 'empowering young people' and 'giving them tools to take control of their lives'. Even teachers often had little comprehension of the theoretical processes at work, regarding the TIE visits as an educational sweetener, a useful visual aid or as predominantly a performance event.

By the end of the 1970s, the cultural hegemony of consumerism and corporatism had become consolidated and pressure developed for an education that served these new values. Robinson (1980: 170–1) identifies the function of theatre as presenting symbols for interrogation rather than merely communicating and points out that the whole purpose of social education is to help children 'understand and reflect on the social values which are pressing on them, and their part in the dialectics of change'. These were beliefs shared by TIE but possibly not by those *funding* TIE. The economic crises of the 1970s had shifted the argument; the nature and purpose of education had come under scrutiny as never before.

With hindsight it is possible to detect a distinct shift to the right in British politics through the 1970s. British voters swung between electing Labour and Conservative governments against a backdrop of the Oil Crisis of 1973, the Miners' Strike of 1974 and the IMF intervention in 1976 (that imposed a move away from interventionist social policies). There was little now to choose between the political philosophies of the main parties and, as we have seen, education and the 'unreasonable' expectations of the working class became the scapegoats for Britain's declining status. Though most of the problems with British industry were more to do with prolonged under-investment, it is certainly true that working-class aspirations had mutated into the bourgeois cultural hegemony predicted by Gramsci in the 1930s.

Thus the potentially socialist working classes that emerged from the Second World War had been turned into consumerist seekers-after bourgeois values. The Tripartite Education System was not delivering the transition to middle-class egalitarianism that most believed was the summit of expectation and the unruly behaviour of the young was blamed variously on cinema, television, popular music and (an easier target) education.

A useful starting point to consider this re-evaluation is the 'Black Paper on Education' that was written in 1969, a time of much social disruption:

Influenced by a variety of psychologists from Freud to Piaget, as well as by educational pioneers from Froebel onwards ... schools have increasingly swung away from the notion ... that education exists to fit certain sorts of people for certain sorts of jobs ... to the idea that people should develop in their own way at their own pace. (Cox & Dyson: 1969: 6)

The socializing approach lauded in the Black Papers found greater favour as economic troubles grew. Thatcher, as Education Minister under Heath, had in 1970 tried to stop the transition to a Comprehensive System and retain selection. However, as most Local Authorities' plans were well advanced this had little effect and by 1975 most areas of Britain had abandoned the Tripartite System and the 11+ examination. Attacks on Comprehensives continued from the right with middle classes fearing the loss of preference that came with a Grammar School education.

The Great Education Debate

By 1976 the Labour prime minister Jim Callaghan in a speech at Ruskin College felt impelled to invite the nation to embark on a 'Great Debate' about education. This led to a new consensus that a centralized, functionalist response to economic imperatives was required. When, three years later, after further industrial troubles, Thatcher's Conservatives were elected, there could be little doubt that things would change. The middle and ruling classes had asserted their right to be protected from trade unions, strikes, declining social values and from an education system that failed to deliver advantage to their children. None of the social reforms were repealed, but attention was immediately paid to trade union 'abuse' of power and then to educational reform. In a pattern that has been much repeated since, education was made the scapegoat for failed socio-economic policies.

Having removed the requirement to introduce Comprehensives, Thatcher went on to allocate scholarships to pay for pupils to attend private schools. In 1984, a combined examination system was introduced. General Certificates of Secondary Education (GCSEs) replaced 'O' Levels and the CSEs (which had been introduced in 1964 as examination qualifications for Secondary Modern Schools). In 1986, the governance of schools was changed to give more power to parents (thus ensuring a middle class hegemony). Such reforms signalled the start of the biggest educational change since the War.

The Education Reform Act

ERA is historically significant because it represents the
culmination of a break with the consensus politics of education.
(Lawton: 1992: 59)

For TIE, ERA represented an attack on the pedagogy, funding,
relationships with schools and content of the work, both contextual
and thematic. There were many aspects to ERA and I will mention
here only those that had a direct impact on the work of TIE companies.
Readers may wish to refer to Geoff Readman's useful summary of
ERA's main requirements and implications (in Jackson: 1993: 273).

Firstly were the reforms that concerned the governance of
schools. If they wished, schools would be enabled to 'opt out' of the
control of the LEA. Even if schools chose to remain within the LEA,
they would have new governing bodies to which would be delegated
funding and recruitment procedures. The aim was clearly to keep
education out of the hands of any left-wing local authorities, but
there was a side effect on TIE funding. In most cases TIE companies
had been able to offer their programmes to schools at no or low
cost; funding of peripatetic services like TIE had previously been
'top-sliced' to provide unified services throughout the area. Under
the Local Management of Schools (LMS), monies were delegated so
that schools could make purchasing decisions – including whether
to buy-in TIE. But a TIE company can only function if a guaranteed
level of funding can be achieved; if only 60 per cent of schools decide
to take a particular project then, under the new system, they would
lose 40 per cent of their education revenue (and an additional 40
per cent of matched Arts Council funding). The possible outcomes
were that companies would have to ensure that all schools wanted
their 'product' (which forced a market judgement on the choice of
material), or they would have to charge schools (which would lead
to pressures to 'perform' to large audiences rather than undertake
participatory work). Given the misunderstanding of TIE that
existed amongst head teachers, parents and governors, the choice
between buying new textbooks or 'having a theatre group in to do a
play' would be straightforward. The distasteful option of charging
schools (i.e. the children) would be discriminatory in favour of
wealthier catchments. Some visionary (or cunning) drama advisors
found ways to circumnavigate this financial challenge. John

Greatorex, in Powys, managed to get the budget for Theatr Powys transferred from the Education to the Community department thus protecting the company for the next twenty years.

Other aspects of ERA would also clearly begin the process of an internal market in education. Schools were encouraged to compete for pupils through a voucher scheme that rewarded numbers enrolled. School catchment areas were abolished, again encouraging schools to market themselves to middle-class parents (with promises of good discipline and examination results) and leaving other schools to become underfunded and socially segregated. For the first time, market forces were deliberately introduced into education.

The National Curriculum

The most significant change, however, was the introduction for the first time in British schools of a National Curriculum. In brief, the National Curriculum set up tested attainment targets at ages 7, 11, 14 and 16 years. There were four accompanying Key Stages and for each stage there was a list of Learning Objectives (LOs) attached to the foundation subjects: Maths, Science, English, Modern Languages, Geography, History, Technology, Art, Music (but not Drama!), Physical Education and Religious Education. Many TIE companies tried to produce teaching packs that cross-referenced the content of their programmes to the LOs for a variety of subjects, hoping to keep the teachers onside and, indeed, lessen their burden by offering a cross-curriculum approach. For others such a compromise with Thatcher's behemoth was anathema. To them, this rewriting of educational purpose was the embodiment of Freire's warning that 'to the oppressor consciousness, the humanization of "others", of the people, appears as subversion, not as the pursuit of full humanity' (Freire: 1972a: 35). David Davis is clear about the political motive behind the exclusion of Drama from the new curriculum:

> It is no accident that drama is not alongside music and art in the foundation subjects. Drama provides the clearest opportunity in the education system for young people to actively investigate the truth of their lives and the world around them in a social, co-operative, feeling way. (Davis: 1988, reprinted 2008: 11)

The view from her Majesty's Inspectorate of Schools was somewhat different:

> To date few companies have attempted to relate the levels and targets of attainment or the programme of study within the national curriculum to their work, but there is an increasing awareness of the potential usefulness of such a process for both company and school. (HMI: 1989: 5)

This 'potential usefulness' involved creating curriculum-orientated work in order to survive in this brave new utilitarian world.

There was one aspect of the National Curriculum's demands that seemed to offer some hope to TIE. References to drama and theatre in the Curriculum are either in terms of their ability to help with verbal and social skills or, in the case of theatre, as an opportunity to learn about production techniques, acting as a craft, and developing skills of analytical criticism to 'understand the educational, cultural and social purposes of drama' (Department of Education and Science: 1989: 2). A visit from the TIE company would facilitate the fulfilment of these LOs. The ACGB was content to go along with this approach, clearly seeing drama in schools the same as teaching theatre:

> Drama in schools offers the same synthesis of skills, creativity and knowledge that might be expected of any other arts subject. The drama curriculum should enable pupils to:
>
> • experience, understand and use creatively dramatic concepts, forms and techniques
>
> • experiment and gain confidence in modes of performance
>
> • encounter a wide range of dramatic materials and texts
>
> • experience and learn about the nature of drama in different periods and cultures
>
> • have access to a wide range of live theatre. (ACGB: 1992: 10)

Rather than offering hope, this was a threat to TIE. Despite nearly twenty-five years of praxis, clearly neither the educational nor the arts purse-holders understood what they had been paying for. It would become increasingly difficult for TIE to argue its case from a philosophical basis in this choice-orientated marketplace. Whether the 'overlooking' of drama in the curriculum is the result of ignorance of its value or fear of its liberating outcomes will depend upon one's political analysis. It is interesting to note, however, that a similar process is happening in the United States:

> As personnel move or retire and funding shifts to other priorities, theatre education is losing ground. Some states are not offering or discontinuing certification of theatre teachers. Despite national and state standards in the arts, theatre as an academic subject is not mandated to be taught, and, in fact, is a classroom subject rarely offered in many states. (Lazarus: 2012: 31)

Some teachers would continue to welcome companies into the schools but, again, the pressure would be to offer performance for large audiences followed by workshops that explored 'how it was done'. This would not be an attractive option for the increasingly pedagogically sophisticated companies of the early nineties. In any case, the decision about whether to pay for a TIE company would be in the hands of head teachers and governors who had never seen TIE at work. As we will see this was to lead to major changes in the nature and format of TIE programmes, though excellence was still to be found through the next twenty-five years to the present.

To end this chapter, I will draw the reader's attention to SCYPT's response to the National Curriculum. In 1992 it offered its own vision:

> Children and young people must know themselves as natural beings; as historical beings; as social beings; as technological beings; as creative beings; as thinking beings. A curriculum that offered materials and knowledge to the young to explore and explain to themselves the diversity and complexity of mankind, would feel the innate capacities and questions that spontaneously emerge out of the experience of living in the world – this is what is needed.
>
> It would be a curriculum for living on the planet – not a *National* Curriculum.
>
> It would be a curriculum for living. (*SCYPT Manifesto* 1992, reprinted in *The Ground on Which We Stand*, 1995: 9)

The introduction of the National Curriculum and the wider implications of ERA were to have a profound effect on the nature and the practice of TIE. It would be presumptuous to assume that these reactionary educational reforms were specifically designed as an attack on TIE, on DIE or even that they were a consciously targeted attempt to corral education into a narrow political schematic. However, implicitly this is what was to happen. The concept of education as an opportunity for children to flourish was subsumed within the need for specific economic roles to be filled. The driver behind this was a hegemonic belief that education is the production line where the labour force of tomorrow is manufactured and nothing more. This clearly suits the traditions and instincts of economic planners, but it closes off radical considerations by making inquiry irrelevant. ERA represented a reversal of the developing ideas about the nature of education that had gained some traction after the Second World War. It was a bold placing of class values at the centre of the educational system that, by proscribing dialogism and prescribing historicism and positivism, was implicitly designed to entrench power in its traditional homelands of wealth and privilege: 'there is a link between knowledge, power and domination' (Giroux: 1997: 43). This audacious attack on authentic education was to be accepted and continued by future Labour governments and is still being extended twenty-five years later. Education has become a commodity. On the face of it, it seems paradoxical to pull curriculum content to the political centre whilst transferring funding to the end providers but there is a logic at work here. If the content of the delivery is sufficiently curriculum-bound, then it becomes possible to give a faux freedom to schools to work within that defined sphere of activity. The assumption is that there is no place for local concerns, local interests or teachers' enthusiasms within the curriculum. This is now accepted; the National Curriculum (with some variations for the home nations) is suitable for all children and there is no need for the policymakers and subject advisors who used to populate County Hall.[2] Money is saved, educational experience is equalized and all students are supposedly uniformly prepared for the world of global economics to which they will be exposed.

TIE had become a flagship for an authentic education that involved scaffolding knowledge for children between what they know and what they are capable of knowing. The medium for this scaffold was theatre, role and a feeling response to objectively placed dilemmas. The commoditization of education almost eliminates the possibility of working in this way. In later chapters I will consider the longer-term effects of ERA, but first I wish to consider examples of the fruits of TIE that were being produced at the time that the new regulations were coming into force.

Notes

1   The Arts Councils in Britain receive a block grant from central government that they distribute according to their own policies. Whilst not totally preventing political interference, the system does offer a certain degree of 'arm's length' security.
2   Since 2011, there has been a shift in this policy with the expansion of 'Academy' schools and 'Free Schools'. These will be described in a later chapter but, ironically, are designed to meet parental choices whilst offering a 'broad curriculum' – not necessarily the National Curriculum.

Afterword

Warwick Dobson

Wooster is, I think, correct to begin his history of the TIE movement by emphasizing the significance of the political watershed that followed the Second World War. Historically, of course, a national system of public education (and, in particular, the education of the working-class) has always posed serious problems for the ruling-class and for the state.

In the decade preceding the passing of the 1870 Education Act, which established the framework for the schooling of all children between the ages of 5 and 13, Dr. James Kay-Shuttleworth (a former Secretary to the Committee of the Privy Council on Education and, subsequently, First Secretary of the Board of Education) warned 'how much the law needs the support of sound economic opinions and higher moral principles among certain classes of workmen' (Kay-Shuttleworth 1873 quoted in Simon: 1974: 357). Six years earlier, he had noted the critical importance of 'promoting the diffusion of that knowledge among the working classes which tends ... to promote the security of property and the maintenance of public order' (Kay-Shuttleworth reprinted 1973: 232). Here then, in the 1860s, we find a former leading civil servant describing one of the twin pillars upon which the new educational system was to be built: the reconciliation of the population to the class divisions of capitalist society.

In 1895, the *Report of the Commission on Secondary Education* claimed that education was not simply the dissemination of knowledge, but 'a process of intellectual training and personal discipline conducted with special regard to the profession or trade to be followed' (Ministry of Education: 1895: 135–6). This invocation of economic necessity established the second pillar upon which this same educational system was built: the provision of a labour force to meet the needs of the economy.

However, a different view of the purposes of education had been in circulation since the late eighteenth-century; and, in 1824, William Thompson published *An Enquiry into the Principles of the Distribution of Wealth most conducive to Human Happiness* in which he saw education as a means of creating a just society. It was, he argued, in the interest of every community, 'to see things as they really are, the real qualities and relations of physical objects, real facts and the consequences of actions, it is their interest to be taught *nothing but the truth*' (my italics) (Thompson 1824 quoted in Simon: 1974: 208). The provision of education for the working-class was also the subject of debate amongst radical reformers throughout the period leading up to the publication of the People's Charter in 1838. Some Chartists saw advantages in collaborating with middle-class reformers on matters relating to education; whereas George Julian Harney insisted on the indissoluble link between the political struggle for universal suffrage and the kind of education necessary for the working-class.

The 1944 Education Act was passed as the Second World War drew to a close. This legislation changed the face of the secondary education system, establishing the Tripartite System, and making schooling free for all children up to the age of 15. The impetus for this reform was the very real fear of the ruling-class that working-class men returning from the war, trained in the use of weapons, posed a serious threat to the economic stability of the nation and the security of the state. Despite the spirit of the act, the twin pillars stood as firm as ever.

The next twenty years saw *some* liberal reforms in education, but it should be noted that the advances made during these years were of an extremely limited nature, and Thatcher's Conservative government, elected in 1979, promptly set about rolling back these gains. Given this political background, it is astonishing that the TIE movement was able to establish itself and consolidate its position during the twenty-five years between the first experiments in the mid-sixties and the passing of the reactionary ERA of 1988.

The real strength of TIE was that it took up the substance of the concerns expressed by the nineteenth-century radicals: in particular, Thompson's call for an education that teaches the young to 'see things as they really are'; and Harley's recognition that politics and education are inextricably intertwined. The *SCYPT Manifesto* reiterated both of these points: stating that one of the most pressing needs of young people is for 'a knowledge about the world and themselves in it' (*SCYPT Manifesto* 1992, reprinted in *The Ground on Which We Stand*: 1995: 4); the 'End Piece' in the same publication draws attention to the fact that the decimation of TIE is part of a broader pattern of political attacks 'on all publicly provided services' (*SCYPT Manifesto*: 1992: 30).

Wooster well understands that any historical account of the TIE movement must acknowledge the enormous significance of SCYPT; and, as Ian Yeoman states, 'the founding of SCYPT was the practical recognition of the necessity for a social, national and international struggle for theory' (Yeoman: 1994: 46). It was the development of SCYPT as a committed, rigorous and dynamic professional organization that created the conditions for the enrichment of the practice of TIE. In any discussion of SCYPT, it has become the tiresome custom to exaggerate the organization's connection with the Workers' Revolutionary Party. Whilst it is true that *some* leading members of SCYPT shared an affiliation with the WRP, this tendency diminishes, devalues and distorts the very real advances that the organization fostered in the work of its member companies.

During the course of the 1980's, SCYPT companies divided into two camps. The first might be characterized as those espousing an issue-based approach; and the second, those committed to a concept-based approach. At the heart of this division is a fundamental philosophical difference; the former begins from an idealist position, the latter from materialism. Issue-based theatre derives from the single-issue politics that were so pervasive during that decade. This approach is idealist because it begins with human consciousness, and concerns itself with morality (right and wrong) and values (whose values?). These programmes aim to alter students' attitudes (e.g. racism is a bad thing, be accepting of difference); the amendment of racist tendencies makes the world more tolerable. Students are presented with the company's interpretation of the world and are encouraged to embrace it.

The materialist approach begins not with human consciousness, but with the material world. It is concerned primarily with what *is* (in Thompson's words, seeing things 'as they really are'). This is not straightforward. Ideology, which seeks to reproduce in human subjects the ruling ideas of capitalism, functions to mystify. It does this by making it difficult to distinguish between the appearance and essence of phenomena. Concept-based theatre seeks to help students penetrate the appearance of an idea in order to understand its essence. An exploration of the concept of prejudice, and where its roots might lie, provides a useful counter-example to the kind of anti-racist programmes that were so popular in the eighties. Here, the object is not to *amend* racist attitudes; but to enable students to look beneath the surface of prejudice to *understand* how it serves the interests of the state.

This difference of approach is not a parochial example of educational in-fighting; rather, it represents a fundamental philosophical difference between two orientations within SCYPT. The most lucid account of this difference remains Geoff Gillham's defence of Cockpit TIE's programme, *The Pitcher Plant* (Gillham in *SCYPT Journal 13*: 44–56). Gillham, of course, well understood how durable the twin pillars are. That is why he spent his life fighting for a pedagogy that would offer young people knowledge that would help them to 'explore and explain to themselves the diversity and complexity of humankind' (*SCYPT Manifesto*: reprinted 1995: 9). He knew that what young people need is not a National Curriculum, as enshrined within the provisions of the 1989 ERA, but a Curriculum for Living that has two cardinal orientations: 'the orientation to understand the objective laws of nature' and 'the orientation to understanding ourselves'; the synthesis of these two orientations helps students understand 'the relationship between human beings (ourselves, society) and the objective laws of nature' (Gillham: 1999: 49). The need for a Curriculum for Living remains as pressing as ever.

PART TWO
Fruits

CHAPTER FIVE

Case Study: *Careless Talk*

To clarify and demonstrate pre-ERA approaches I will consider *Careless Talk*, a participatory project devised in 1986 by Theatr Powys, based in rural Wales. This was a full-day project, designed for one class of about thirty children. The target age group was top juniors (10 and 11 year olds). The performance and workshop techniques were devised by the company: Tessa Gearing, Dave Lynn, Carol McGuigan and Louise Osborn (who also directed). For several years, the company had been developing work using Heathcote's approaches. The subject of the programme, the Second World War , was selected by the company in consultation with schools. The children had been studying the War and had a framework of knowledge that they were able to bring to the programme.

The story

Mother, son and daughter live on a family farm. As a farmer, the son (Gethin) is excused military service; farming is a 'reserved occupation'. The daughter (Lizzie) is still at school. To this school, and to Lizzie's house, comes Kathleen, evacuated to the safety of the Welsh countryside from Liverpool. Gethin has been caught up in the patriotic fervour and has enlisted despite his mother's objections. Kathleen finds it difficult to settle in to her new surroundings and, in a series of flashbacks, we see the closeness of her relationship with her grandfather. Later in the story, the grandfather is killed in a bombing raid leaving her desperate with grief. Gethin returns from the war disillusioned, confused and bitter about what he has seen and done.

The themes of the programme

- War. Why we go to war. Where loyalties begin and end. Patriotism.

- Friendship. What makes friends?

- Teasing and Bullying. The relationship between this and ...

- ... Racism, Fascism, Nazism. The drive to feel powerful at someone else's expense.

- Death, loss, coping with bereavement. Empathy.

- Responsibility as friends, as citizens, as siblings, as parents and as children of parents.

In working through selected sections of the programme, I aim to explicate the techniques and the sensitivity with which they are being applied. Teachers were expecting (and received) a dramatic presentation with a good deal of contextualized historical information, but the themes above additionally address questions about the nature of education, specifically: why do we learn history? From the classroom teacher and research with their families, children were gaining factual knowledge, but authentic education is more ambitious and seeks to understand events. What is there in human nature that makes us resort to confrontation and violence? Children are not expert at these things, but they are expert at being children. It is within the power of a TIE programme to harness that expertise and allow a melding of their understanding of human motivations, with those they can observe in the adults who take citizens to war. They will be working in Vygotsky's ZPD where they will be allowed to connect their own knowledge, understanding and intuition about the world with the complex realities of international conflict. In Heathcote's terms, they will be being enabled to connect an understanding of a particular issue played out before and by them, with an understanding of the universals contained within that particular moment.

The initial session takes place in the classroom where the children meet the company members and tell them about the schoolwork they have been doing on the Second World War. The children wear name badges and this enables the actor/teachers to quickly develop an informal rapport. The lead facilitator introduces the project. The children will be told a story about a farm during the War. A photograph album helps illustrate her introduction. Many of the children themselves live on farms and the buildings look both quaint and familiar. Sometimes lively discussion breaks out discussing life on a farm in 1939, for the children have been encouraged to talk to their grandparents about life in the 'olden days'. The facilitator takes the children through photographs which they can see are of the actors standing in front of them and that 'there are only four of us and we will be being different people in the story. Do you know what I mean by that?' The children know very well. Not only have they seen Theatr Powys before, but in their own play they too will be different people as the game requires. The children are invited to speculate about the people in the album, but this is not a guessing game with right and wrong answers. The facilitator is inviting ideas so that the children invest in finding out whilst bringing their own knowledge to the process. Heightened mystery is also introduced by one photograph at the end of the album, of previously unseen characters who resemble none of the actors. The photograph is dog-eared and has some German writing on it. This, and all the other mysteries of the album, sets up expectation and anticipation. There is so much for the children to help find out! The facilitator, taking a deep breath and with a tone of genuine enquiry asks, 'we thought that an exciting way of finding out would be for you (she pauses – perhaps this is too much to ask) to come back in time with us to 1939 and actually be in the story with us'. The children are already assenting but she goes on:

> We wondered if you would like to be the schoolchildren who were in Mrs Evans' class at the school in the village where Lizzie and Gethin live. Would you like to do that?

The excitement is clear and many are already on their feet but the facilitator adds a word of warning:

Sometimes in the day the story is quite sad. But don't worry, it's quite alright to cry if you want to. If you feel sad you can always come and sit by me and we can stop the story.

There are several important things going on here. The first is that a *contract* is being made with the child that has only emerged after a period of *edging in*. Should any child be reluctant to 'sign' the contract, they would be invited to stay on the periphery with the teacher and to join in when they felt able. Secondly, the children have *not* been invited to act or perform; they have been invited to 'be the children in the class'. Additionally, the children are alerted to the fact that some scenes will be sad and their responses to that are validated. For the children this creates a frisson of anticipation. They have difficult and exciting work to do and a final word from the facilitator confirms this:

During the day we will be stopping the story to see what we have found out so far – like detective work.

As the children leave the classroom for the hall, the facilitator reminds them that their teacher in 1939 will be very strict. When she says 'good morning' to them they will be expected to reply 'Good morning Mrs Evans' and stand with backs straight until invited to sit down. A useful control device is thus introduced which is both historically accurate and will give the children a 'way in' to their role from the outset.

On arriving in the hall they are greeted by Lizzie, 'a fellow pupil' (an actor/teacher in period costume) and she greets them as friends, talking to them about the recent summer vacation, about her brother, Gethin (who has a big secret!), and tells them about the den in the hayloft. The excitement is interrupted by the arrival of Mrs Evans and, taking their cue from Lizzie, the children immediately become quiet and respond to her 'good morning' as previously primed. The schoolroom is dominated by a blackboard, a map of Europe and a period radio. Mrs Evans looks severe, wears spectacles and carries a cane. Throughout the next session the actor/teacher playing Mrs Evans has to be alert to what Heathcote calls 'the social health' of the group so that she can push their role-engagement as fully as possible without causing fear or embarrassment. It is a development of the approach that all actors have to take – to be another character whilst remaining in control. Janice Jarvis, in an interview about acting in TIE, puts it thus:

> Both aspects of my brain have to be functioning very acutely in order to maintain both the right level of reality of the character, **and** my function as a teacher in enabling the kids to pursue and develop their own lines of thought. (*SCYPT Journal 11*: 1983: 23)

Mrs Evans may note with approval that the boys are wearing strong boots ready for the winter and inform them that the school stove will be lit next month to help dry their clothes after their long walk to school across the fields. If the actor/teacher judges them ready she will push further: 'Is your brother's whooping cough better?'; 'Did you pick many blackberries this year?'; 'What did you make with them?'; 'I hope you all helped with the harvest'; 'What did you do, Dafydd?' – and so on. Socio-historical information is being given, collective story telling invited and the role of the children being deepened. This technique is applied at moments throughout the day.

A child volunteers to write the date on the blackboard and the children share their knowledge of the outbreak of the War. Mrs Evans also reads from the newspaper of 3 September 1939 and the children discuss who Hitler is and how Britain is responding to events. Gas mask and blackout regulations are discussed and the importance of not talking to strangers: Careless Talk Costs Lives! In this sequence children learn and share much about the minutiae of wartime living until the session is interrupted by the arrival of Gethin, ready to go off to war. Mrs Evans has prepared the class for this by distributing Union Flags and suggesting that they give him a rousing chorus of *Onward Christian Soldiers*. Gethin enters and gives a patriotic account of why he joined up:

> I responded to the call! ... Those Germans have invaded Poland, then it'll be France and then it'll be our turn ... unless we say 'no' ... we've got to put a stop to this now! ... Every time I kill a German, I'm going to put a notch on my gun and when I come back I can show you what I've done for my country .... My mam has given her consent and wished me luck .... I'm fighting for my valley, for Wales and for Britain ... God save the king!

FIGURE 5.1 Careless Talk *(Theatr Powys 1986). The children accept their role. Photo: Keith Morris (www.artswebwales.com) and with permission of Powys County Council.*

The children sing the hymn and wave the flags. They have genuinely been caught up in the patriotic fervour – as clearly Gethin has been. It is worth noting that in his speech Gethin refers only to 'Germans' for in his ignorance (which reflects the children's) he has not yet learned that there is a difference between 'German' and 'Nazi'. The nicety of the phrase 'mam has given her consent' also resonates with some alert children.

A key technique now comes into play. Through the simple action of removing her spectacles, Mrs Evans becomes again the facilitator and, leaving Gethin 'frozen' in depiction, says: 'let's stop the story there for a moment. We are outside the story now'. The image of Gethin is analysed. The facilitator will follow up the responses of the children, but here are some initial questions that were used. They are 'open' questions and the facilitator will not 'correct' the children but seek to develop their understanding through a Socratic approach:

How is Gethin Feeling?
What might he be thinking?
How do you think he feels about his gun and his uniform?
What makes someone feel proud I wonder?
What do you think it is that makes someone want to go and fight for their country?
How did it make you feel singing the song and shaking hands with Gethin?
How do you think his mother would have felt when he told her he was going away to fight for his country? [An opportunity for the 'given her consent' remark to be examined.]
Who decides if a country should fight?
I wonder what happens if someone doesn't want to fight?

This mode of questioning is very much based on Heathcote (see Wagner: 1979: Chapter Six) and the musing 'I wonder why/what' is particularly useful in inviting responses in this sort of facilitation. The children are allowed to give opinions, without judgement, about a variety of themes that will recur during the day. One child noted: 'I think Gethin is brave on the outside and frightened on the inside' and the facilitator 'wondered' whether we all feel like that sometimes.

The discussion about how the mother might have felt when Gethin told her of his intention to sign-up leads to the next scene. The children are invited (as *audience*) to observe a flashback of the day Gethin gave the news. They observe a domestic depiction of Lizzie struggling with homework, Mam darning and Gethin polishing an oil lamp but clearly preoccupied. The children discuss, with a facilitator, what they think they know about the characters and their thoughts. The picture is brought to life to see if their speculation has been correct. There is an intense and emotional argument between son and mother about joining up with Lizzie offering immature yet enthusiastic support for Gethin. The story is again stopped.

This frequent stopping of the story during the day is not disruptive to the children's engagement. As has been previously pointed out, a key point of divergence between TIE and theatre, even Brechtian theatre, is the offering of space for *reflection*. Children relish the opportunity to take a moment to think properly about the complicated issues before them. Freed from the tyranny of 'what happens next', they can address the far more interesting question of 'why does what happen, happen?' This is the learning environment that the educationalists considered in earlier chapters have been keen to create, to give time to allow children to climb the scaffold from what they already know to what they are capable of knowing. It is also a creative twist to the usual application of dramatic irony, for the children know what will happen and yet are able to voice their desire to control the action. Brecht would want us to be aware of the truth of a situation that the characters are unable to see and, in this TIE technique, this is taken further, allowing the 'audience' to explore objectively and securely the decisions the characters make. While the story is paused here, they are asked to consider what arguments the son might employ to convince his mother and how the mother might convince the son. This is a flashback, so the children already know the outcome. They are being given the space to reflect upon and verbalize the issues dialogically. The 'frozen' actors listen carefully to the children's ideas and when the story is restarted they use the children's words in their arguments, validating their contributions. But Gethin is going to war, and because we already know that, even the children whose arguments have 'lost' are not disappointed. What has been important is the dialectical argument that the children have identified.

After a break the children are back in role in the classroom in May 1940. Mrs Evans and the children listen to a radio broadcast by Winston Churchill. They say a prayer for the war effort and everyone shuts their eyes. When they open them again the bedraggled evacuee, Kathleen, is standing at the front of the class, frightened and alone. In her solitude she is defensive and aggressive. She has a strong Liverpool accent and seems unlike the other children in every way. She has been placed with Lizzie's family and Lizzie is clearly not happy about it. Again the story is stopped and the children invited to investigate Kathleen's character, social status and feelings.

The children identify her poverty, alienation and fear. From her rosary they learn she is Catholic – another source of alienation from these Welsh chapelgoers. She is of Irish extraction and the facilitator discusses with the children why people emigrate from one place to another. The children share feelings about belonging and what it is like to move to new places. Back in the story, Mrs Evans leaves the class to look after Kathleen. The situation soon deteriorates in the face of her defensive aggression and boastful fantasizing, and the children – despite the theoretical empathy they have shown in discussion – soon find themselves teasing the evacuee, convincing her that frogspawn is a sort of confectionary. Things get worse when Mrs Evans returns and Kathleen runs from the room when asked to write her name on the board. Out of the story, the children admit to teasing and using their superior knowledge to make her feel bad. They identify that Kathleen is illiterate and discuss how to help her. They are invited to see a flashback of Kathleen in Liverpool with her granddad in order to understand her better.

This Kathleen is very different – happy and loving though desperately worried about being sent to Wales. Before the scene starts, the children discuss what they think they know about the depicted granddad and become alerted to aspects of the story that they could investigate. They find out that Kathleen has troubles at home, with everyone in her large family arguing about the War. She works herself up hysterically but is eventually pacified by the gentle granddad. The thematic content of the scene deals with anti-Semitism and fear of 'other-ness' as the evacuation to Wales and the War are discussed. The gentle grandparent can talk to Kathleen in simple terms, reassuring her about her fears:

Granddad	They don't all speak Welsh .... I knew some Welsh boys in the First War ... they spoke English better than me.
(pause)	
Kathleen	But you're Irish.
Granddad	You know what I mean.
Kathleen	They'll laugh at me because I'm different to them and I'll sound funny ... like the Jew boy that came ...
Granddad	Jewish boy ...
Kathleen	Like the Jewish boy that came to our street from Germany.

The children are aware that they behaved to Kathleen exactly as she had feared. The mantra that granddad now repeats sets what has happened in context:

Granddad	What do we do if we know that something's wrong?
Kathleen	Put it right.
Granddad	How do we do it?
Kathleen	Stand firm and tell the truth.

Kathleen and granddad are left in depiction as the facilitator examines these issues with the children. Why do people tease? How does it make you feel? The parallels between anti-Semitism and bullying are brought out. Why does it seem alright to tease people if others are doing it? A child responds that if you don't join in you might get picked on too. The educational strands are coming together, for here is an insight into how an ideology like fascism takes hold and that the only strength we have as individuals is to 'stand firm and tell the truth'. The facilitator draws the children's ideas together and introduces examples of contemporary racism using South African apartheid as an example. The particular example of fear of going to Wales and being a stranger is linked to the irrational fear of Jewish people and to the contemporary existence of apartheid.

The children are once again asked for suggestions for granddad to use to persuade Kathleen to go to Wales and these are picked up by the actors. The children *know* that Kathleen goes; what is interesting is why she agrees to go. Granddad also introduces a simple metaphor for Kathleen (and the children) to engage with, as to how fascism must be dealt with. Hitler is likened to a weed in a garden that needs to be eradicated before it spreads:

> You've got to dig it out and throw it away … and afterwards you've got to remember what the weed looks like … in case it tries to grow again.

In a touching moment, Kathleen agrees to go to Wales and granddad asks her to look after his watch as he 'keeps forgetting to wind it'. The events of the scene are reflected upon with the facilitator and the children:

How do you think she feels about going to Wales now?
What do you think Granddad feels about the War? It is
different from how Gethin feels about it?
'Hitler is a bad weed.' What does that mean? Gethin said
Hitler was madman. How do you think he was able to get
so many German people on his side?
I wonder what makes one country want to invade another?
Granddad asked Kathy to do him a favour and look after
the watch. Why did he want her to have the watch, I
wonder?

Before the final session they recap what they have discovered
and discuss how the war might have changed Gethin. Back in the
1940s classroom, Kathleen has clearly settled in and is at ease with
her classmates. The mood is darkened when Kathleen receives a
letter. Kathleen cannot read and we watch her puzzle over the
contents later that day in the barn. She hides the letter when she
hears others coming and, with the facilitator, the children read the
contents. It contains news of the death of her grandfather and they
discuss how she will react when she finds out. They are reminded
that if the scene gets too sad, they can sit by the facilitator or
the teacher. What happens is worse than anticipated. The children
(Lizzie and a new character, Billy) are playing ghosts, trying to
frighten Kathleen and things get out of hand. They start teasing
her about her religion and her poverty and this becomes a bullying
game in which they tie her up and put her in a hamper. She gets
very frightened and cries out, 'you pigs, you Nazis. You're just like
them you are!'

As she climbs out of the basket the letter is discovered and Lizzie
starts mockingly to read it. As she realizes what she is reading she
trails off into silence and Kathleen becomes hysterical. Billy makes
his excuses and leaves. Lizzie manages to calm Kathleen, sharing
with her memories of her father who died of TB when she was seven.
She suggests, after a time, that Kathleen could bury Granddad's
watch with a letter and say a prayer – 'a Catholic one' she adds,
diplomatically. Kathleen decides to keep the watch but agrees to
write a letter and bury it. With the help of the village children,
a prayer/letter is written and Kathleen is supported through her
grief. The children have brought their instincts about dealing with
bereavement to the story in a safe way, protected into these feelings

FIGURE 5.2 Careless Talk *(Theatr Powys 1986). Lizzie reads Kathleen's letter. Photo: Keith Morris (www.artswebwales.com) and with permission of Powys County Council.*

by the objectivity of theatre yet engaged through the empathy of their role.

Gethin is due home and the house is in turmoil as a big welcome is prepared for him. The girls get ready to spring a surprise as the children observe a touchingly underplayed scene between mother and son. Neither says what they need to say, the mother filling the emptiness with chatter. The children have become a highly intelligent audience and are interpreting every sign and nuance. The raucous girls interrupt the mood and Gethin clearly cannot cope. Lizzie has kept an imaginary diary of Gethin's gory adventures and when he tears it up, she is distraught: 'It wasn't meant to be like this!' Desperate to explain, Gethin takes out the photograph of the German family which he 'took off a dead German'. He is unable to cope with the fact that he killed someone who had family and loved ones. Kathleen explains her understanding (gleaned from her grandfather) and the rights and wrongs of war are emotionally problematized for the audience.

As with previous scenes, the events, text and subtext are deconstructed with the children and they show themselves able to dialectically understand the complexities of what is going on for each of the characters. They are invited back into the story so that they can explain to the Mam why everyone is so upset; 'you seem to understand it so much better than anyone else'. The children, in taking on this role, know the construct is a pretence. They are not acting; they are being themselves and not-themselves at the same time. They are seriously playing. They are left alone, for the first time without any actor/teacher support, to decide what they will say. This is their opportunity to explain their understanding of the day's work to themselves. Then, to the mam, they explain the anger, the torn diary and the events with the German soldier. They 'play' in deadly earnest – desperate to explain (even though they know – outside the story – that she knows all that they know). They offer support and advice in order to help Gethin recover from his trauma. Having talked to the mother, they then speak to the girls and finally to Gethin. He shows his family the German photograph and tries to explain. The family are reconciled. The story comes to an end and the facilitator thanks the children for explaining things so well and so wisely.

At this time, there were many excellent projects using similar techniques. Readers may be aware of Pit Prop's *Brand of Freedom* (see Jackson: 2007: 169–71) dealing with slavery and the oppression of the Lancashire cotton workers in the nineteenth century. What all such programmes have in common (aside from a range of participatory techniques) is that they empowered the children to approach a historical subject in a feeling way, protected into developing and applying their own humanity to the material facts and events.

In *Careless Talk*, a wide range of techniques culled from drama theorists and from theatre can be observed, and TIE projects such as this represent a highly sophisticated hybrid, the further development of which was to be made increasingly difficult by the changes brought in by ERA. The theatrical conventions adopted clearly owe a lot to Brecht. As well as the use of *gestus* in the form of depictions that allowed analysis, there is the flexible use of role and the playing of multiple characters by the actors. Another theatrical device that *Careless Talk* uses to great effect is manipulation of the timeline through flashbacks. This allows children to concentrate on the 'whys?' of a situation and also can be used to pre-empt any tendency to moderate their own behaviour in role that might evade the issues. For example, they have already teased Kathleen when they find out that that is what she most feared.

Progressive ideas about education and how children learn, though they had not always been closely studied by actor/teachers, were demonstrating that education should be about starting from where the child is in order to allow authentic learning to take place into the next level of educational possibility. If education is about understanding the world and being empowered to make it better, it means finding the space for safely offered reflection and analysis. In TIE, this space is the fictive world of a theatrical construct. With this accepted fiction in place, children can relate their own particular knowledge to it and build from it an understanding of universal issues.

Many of the techniques have come from DIE, itself built upon the pivotal premise that humans learn through play. Through this case study we see that this has to be accomplished sensitively, without patronizing the children, giving full value to their ideas without prejudicial comment and by gently 'edging in' to a brokered 'contract' in which all parties agree to suspend disbelief and engage with the material. Questions have to be genuine with an open expectation of responses. This is further bolstered by collective storytelling, the acceptance of role and clarity about the status of the adults.

We also see in this project the close involvement of schools in the choice of subject matter, in the children's preparation and the possibilities for further project work following the visit. At this time, schools were usually ready and able to come 'off timetable' for the day to facilitate the work and exploit cross-curricula possibilities. The regular contact with schools and the slow turnover of practitioners meant that professional and trusting relationships could be established and maintained. However, especially in the secondary sector, working within a strict examination-focussed environment was more of a challenge, and it was here that performance-based projects became the norm and required different 'participatory' approaches. The second case study is an example of this methodological approach.

CHAPTER SIX

Case Study: *When Sleeping Dogs Awake*

There is a great deal of difference between being nearly 11 and being nearly 13 years old. Aside from the hormonal attack on the psyches of the fledgeling adults, the school environment also changes radically. At Junior School they were 'top dogs', generally secure in their place in the hierarchy of life. They had had contact with the same peer group all their educational lives, played and learned with them to find their place and themselves. In each year of their schooling, they had had contact with one main teacher with whom they might have built close bonds. The educational environment, though increasingly disturbed by testing and assessment, also offered degrees of flexibility which good teachers were able to exploit. All this changes with the move to Secondary School where the regime is one of obedience to the bell and traipsing between specialized teaching spaces and specialized teachers. From being in a school of maybe a few score, they may now be one amongst thousands where it is easy to get lost literally and emotionally. No longer top dogs, the adjustment to being looked down upon by older pupils maybe daunting. From the start, their lives are ruled by inflexible timetables, preparation for the next Standard Assessment Tests (SATs), examinations and the pressures to conform to a range of constructs from fashion to social attitudes. For some this can be truly traumatic.

These changes have to be considered by a TIE company working with Secondary School pupils. Young people do not lose their ability to learn through play, to use their 'what if' skills to investigate fictive situations, but it now becomes difficult for them to do so. They are beginning to learn that 'pretending' is beneath them and that they are too sophisticated to undertake the roles that they might have willingly accepted even a year before. Techniques for making role-playing ideas age-appropriate (through the use of 'frame' and the application of Forum Theatre, for example) have been discussed in an earlier chapter. Another approach is used in the programme I wish to offer as a second exemplar for the 'Fruits' section of this book. *When Sleeping Dogs Awake* was written by Geoff Gillham in collaboration with the devising team of actors at, once again, Belgrade TIE company, in 1988. The development of the project is described by Louise Townend (Townend in Grady & O'Sullivan: 1998: 78–86). She relates that the company's brief was to produce a show about racism for 10–12 year olds for Secondary Schools and their feeder Junior Schools. Performances took place on Mondays and Tuesdays followed by workshops. Further work was then undertaken by teachers prior to a public performance on the Friday evening when the follow-up material of the young people was also exhibited.

I will discuss later the dangers of presenting 'message-based' work, but here there would seem to be little area for concern though there is little value in a project that tells you what you already know. What is required educationally is an analysis that builds upon what the children know (or think they know) and enables them to sophisticate their understanding. The Belgrade project did this by delineating, in their devising, the distinction between 'street racism' (perpetrated by ordinary people in their everyday lives) and the endemic racist ideology that is part of the capitalist processes of exploitation and control – 'systemic racism' (Grady & O'Sullivan: 1998: 79). The aim was to identify where attitudes come from. Immediately it is clear that we are stepping into politically contentious areas. In devising, the company looked at the links between street and systemic racism and set itself the goal of offering the young people a path towards understanding. Notes in the Belgrade's archives indicate that the company sought to trace the relationship between racist ideology and the 'actual mechanics of capitalism, colonialism and imperialism' (Belgrade Archive, Herbert Museum, Coventry).

In the exploratory sessions, Gillham and the company deconstructed a variety of images (Townend: 1998: 80). One of these concerned a guesthouse sign which declared 'No blacks, no Jews, no dogs'. It is perhaps the equivalence given to 'blacks, Jews and dogs' that was one of the seeds of the final project. Another strand was the image of 'rope' that can be used to bind, to secure, to restrain or to lead. It can be tied and untied – or cut. 'Dogs' and 'ropes' became the unlikely symbolic tropes of the devising process and the thematic issues had become:

1   How do material conditions affect people's thoughts and actions?

2   How is it that people frequently hold ideas contrary to their real interests? (Townend: 1998: 82)

So it was that the performance section of the TIE programme *When Sleeping Dogs Awake* consisted of the team of actors playing stray dogs on derelict land. Though some teachers were concerned that the metaphor was too opaque for some of their students (Teachers' Feedback Sheets: Belgrade Archive), I contend that this was an inspired choice in that it appealed to the still-accessible child within the young adult but also offered a challenging theatrical allegory that would demand a mature level of interpretive processing. The play would intrigue and even amuse whilst presenting complex ideas. Humans playing dogs has innate humour, as does the idea of dogs reflecting human responses and values, but there is also liminal educational potential where these two absurdities meet and offer the 'opportunity for learning in an economic form' (Townend: 1998: 83). Gillham was later to describe such an approach as a 'productive distraction' where 'reality is dealt with in the form of symbolization' (2001: 67). *Sleeping Dogs* was a successful project because it tapped into a symbolic world to which the audience could relate and develop a drive to understand. It is another (more age-appropriate) way of offering the same opportunity to be safely distanced from the issues in order to objectively deconstruct them, as was offered to the child-participants of *Careless Talk* in their 'myself-as-someone-else' role. Effective TIE depends on the unification of experiential with the reflective. With a project such as this, a workshop becomes necessary in order for it to be 'affective and analytical' revealing 'real or "embedded" *understanding*' (Gillham: 2001: 68). But, what of the programme itself? I should point out from the outset, lest the reader creates an image in their mind of actors scurrying around in pantomime fake-fur costumes, that the characters were clearly human but with dog-traits. Goldie, the Labrador, has an even temper, a peace-maker; Precious, the poodle, is vain and self-delusory; Lucky the spaniel has high energy but tends to act before s/he speaks – and so on. An inventive designer would find additional ways of suggesting the 'dogness' within the humanness (or vice versa) of the characters.

The story

At the beginning of the play, the stray dogs hear that a member of the group has killed one of their number. How to deal with this murder exercises the pack and displays the various natures of the different breeds, from impetuosity to appeasement. Some wish for speedy retribution and others want to avoid confrontation. The nature, causes and repercussions of the murder are examined in a series of flashbacks, performed by the dogs themselves. By the end of the play, they are still arguing about what to do about the murderer and only come to the realization too late that the real enemy lies beyond the dog-world, amongst the humans who are arriving to destroy them. Though never explicitly stated, it is clear that the stray dogs are a metaphor for all those with a common class interest, across race, orientation and intelligence. They are all the victims of oppression by the capital-owning humans who exist as a threat at the edge of the dog-world. It should also be noted that the casting is explicitly gender-neutral and any gender-specific pronouns in the examples below follow the published text (Gillham: 2011) which itself emphasizes that choices are arbitrary.

The themes of the programme

- Street racism
- Systemic racism (and the ideological relationship between the two)
- What do we need to know to act in our own best interest?
- What prevents us from knowing what we need to know?

These themes are, of course, extremely complicated to unravel, but this is where the street-dog metaphor plays its part. It enables a boiling down to essentials and permits a sideways look at issues freed from the subjective baggage of one's own colour, behaviour, political attitudes and inherited beliefs. It leaves the audience with questions about what the dogs did or didn't do and it will be in the workshop and follow-up that the thematic issues can be explicitly brought into the light.

There is a tabloid tendency which characterizes any particularly heinous human act as having been perpetrated by an 'animal'. An early example of this from *Sleeping Dogs* brings forward a note of humour (for, yes, he *is* an animal) but also starts an internal re-wiring of our spectator brains as we become aware that our normal perspectives and assumptions are going to be challenged:

Target enters, blood on her clothes, face and hands

Pug   Now perhaps you'll believe me.

Silence

Lucky   Murderer! Murderer!

Pug   Animal. (Gillham: 2011: 81)

Similarly the racial arguments that can be heard on the streets and in the right-wing press slip into the dogs' arguments setting up further resonances that may be examined in the workshop section:

Bernard You can't go around killing every dog that insults you.

Target   What was I supposed to do then?

Pug   Not come here in the first place.

Target   I was born here!

Pug   Don't give me that stuff. Nothing but an animal. (Gillham: 2011: 82)

Pug's racist analysis continues:

Pug   But you still haven't got it, have you! (*to all*) They aren't like us. When we discovered Shortlands, them Targets were just living wild, fighting each other; they didn't know anything. They didn't even know how to eat out of bowls. The ... humans had to teach them everything. Go on, I'll show you. You lot be the natives. (Gillham: 2011: 83)

The character of Pug then introduces the first of what will be a series of enactments that either fill-in aspects of the narrative not portrayed on stage or demonstrate the ideology (in this case) of the racist. The dogs act out the accepted 'truth' that dogs from the 'Shortlands' were uncivilized until 'discovered' by humans (i.e. the colonialist explorers of the previous centuries). Pug explains that eventually the native Shortlanders were civilized (though their nature 'was always there') and they were issued with identity tags that allowed them to 'come over here'. The 'sly little beasts' came over in their thousands and were treated to preferential treatment because the humans wanted to use them as cheap labour – 'you could keep two of them for one of us. So they got the best owner's and the best kennels'. Pug's analysis is completed with a call for justice against these ingrates who are nothing but savages, 'just animals'.

Target posits her view of history in response. She explains that in fact the Shortlanders weren't fighting all the time but lived in packs working cooperatively in a mutually supportive way. Under Target's direction some of the dogs enact her world and into this idyll Target introduces the human visitation and shows how the dogs were driven off their land with guns as the humans fenced it and searched it for resources. As a result, explains Target, the dogs were driven to the poorest land where they became starved and weak. The next section of text introduces an important ideological link in the explication of the metaphor:

Target   Then they had an idea ...

Flick   [in human role] 'Supposing we could train those dogs ... Like the ones back home ...'

Bernard   [in human role] 'They're killers Arnold.'

Flick   'I know. But why not get them to kill for us ...' (Gillham: 2011: 85)

And Target, with Flick and Bernard's help, demonstrate how the dogs were trained to kill and get food so the humans didn't have to. The play is carefully indicating the common interests between the Shortlands', colonized, dogs and those who have traditionally offered up their labour for the benefit of the human ruling classes.

When street racism is present it is often dismissed (by the perpetrators) as 'banter' or 'just having a laugh'. And, despite the existence of rules in a 'civilized society' such behaviour is tolerated, as when Target had been previously attacked:

Target   And you lot, what did you do?

Lucky   Nothing, we didn't do anything.

Target   No, you just stood and watched it happen. I didn't hear anyone talking about 'rules' then! (Gillham: 2011: 89)

There is a danger that the causes of racism become over-simplified through this use of symbol. This danger is addressed and the

FIGURE 6.1 When Sleeping Dogs Awake *by Geoff Gillham (Belgrade Theatre: 1988). Courtesy of Belgrade Theatre Archives (photographer unknown).*

situation problematized just before the end of the first act when Bullet (who Target killed in retaliation for the persecution she received from him) has his back-story played out by some of the dogs. We see that Bullet too (representing the indigenous working class) has been exploited, abused and made savage by the treatment he has had at the hands of his human owner. Bullet too was kicked out (made unemployed?). That's what made him aggressive towards Target. But the dogs are unconvinced and argue about whether it is nature or environment that creates behaviour and consider whether, if it is all down to nature, then killing is inevitable. Precious sums up the message as he sees it: 'that's why we need owners – to keep us in order'.

The second act continues the philosophical debate about nature versus nurture and the need for laws and control that, in the context of the metaphor, are symbolized by the dog-lead and the dogcatcher. Bernard posits the view that what is needed is for us not to wear leads but to *behave* as though we were: to choose between good and evil. Many sophisticated ideas are being brought to the surface here concerning not only racism but also the nature of government, religion and ethics. The relationships, correspondences and contradictions are fuelling new ways of understanding. Flick, in frustration, stumbles across a Gramscian view of the world:

> Flick   They train us, make us do what they want from the moment we're born. They train us so well we don't even know what we think. We think what we want is what we want. But it isn't. What we want is what they want us to want. (Gillham: 2011: 95)

Flick has arrived at a moment of insight, shared perhaps by some of the audience, that it is in the humans' interests to keep the dogs divided amongst themselves and even the murder of Bullet serves these interests since it shows the need for strong authority.

Within the narrative the problem of what to do with Target, the murderer, remains. The humans will soon discover the crime and will seek to impose their justice on these animals operating outside society. The lack of solidarity amongst those with a common interest is shown by one of the dogs suggesting that they tie Target (rope again) to a post near the body, offering her up to human authority.

Other voices dissent and point out that the majority would still not be safe from the humans as notices have gone up that 'all dogs must be kept on leads'. The humans will still come after them. Despite increasing ideological awareness amongst the dogs of the threat they are all under, some refuse to acknowledge the truth. Bernard just hopes that 'nothing will happen'. Precious points out that the signs were written for humans, not dogs and, as they haven't got owners to keep them on leads, then the notice doesn't apply to them. A scene is re-enacted in which an 'owned' dog was captured by the dog warden and then rescued by its owner. That would not be their fate!

There is one dog, Goldie, who has always been side-lined by the others, preoccupied by what she knows, who finally gets her voice heard. She reports an overheard conversation amongst the humans discussing the 'stray dog problem'. There are those humans who appear understanding of the stray dogs and that they have been let down by humans. Other humans want to proactively tackle the problem, rounding them up and locking them away. But that would cost money. Putting them down would be a better, final, solution. It would be 'a kindness' says Pug in role as a human. But Lucky, as one of the 'understanding humans' dissents:

Lucky   'I couldn't go along with that. We fought the Nazis to stop things like that!'

Pug   'They're only dogs; for God's sake!' (Gillham: 2011: 104)

This brief interaction contains humour but also softens the line between the dog/human metaphor whilst still allowing the represented human to distance himself from fascist attitudes. It is supremely ironic and provides a rich source of material for the pupils to cope with either now or in the later workshop.

The humans have decided on a compromise which is to round the dogs up and 'dispose' of them, the nature of that 'disposal' being left undefined. The final piece of information from Goldie makes the impending danger explicit. She heard two of the human committee members secretly agreeing to get a van ready for the round-up and to 'make sure it is airtight', though she doesn't understand what the implications of that are. Target spells it out. General panic threatens and a total lack of solidarity is evident. Precious, in his child-like innocence finds a rope and puts it around his own neck. It is a deeply pathetic moment when we, as audience, can see the ideological truth to which Precious is blind. We see the dogs misreading the symbolism of the leashes, and we feel a desire to intervene. It is taking the power of dramatic irony and empowering us to identify the changes that need to happen. In the play, for lack of any better plan, some of the other dogs follow Precious' example, tying themselves up in a startling theatrical image: the oppressed fully taking ownership of their own oppression in a vain attempt to survive. Inevitably the wardens arrive to find that the dogs are behaving in their usual rowdy anarchic way and that some of them 'have even tied themselves up for us'. Flick's last line is 'we didn't understand in time'.

Clearly Gillham's work has a Marxist perspective and his Trotskyism frequently set him at odds with funders, education authorities and even some colleagues throughout his working life (he died in 2001). Notes from the end of tour debrief refer to the issues that the company met along the way. Whilst acknowledging that the project was very 'fruitful' and that the success of the project made any problems 'ultimately insignificant' the Belgrade team took itself to task for 'protecting the liberal interests of the company' and backing out of 'fighting for a truthful analysis and real struggle for social change' (Belgrade Archive). This is perhaps the obverse side of the criticism raised by a few teachers in their feedback that the meanings of the play were at times too subtle (Belgrade Archive). Personally I feel that both the company and the teachers have underestimated the resilience of the understanding that was being placed with the pupils. Edward Bond, in his Foreword to Davis' edition of six Gillham plays comments that Gillham 'saw life as an emergency' (Bond in Gillham: 2011: ix) and Davis himself sees him as a passionate believer in the 'power of theatre to humanise and in doing so become a force for change in the world' (Gillham: 2011: xi).

I contend that Sleeping Dogs is in not polemical. We have already seen (Chapter Three) how Gillham made conscious efforts to develop his work away from its agit-prop roots and, using Vygotsky and Bruner's ideas, to create valid learning situations. Cooper (Gillham: 2011: 76) describes this as a move away 'from a more didactic theatre towards showing rather than telling' in which 'the use of metaphor is of particular importance'. If one is dealing with issues of racism in society it is insufficient to just point out that it is bad (at least, it is a waste of good theatre). In Vygotskian terms, real education needs to offer that scaffolding between what the children know, or think they know and the larger understanding of which they are becoming capable. In this case they will be aware of the street racism that they live with (perpetrate? suffer?) each day but are capable of being offered a context of understanding of the systemic racism that is both the cause and effect of street racism. It may be that, in the workshop, they will want to defend hitherto held positions, but they will have to do so in the light of an analysis offered by the metaphor of the stray dogs. They will have to think.

[Education] is the moving interface between the development of the children ... and the requirements of society. (Gillham in *SCYPT 30*: 1995: 47)

However, by 'society' Gillham means '... not the narrow confines of a nation, but the totality of human society'. He goes on:

To plan for the future is to understand the present. To understand the present is to comprehend the past and how it is contained within the present. (Gillham in *SCYPT 30: 1995*: 54)

The argument for including this project as an example of the 'fruits' of TIE practice by the end of the 1980s, is that it offers a genuine education that is appropriate to the learning skills that 10–12 year olds are needing (and are able) to cultivate at this point in their development. This is more than their education will usually have expected of them and it is not necessarily what the Primary or Secondary School curriculum requires. It is arguable whether there is space within the accepted secondary framework for these 'tools' of the mind to be operated. Does society want young people to be intelligently investigative, 'to be able to arrive at explanations, to knowing and to knowing what you know' (Gillham in *SCYPT 30*: 1995: 58)?

In the same document Gillham quotes Heathcote on the need 'to keep explaining to each other' for, until we do 'we cannot really own the knowledge' (Gillham in *SCYPT 30*: 1995: 60–1). In a project such as *Careless Talk* this can fairly effortlessly be achieved with the children in participatory role interacting with the characters and each other even to the point where the children can be left alone to sustain and carry out discussions in role. This is less easily achieved with 'lowly' Secondary School pupils who may not only be reluctant to adopt a role but may even be losing the power to communicate openly with their peers at all, especially across gender or ethnicity. There is too much face to be lost and ways have to be found to open up the dialogue between pupils and company and amongst the young people themselves. In a participatory project, a combination of role, depiction and reflection can be used to look at the issues 'sideways'. In *Sleeping Dogs*, there is a need to differentiate between 'knowledge' as a memorizing of someone else's knowledge and a personal knowledge that 'is deduced or constructed from the process of the fiction itself' (Gillham: 2001: 68). Gillham demands that TIE must have a task that demands thinking, problem solving, collaboration and communication. There is no place, in Gillham's TIE world, for a workshop that merely acts as a measure of the extent to which the pupils have absorbed and accepted the message. That is akin to assessment at the end of a lesson and is often a feature of Theatre in Health Education programmes that will be considered later.

The workshop for this programme demanded collaboration, explication and communication of the themes of the play, but it did not rely on the pupils having (or using) dextrous verbal skills. It recognizes, as Gardner (1993) was later to point out, that there are intelligences that may not be recognized through literacy or verbal skills. Following workshops involving teams of actor/teachers and the school subject teachers, they are engaged in the setting up of a memorial exhibition with the 'task' of warning other dogs about the perilousness of the situation. Their understanding can be demonstrated in whatever creative form they feel competent. This exhibition was then presented to the public together with a performance of the play. Townend (in Grady & O'Sullivan: 1998: 85–6) gives an analysis of the exhibition workshop. Through the workshop, she observes, they are processing for themselves the new knowledge they have obtained by watching the play. The metaphor acts as a gateway to understanding their own world and the action they can take in it. They are working in Vygotsky's ZPD, mediating the stray dogs' existence through their own knowledge into an understanding of the society of which they are an important part. The ZPD has been created by the TIE play offering knowledge that is just beyond them but yet attainable:

There is an obvious similarity here between the action in the play, and the action that the pupils involved in the theatre programme will be engaged in …. The pupils will be addressing the universal questions through the concrete actions they take and the decisions they make concerning the production of the exhibition. (Grady & O'Sullivan: 1998: 85)

The pupils are to use their own affective response to the play that can then be connected to their understanding of racism. A real understanding of events is firstly 'felt' before it can become part of the human being's knowledge. Affective engagement opens the door to effective perception moving us from the objective observation of an event (the play) to the appreciation of the need for change. It is the symbiosis of play and workshop that allow the dramatic meaning to emerge. Discussing DIE, O'Toole talks of a 'many-layered dynamic' (O'Toole: 1992: 43) being established allowing negotiation and renegotiation. In the same way a TIE workshop is not there to make sure the 'message' is received and understood; it is there to allow this negotiation to take place in and between each of the spectators.

CHAPTER SEVEN

The Aesthetics of TIE

Low esteem

Throughout its fifty-year history TIE has had to fend off accusations and respond to the prejudice that it in some way lacks aesthetic value. John O'Toole in 1976 seemed to have these concerns, noting that performers in this new genre of theatre were called 'with heavy accuracy' actor/teachers (O'Toole: 1976: 14). He goes on to note that TIE's 'overall primary aim is always educational' (O'Toole: 1976: 16) with an apparent implication that this negated artistic value. By 2006 though, he agreed that 'TIE brought radical innovation' (O'Toole: 2009: 480). Here I argue that not only does educational function not preclude aesthetics but that the aesthetic function is actually essential to successful teaching. In this O'Toole would agree, observing that 'the better the artistry, the better the learning' (O'Toole: 2009: 484), an argument he had previously made in 1992:

> The TIE team *must* satisfy the aesthetic demands of the audience if the instrumental aims are to be considered. (O'Toole: 1992: 125)

The examples I have given in the preceding chapters are but two amongst many examples of programmes the performances of which should free TIE from suspicion of failing to meet aesthetic expectations. With undergraduates I continually stress the hybrid nature of TIE and that the 'theatre' in 'theatre in education' needs to be a good as they are capable of; they may be introducing a child to the art form of theatre and the responsibility is a weighty one.

O'Toole (O'Toole: 1992: 125) also points out that aesthetic experience is high on the list of expectations of schools. There will be demanding deviation from the normal school routine and if a fee is being paid, then the company must come up with the goods. I believe that most artists would want to fulfil aesthetic expectations however they were funded, but we can take O'Toole's point: to survive, a company must have high artistic standards and he is right to alert us to the danger that pedagogical aims might overwhelm aesthetics and create negative attitudes towards theatre.

The origins of the low esteem afforded TIE may be due to the fact that, in the earliest days, many actor/teachers were *not* trained nor experienced actors though this quickly became the norm. Secondly, there is the previously mentioned tendency for young actors to view TIE as an 'easy' way into the profession or to unionization (at one time so important). For actors with this attitude TIE is a stopgap until the next telly, advert or main house theatre opportunity arises. I have met some of these actors along the way but rarely. Indeed, some who came into TIE with such attitudes became converted and made their careers there. I don't remember ever hearing a TIE actor saying after an unsatisfactory performance, 'doesn't matter; they're just kids': I *have* heard seasoned theatre actors say this having given a lack-lustre matinee performance.

TIE and design

There have been (and increasingly so I fear) TIE programmes with questionable aesthetic values, but this is true of all forms of theatre. There is nothing intrinsically anti-aesthetical in TIE. Critics of TIE are, perhaps, failing to appreciate just *what* the aesthetic is that is at work. In design terms, for example, you are never going to get the audience gasp and applause that might attend the raising of the red velvet curtain at a West End show revealing a lavishly naturalistic reproduction of an eighteenth-century ballroom, but then you cannot aspire to such opulence in any touring theatre production. TIE has taken its approach to design from Brecht, from touring and alternative theatre in what O'Toole calls 'a conscious renegotiation of the appropriateness of certain spaces' (O'Toole: 1992: 35). Where once comfortably seated audiences required the opulent ballroom (requiring little of our ability to suspend our disbelief), we now rejoice in the demanding semiotic creativity of the minimal indicator. And certainly children are incredibly athletic at making such creative leaps, having no issue with accepting their school hall transported to other times and places. I have seen children totally enthralled, learning from a centurion about Roman culture, even though the exchange took place in a cloakroom. Though O'Toole (O'Toole: 1992: 50) feels that school settings 'actively mediate against the ready suspension of disbelief', *my* experience has been of children transported to a Celtic village with no more than a circle of chairs covered in hessian in their gymnasium to trigger belief. I would not accept that these are examples of low aesthetics but rather a justification of how the child's ability to play is combined with the actor's ability to 'play' within a frame that is both a theatrical and learning schematic:

> Invoking the *voluntary* suspension of disbelief is a powerful construct of both aesthetic and learning potency. (O'Toole: 2009: 485)

The creators of a TIE project have to consider the essential symbols that will facilitate entrance into this fictive world. In *Careless Talk*, for example, the home scene has the historically accurate tea-set, the oil lamp and other minimal but resonant dressing. The scene with the grandfather is based around the sharing of precious confectionary and the pocket watch, each item carefully chosen for its totemistic value within the programme rather than for 'dressing'. In theatre, though not in film, design will include only what is required: it is part of the mediation with the audience. If there is a gun in Act One it will be used in Act Five; if there is a telephone then it will ring. To have on stage what you need and no more is part of a theatre language that most of us accept and relish. Costume is equally important, as historical accuracy may be a significant part of the programme's educational value. If the children are participants in the drama it may help for them to have some costume signifier, though they will not need much to enhance their engagement; if a stick can be a horse or a sword, then an apron can transport them to being an eighteenth-century millworker. Usually not even this is required. DIE uses minimal symbols in the same way. Heathcote, in her Mantle of the Expert, will prepare semiotic documents and other stimuli; even a telephone will be represented by a piece of paper with a phone drawn on it. As early as 1980, Gavin Bolton wrote of the power of objects as symbols to 'encapsulate a thematic meaning of the drama; representing a feature of the context [and] engaging the feelings of the group' (in *SCYPT Journal*: 1980: 7). More recently John Somers has built on such ideas, developing an approach using a 'compound stimulus' to facilitate children's engagement in creating a drama (see Somers: 2008: 68).

TIE and the aesthetics of performance

The criticism of TIE's aesthetics may be based in any or none of these visual aspects. The most serious charge would be a lack of performance quality and it is this charge that can be the most misplaced and the most indicative of a misunderstanding about the nature of TIE. TIE is not just acting out a play with a message. We have seen that the TIE actor is using his or her skill, in interaction with the learning-through-play instincts of the children, to create and develop knowledge grounded in an empathetic analysis of emotional 'particular circumstances' that the children are then enabled to use as a bridge to a knowledge of the world. This is achieved through the exploitation by the actors of 'play' in both performance and workshop contexts.

The TIE actor has, in fact, to be in command of a highly complex performance aesthetic that ranges from full engagement to working outside their character as a facilitator of learning. The range of acting 'depth' will be somewhere on the following spectrum:

- Fully engaged as the character ('naturalistic' acting).

- A Brechtian approach where the actor has emotional distance from the character in order to facilitate spectatorship in the audience.

- A 'twilight' performance style that frees the actor to make more overtly pedagogical decisions *from within* the character.

- As facilitator, where the mask of the character is abandoned completely and the children are communicated with 'outside the story'.

Using the two case studies as examples, I would suggest that *Careless Talk* uses all these approaches at different points. The performance at times is highly intense and 'truthful' and at other times offers more demonstration in a carefully directed structure, using 'signing' as explained by Heathcote (*SCYPT Journal No. 9*, 'Signs (and Portents?)' and described in Chapter Three). At other times, as in the final scene where the participants (in role as the children of the village) converse with the mother and explain events, the actor/teacher is taking more of a twilight role. The project requires that the actor/teachers segue seamlessly between the acting styles. When 'twilighting', the actor moderates responses based on her character in order to deepen the children's analysis. A consideration of the use of 'hotseating' may help amplify this 'twilighting'. Those who have used hotseating as a rehearsal exercise, to create and deepen character, will know that faced with difficult questions a particular character (truthfully) might swear, threaten violence or leave the room as an accurately observed response. This would not be useful in a TIE workshop. Instead the actor/teacher has to adjust response to ensure the enhancement of learning. Rather than responding to the question 'Why don't you talk to your mum?' with a (truthful) 'Mind your own business!', the actor might feel it is more helpful to reply: 'What on earth could I say to her?' In such ways, actor/teachers can adjust their characters (*not* abandon them) in order to engage the participants through character-rooted Socratic questions. As with a teacher using DIE, children have no problem interacting with the role and then explaining that interaction to the same person out of role. All actors have to maintain a 'cold strip' where they control the character and in the actor/teacher, these skills have to be finely honed. Something akin to Boal's *metaxis* is at work and child-player and actor are aware of the action and involved in it at the same time. Indeed, all artistic endeavour, as creator or spectator, requires aesthetic distance or it becomes part of our reality without any opportunity to mediate it. I am highly critical of the fashion that existed in some TIE programmes for the children to be actually encouraged to believe that the fiction was a reality. In this way companies sought to get a 'true emotional response'. I was involved in such projects myself in the late 1970s and what actually occurs is that the children are left confused (is this real or not?) and stripped of the ability to respond objectively to the situation; the responsibility of the decisions that have to be made is too great. The children must not be 'reacting in real life' (O'Toole: 1976: 137); they must remain aware that they are reacting within a fictive context that allows them to explore reality in terms of play.

In *Sleeping Dogs*, the very nature of actors playing dogs is a quintessentially Brechtian *Verfremdungseffekt*; a 'making strange' that distances the audience from the events and requires fine artistic judgement and physical/vocal control. In the workshop, the play is virtually left behind as the actor/teachers engage in practical explorations. Certainly it is possible to direct and act this (or any other) play badly, but the internal aesthetics of narrative, flashbacks and the insightful paralleling of the human and dog worlds make it an exceptionally satisfying piece aesthetically.

In participatory projects, the children are undertaking none of these levels of performance. They remain themselves whilst in a 'play' (all senses of the word) situation. In the programme the notions of play come together. The actors know their characters and the limits of their flexibility and they are acting alongside the children who are 'living through' the situation and learning in the process. Jackson (2007: 138ff and 145ff) confronts the question of whether the use of participation is possible without destroying the aesthetic distance required for successful theatre. The fundamental problem is that if the audience can decide outcomes, then the ability of the artist to frame the narrative, mould super-objectives and craft conclusions is compromised; if the audience are totally immersed in a series of events, then where is the art? Perhaps we would be better improvising a piece of Applied Theatre? This is to misunderstand the function and misconstrue the methodology. If you are performing a history project then – factually – we know the outcome and we cannot change it. In *Careless Talk*, the children *know* that Gethin goes to war – but that does not stop them being able to engage with the actors in creating the arguments for and against his going. Participatory TIE allows for exploration of knowledge within a structured narrative, as Jackson relates from his conversation with a pupil:

> [The TIE programme] was not just a rather elaborate form of play which could have gone anywhere, but a narrative with a clear strong structure .... He could not make the story go his way, but he was a contributor to it, not a passive receiver of an already finished product. (Jackson: 2007: 147)

These are the elements that the TIE piece must intrinsically have – to attain aesthetic completeness that respects the children's inputs (their knowledge) and the objective facts. In this respect, therefore, O'Toole, in 1976, had not yet come to a full understanding of how TIE operates:

> In practice, the benefits of a participation that is momentary and superficial may well be outweighed by the disadvantage that it merely arouses a shallow excitement it cannot satisfy. (O'Toole: 1976: 97)

He feared that children are just extras fulfilling a place within a play with predetermined outcomes. Later contributions by O'Toole indicate that he came to appreciate the way in which TIE should work. He acknowledges (in 1992) that a 'sophisticated definition of learning is evident':

> ... when it seeks not only to acquaint students with 'surface', reproductive knowledge, but ... using identification with a **fictional context** as a way of assisting them to discover aspects of that situation, by 'putting children into others' shoes'. (O'Toole: 1992: 45)

As in any theatre, there can be bad acting in TIE: and bad design, bad writing and bad direction. Landy refers us to O'Toole's observation that TIE 'was not universally embraced nor was it always well done' (Landy & Montgomery: 2012: 102). Some companies, they report:

> ... put forth theatre that was poorly produced, unrelated to children's interests and, in some cases, exploitative. (Landy & Montgomery: 2012: 102)

I think the reference here is to some early, unstructured and poorly theorized TIE work, though I would reserve similar criticisms for some of the work that emerged in the later 1990s and into the twenty-first century. The later 1980s, however, offered the fruits of a highly complex genre of theatre which required flexible and powerful authority over a range of acting styles and which demanded that these be blended with a minute consideration of the use of symbol and efficient design. Jackson (2007) poses the question whether the aesthetic and social functions of TIE can ever fit together and comes to the conclusion that being part of a participatory project can indeed be an aesthetic experience. In agreeing with him I offer the following additional example of a project I once observed.[1] Based on *Romeo and Juliet* it used few semiotically precise props alongside powerful performances. The audience were in role as a Board of Enquiry deciding what should be the fate of the apothecary who provided the drug that facilitates the tragedy. At the end of the project even less verbal members of the pupil group could de-problematize their knowledge by arranging the props in relation to each other, thus summing up their analysis of the play. Carefully and thoughtfully different arrangements of the dagger, the money, the drug vial, the wedding rings and the bible were contemplated. The actor/teachers needed hardly to say a word. These may not be the aesthetics of other forms of theatre but they offered, nonetheless, a striking approach to the theatre aesthetics' lexicon. Not all 'TIE' lives up to the genre's potential and I will happily join in the criticism of those programmes that lack proper consideration and integration of production, performance and workshop decisions. However, by the late 1980s there were many projects that demonstrated this attention to artistic and pedagogical detail and remain key fruits of this period of TIE:

TIE will be effective educationally only *if* it's effective aesthetically. (Jackson: 2007: 160)

Note

1   The project was *The Apothecary's Story* by Theatr Powys (1999).

CHAPTER EIGHT

Making It and Making It Work

In earlier chapters I have argued that the phylogenetics of TIE are based in the unique socio-political, economic and educational environment in the mid-1960s. I want now to contemplate how these circumstances affected the way in which TIE was created by considering structures, working processes and contractual arrangements. The nature and quality of the TIE of the time owes much to these working practices and I consider them to be amongst the 'fruits' of the contribution brought by TIE companies to ways in which artists organize themselves and create their work.

Actors or teachers?

The actor/teacher is an unusual creature having to display aspects of both genera. As has been shown, early actor/teachers came from the separate disciplines and initially there was a demarcation between the skills they offered. Those from the teaching profession offered the workshop elements of a programme, whilst the actors (often seconded from main house theatres) would undertake the theatrical elements. At Perspectives TIE (1972) all members were trained teachers, post-graduates from Bretton Hall, though Colin Hicks recalls (interview: 18 June 2014) that 'we were mostly very good from the neck up', meaning that they were more confident in their manipulation of text than the body. Many TIE companies until the 1980s demanded, or even prioritized, teacher training in their recruitment. The separation of skills became blurred and then disappeared as the techniques became more sophisticated and 'actor/ teachers' more adept across disciplines. This in turn was a result of teams growing their expertise over a period of years. A great deal of 'on-the-job' training and mutual discovery was taking place. When company members did move on, their expertise became diffused through the next group with which they worked.

By the mid-1970s, though the requirement to be teacher trained was waning, such expertise usually resided somewhere in the company and it was upon the drive of the director that the responsibility to weld together the artistic, educational, practical and theoretical spine of the work often depended. Actor/teachers would then be encouraged to undertake research and the hard work of grappling with theory. For Yeoman, the 'socially organised opportunities offered by SCYPT regional and national conferences were invaluable'. In Bennett's *Theatre for Children and Young People* (2005), Anthony Haddon (then director of Blah Blah Blah Theatre Company) asks whether it is easier for teachers to act or for actors to teach. He argues for the 'conviction' that actors can bring but also respects the engaging power of a teacher working in role and concludes that 'the best team is a mixture of actors and teachers' (Haddon in Bennett: 2005: 165).

The fact that both teaching- and acting-trained young people were attracted to this new genre of work reflects the social optimism of the time. For drama teachers, this new approach called 'TIE' offered more opportunity to implement radical teaching philosophies in a working environment freed from much of the school bureaucracy. For young actors with left-wing sensibilities, TIE offered a fresh approach to theatre's place in society: an opportunity to use theatre as an implement of change and a freedom from the claustrophobic world of traditional velvet-curtain theatre. It also offered opportunities for those with less experience to get 'a foot in the door' and to acquire the elusive Equity (union) card.[1] In later years (and until 'closed shop' arrangements were outlawed in 1982), this became something of an issue for the TIE movement as auditions would sometimes attract those seeking 'easy' entrance into the acting profession. Colin Hicks (interview: 18 June 2014) recalls the struggle they had getting Equity cards for Perspectives

TIE company when it was set up in 1972 because tight quota arrangements were in place.

In the 1970s, it was common practice when auditioning to demand training or professional experience as an actor *and* the possession of a teaching qualification. In Theatr Powys and Action PIE, for example, one of the first stages in trying to whittle down the hundreds of applicants to a shortlist was to eliminate those without teacher training. That situation changed radically in the following decade and acting training became the priority for all companies, though rigorous interview and workshop exercises would be used to seek out those with genuine interest in and sympathy for the work.

In search of a democratic working process

Whichever discipline the new TIE workers came from, they shared a desire to find new ways of working reflecting their view of how the world of work should be. Having implicitly rejected the strictures of the education status quo, and/or having rebelled against dusty theatre hierarchies, they wanted to work in systems that reflected their political worldview. It was part of the new vision of theatre within education that was emerging. Belgrade was set up in this way and most companies that are mentioned in these pages attempted to tread the same path. Even companies not originally set up as cooperatives (for example, Theatr Powys) tried to move towards collaborative processes under SCYPT's influence.

Anyone who has worked in such an environment will know that the utopia is elusive but one could not press for personal growth and independence of mind through your TIE programmes if one could not afford oneself the same freedom in the creation of the work. With various degrees of success, companies attempted to create democratic structures through which the voices of all contributing artists could be heard.

Yeoman (interview: 28 May 2014) offers a particular example of the pain that can come with the democratic freedoms of cooperative decision-making. He recalls working for a company that, under extreme financial pressure in the 1980s, had to make a redundancy. In the spirit of openness, each company member had to justify his or her role professionally. The company would then vote who would go. Worse still, having been through this process it was found that there was a need for a second redundancy, so another person previously reprieved also had to be sacked. This 'entirely contradictory experience' has, he says, informed all of his subsequent approaches to trade unionism, management and workers' rights. Such processes are deadly to working relationships. Was there a fairer way of making these cuts? Would the autocracy of traditional management have been less painful? Kevin Dyer writes about the theoretical contradictions of trying to work as a cooperative that lead to 'discrepancy between policy and practice in socialist theatre management' (Dyer: 1988: 15). He recalls the pressure that his company (Avon Touring Theatre Company) had from funders and the Charity Commission who clearly disapproved of collective working but argues that the problems encountered by cooperative companies go beyond these clashes with traditional structures (Dyer: 1988: 16). The director tends to have control despite any stated policy to the contrary and a worker without control over their work is not, clearly, working in a cooperative. The resolution to these issues resides in the ability to define role boundaries and respect the expertise of different jobs, but Dyer is right in alerting us to the fact that this is not easily done and he argues persuasively for commitment to real cooperative working, despite the consequences. All of the practitioners I interviewed conceded that ultimate power usually rested with the director though Chris Vine (interview: 21 September 2014) maintains that Perspectives (in 1974) was 'genuinely a collective' with parity of wages, policy influence and choice of material. Warwick Dobson describes the attempted collectivism at the Duke's Playhouse TIE as a 'bold attempt' though he recognizes the difficulty of finding the line between democracy and leadership. He remembers that the company trusted 'to the collective and something would happen (and sometimes it didn't)' (interview: 8 October 2014). Dyer's experience, some fifteen years later, was less relaxed and as time went on he notes that there was a tendency for long-established companies to be protective of their work practices by limiting the voting rights of new members. Some, in these cooperatives, were less equal than others.

Tony Coult, in 1980, interviewed a variety of TIE workers about collective working, including several voices already mentioned in these pages (Coult in *SCYPT Journal No. 5*: 1980: 40–8). Chris Vine felt that collectivism was the ideal but it could not always be lived up to. There would be those who involved themselves more deeply in their theoretical understanding or whose contribution would be shaped by the nature of their role in the company. This would include the role of director and it was 'absolutely essential that there are people there in the work who are capable of directing an artistic experience ... I don't think that can be found cooperatively' (Coult in *SCYPT Journal No. 5*: 1980: 41). Vine also identified the need to be able to take criticism and, indeed, to be self-critical. An actor with Cockpit TIE at the time, Harry Miller, describes the struggle the team had with developing a political analysis of the work but notes that voting was rarely necessary and work was carried out on a basis of trust and consensus (*Coult in SCYPT Journal No. 5*: 1980: 41–2). Pammenter, however, acknowledges the occasional need for voting which may occur when a group of 'village elders' decide they no longer need a dialectical process because they have the answer. This he describes as 'paternalistic' and a vote may be needed to force discussion. Pammenter identifies an additional problem, which is that those with experience and who are articulate can undermine the democratic process and Vine adds that articulacy can actually be a danger if one abuses it 'to bamboozle everybody'. Sue Hill, an actress with Perspectives at the time, saw another issue with company democracy – the assumption that everyone would be good at their job and could be trusted to do it. She felt that the larger the group, the more statistically probable it would be that someone would *not* be good at their job and then it is 'very difficult to allow them the kind of power and responsibility that they should be democratically allowed' (Coult in *SCYPT Journal No. 5*: 1980: 45). A further issue identified by Hill was the way in which male-orientated debating traditions tended to exclude female members. She found she had to be pushy and aggressive to survive which, she admits, led to her being accused of 'using male methods to take part in company organization' (Coult in *SCYPT Journal No. 5: 1980*: 46).

On a very different level, deeply held moral (rather than political) views can cause disruption in the collectivist idyll. Murphy (1975: 22–3) relates how the employment of a Catholic actor/teacher stalled the improvisation of *Sweetie Pie* (a performance TIE piece play about women's rights, including discussion of the right to choose to have an abortion) and led to unsatisfactory compromises in the final scenes of the play which clearly needed, and failed, to offer the audience opportunity to discuss 'choice' issues. Perhaps he should not have been employed into a company likely to deal with such matters? The idea of including questions about religion and morality in auditions, however, would be highly problematic. For all the artistic power collectivism gives, it is clear that there are structural weaknesses that could easily fracture under financial or artistic pressure.

As with theoretical and political consciousness, it was SCYPT that ensured such issues were considered by affiliated companies. The conference in 1976 devoted a whole day to the discussion of company structure (Redington: 1983: 119) and as a result many prioritized a reconsideration of their working arrangements, employment, role-designation and contractual policies. This was not always easily achieved for companies working within local government frameworks.

Working cooperatively within a hierarchy

Complications emerged as funding settlements became more secure, for this very security usually meant that the TIE companies had to fit into the mindset of organizations that did not share (or understand) these working practices. TIE was spending public money and had to be correctly overseen and audited. This is what traditional structures are designed to assure. In the early years this was often achieved through the companies' attachment to main house theatres, using their governance to legitimize their own. Others, independent of theatres, operated as educational charities with a board of trustees offering oversight and ultimate public accountability. This remains a popular structure and is indeed necessary in order to be eligible for funds from trusts and foundations. Companies can also be set up as limited companies (limiting the personal liability of members in the case of financial collapse) but these are less common as their ability to attract sponsorship is narrower. There are also many (usually set up by recent acting graduates) who offer work to schools on a 'profit-share' (for which one may usually read 'loss-share') basis. These companies are sometimes more about gaining experience and expanding CVs or résumés than they are about developing a philosophy of working practice.

Whichever legal structure was adopted the most common model of funding at this time was that of match-funding from Arts

Councils, Arts Associations and the Local Education Authorities. To receive monies companies would have to have an interface between themselves and the funders. Prior (interview: 27 May 2014) recalls that in setting up Action PIE he was required to create a management 'advisory' panel of teachers and counsellors in order to access Arts Council funds. Whatever the structure it became common to have advisory boards/panels/management committees offering financial reassurance, though the degree to which these panels were involved with the TIE work varied. Theatr Powys, for example, was created as a section of the education department under the leadership (and subject to the scrutiny) of the Drama Advisor – a Local Education Authority role. The activities of the company would be reviewed by a Management Panel that would also approve future plans. The Drama Advisor would attend Panel meetings perhaps accompanied by the Administrator and/or Director of the company (as observers) who could answer questions.

Such external management arrangements were fraught with potential problems, often related to ignorance of the work on the part of those doing the managing. If teachers themselves found it difficult to comprehend the nature of TIE, what hope was there that councillors and education bureaucrats would have a better understanding? Often a strange binary process developed where, externally, governance was traditionally structured and beyond reproach whilst internally companies were struggling to forge democratic processes.

At Lancaster TIE, from 1983 there was a structure in existence that had been common in previous years. The company was attached to the Duke's Playhouse theatre and the education director was part of the theatre's Management Panel. This panel in turn had a sub-committee concerned solely with the work of the TIE company and which contained a representative of the main house theatre. In this structure, company members were involved in recruitment decisions and, though unusual, this was a comparatively minor issue for a company based within a traditional theatre.

At Theatr Powys a more translucent game was played. When new appointments were made applicants would be applying for a teacher contract post that had to be made by officials of the LEA, i.e. the management panel. If the appointment was to be successful, it would clearly be important that the appointee would be able to work with existing company members and be in tune with their working methodology. To the Local Authority the idea of involving actor/teachers in the appointment of a fellow worker or, in the case of a director, their 'boss', was an idea beyond comprehension. The rather awkward compromise would be for company members to produce the shortlist and to workshop/audition the applicants who would then have a formal interview with the management panel at which the preferences of the company would be conveyed by the Drama Advisor. A high-risk way of doing business but, as I recall, it seemed to work, though I was never quite sure of the extent to which the panel knew they were involved in a façade. Whatever mode of governance was employed, there would always be the potential for misunderstanding and political interference:

> Leaders must be selected and appointed by someone who also has the authority to supervise and even fire them [but] these tasks should be the responsibility of an autonomous board ... because an autonomous board will first and foremost have the interests of the organisation in view, whereas a political body ... will be guided by primarily political considerations. (Klaic: 2012: 162)

'There will be a meeting' (*Fanshen*, David Hare)

The main issue with collective working can be the stifling amount of time that has to be devoted to company meetings. As Theatr Powys expanded and pursued collaborative policies, the necessity grew for regular meetings to facilitate proper communication and these took an increasing amount of time. It became difficult to know which decisions could be left to designated roles and which required company approval. Circular arguments about resource priorities would surface whilst the administrator was having to delay urgent responses to schools or funders because the company had not yet discussed them. Even in small companies the clash of egos can be bruising. 'There were endless meetings', recalls Hicks of Perspectives, 'we slugged it out', though he adds that it was 'not a major problem – we were effective devisers and there was a lot of convergence about the motives for doing it.' A similar pattern was to be found across the TIE landscape. Despite contradictions,

Yeoman recalls that at both M6 in the early 1970s and at Lancaster TIE from the 1980s to the early 1990s, there was a constant struggle to use democratic meeting structures to underpin the validity of the work; 'company meetings were the highest forum for decisions and involved the whole company'.

It is because of this positive attitude that, despite inherent problems of democratic working, this search for new structures may be lauded. For the actor/teachers, and potentially for the whole workforce, they offered a refreshing opportunity to engage with the work through camaraderie leading to ownership. For this to truly work however, *all* company members have to be engaged in the philosophical decisions surrounding the work. The companies who achieved this most successfully would see not only actor/teachers at SCYPT conferences but also stage managers, designers and administrators. This was not always financially feasible nor did non-performing individuals always feel the necessity. Schisms could develop in companies based on the implication that there were 'producers' of the work and 'support staff'. When this occurred, collaborative working became more problematic and the meetings more tedious and less fruitful. As Klaic (2012) has observed, development of ideas and confidence inherently brings with it:

> new aspirations, opportunities and predilections ... which cannot any longer be contained by the group's identity and working process .... Factions emerge, fight, split, restructure on their own terms or disband. (Klaic: 2012: 47)

This process can be seen as a brutal but fruitful way for artistic endeavour to evolve. Dobson fondly recalls Gillham's aphorism that 'if you've got six people in a room agreeing, then five of them are redundant'.

Creating the work

In the rehearsal studio cooperative working offered a frustrating liberation that engendered exhilaration and migraines in equal measure. It is genuinely inspiring to have the freedom to forge ideas as part of a team – a freedom denied most teachers and many actors. In most companies ideas could come from anywhere, but one had to be prepared to be knocked back. Yeoman relates how at M6, under the guest directorship of David Pammenter, he wanted to do a project about El Salvador and the Contras. Pammenter wanted to do something on the Irish Republican hunger strikes. Both projects were presented and voted on and the hunger strikes project won out. Yeoman recalls feeling bruised but came to accept the decision as having been the right one for the company at that time. Working together creatively with the same group of people for perhaps years will create tensions that will lead at times to heady confrontation. Nicolson refers us to Bolton TIE's project about sexism, *Sweetie Pie* (1972, cited above) in the devising of which many male members of the company found themselves forced to address their own internalized sexism (Nicolson: 2009: 27. See also Murphy: 1975: 15ff).

As Pammenter points out (in Jackson: 1993: 53ff), it is impossible to describe all the possible ways of devising TIE; each company, director or writer will have their own approach. For Dobson (interview: 8 October 2014), one of the most valuable experiments was having different 'directors' for the devising process and the rehearsal of the emerging text. If there are contradictions between the themes being worked on and the attitudes of the group members there will be the opportunity for personal growth but also the potential to resist ideas. Murphy's description of the devising process for *Sweetie Pie* is illustrative of this. Devising was, from the earliest TIE adventures, the norm for creating work. There was a professional passion in working from thoughts on a whiteboard to a finished programme. Few companies initially used writers (though this did change as funding opportunities developed) and some, for example Perspectives, eschewed the employment of a writer (and even a director), preferring to allocate new monies to employing a designer.

Even when writers were employed, they would be required to craft the ideas and possibilities devised by the actor/teachers. Devising is not an easy option:

It demands ... an understanding of its potential audience/ participants; objectivity, clarity and analysis in the researching process; creativity, vision and vitality in the structuring and writing process; and, at every stage, a sense of theatre and dramatic order. (Pammenter in Jackson: 1993: 53)

Often, the initial impetus would come from a theme (for example, 'racism' in *When Sleeping Dogs Awake*). At other times the starting point might be schools' requests for a project about, for example, the Second World War, and a company would then set about unpacking the possible themes within such a programme (for example, *Careless Talk*). Another, more nebulous approach might arise when a company member would present a newspaper article, a poem, an image or a historical event which contains something that they are unable to identify but which their professional instincts tell them is worth investigating. In a democratic company, such ideas would be tested out through practical exploration, and yes, through discussion.

It is at this stage in the process that it can be hard to move beyond traditional working structures. For an idea originating in any of the above ways, there will need to be, at some point if not immediately, a guiding gut to frame the explorations. This is normally the role of the Director (which gives them the inherent power within the company), but in a cooperatively operating company, the direction will take account of alternative approaches coming from the rehearsal floor. The process requires two-way communication, trust – and a willingness, when necessary, to let go of an idea that no longer belongs to you alone.

Townend does not relate from where the theme of 'racism' emerged for *When Sleeping Dogs Awake*. She does though describe the devising process (Grady & O'Sullivan: 1998: 79ff). Here, clearly, the lead is being taken by the director who starts by getting the actors to depict historic images from the Indian Mutiny. They are: the tying of a mutineer to a cannon by a fellow Indian soldier watched by a British officer; the moment after the canon is fired; and the Indian soldier, alone, cleaning the cannon afterwards. These images have no place in the final play but they bring forward key themes that will emerge (Chapter Six) such as 'what makes us act against our own interest?' and the image of the rope that binds. This exploration provided a contextual group framework in which further investigation could take place and Townend describes how the onus is turned back to the actor/teachers by asking them to create their own race-depictions. This was to offer up the image of the sign reading 'no blacks, no Jews, no dogs' and though, again, this has no appearance in the narrative of the play, it brought forward the notion of dogs as symbols of despised creatures. In this way the director, in his/her role as shepherd of ideas, has to be both an equal company member and also offer their particular skill of analysis and synthesis.

The task of being artistic leader and democratic company member is a tricky one. Can you create art collaboratively? Most directors have the ultimate power and will use it; theirs is the final vision. John Prior recalls that when working at Stoke-on-Trent in the early 1970s Stuart Bennett as Artistic Director maintained that the company worked cooperatively but was not under workers' control; he had the final word. Jackson (interview: 24 June 2014) shares the view that, de facto, directors hold ultimate power. When Prior went on to set up Action PIE, he insisted to funders that the company would have to work as a democracy and a key resource was to be a round table for discussions! At nearby Abergavenny, however, Theatr Gwent was structured as part of the Local Authority Youth Service and the director and administrator were clearly placed at the apex of a hierarchical structure.

The TIE writer

The TIE writer is a role that evolved later. Some companies, as we have seen, preferred to share this key artistic role, but others saw value in the artistic completion offered by a writer, relieving performers of the burden of possessing such skills. As TIE became better funded and more theoretically mature there was a felt need to separate the skills of actor/teacher, director, designer, musician and, for some, writer. However, a playwright is a breed apart and whilst most writers write because they have something to say, the TIE writer is expected to have something to ask; they need to be able to provide a framework in which issues can be examined. Even Brecht knew what he wanted his spectators to think, but good TIE writing goes beyond this to wanting the participants to reflect on and respond to a situation. TIE is about learning not *what* but *how* to think. A particular example of this will be considered with the recent work of Big Brum and Edward Bond in a later chapter, but here I offer a brief example from my own working history. Greg Cullen was a powerful influence in Theatr Powys in the 1980s strongly drawn (from his engagement with the Socialist Worker's Party) to collaborative working and group decision making but often frustrated by the limitations this placed on him as a writer:

> Few, if any company members understood the particular needs
> of a writer …. This led to my serving the company rather than
> developing my own voice. (Cullen in Taylor: 1997: 140)

For Cullen writing was an individual activity that fitted
uncomfortably with the collectivism he aspired to, even though
he was largely responsible for bringing Heathcote's practice to
Theatr Powys' TIE work with *Past Caring* (1984). Writers seem
most happy when they have personal ownership of their work.
The fine TIE work of writers like Charles Way and David Holman
has led them away from the TIE genre into children's theatre,
and the contribution that devising and collective processes had to
honing their skills as writers is not always recognized. Some of the
most memorable TIE work by Holman ('*No Pasaran*', *Drink the
Mercury*) is performance based and this has subsequently become
his standard mode of working. Readman (in Jackson: 1993: 280)
mentions a performance of Holman's *Frankie's Friends* and notes
that the performance piece was followed up by a workshop devised
by freelance workers. Mary Cooper (in Jackson & Vine (eds): 2013:
103) notes that 'few companies have either the time or the "team"
to devise and most work is now left to a designated, even externally
sourced, writer'. Whilst true, it is a little sad that one of the fruits
of the TIE experiment (work created with dedication and passion
by the group) should now be regularly outsourced, notwithstanding
the fact that many fine pieces of work are produced through this
approach. The comments of Jim Mirrione (of the Creative Arts Team
in New York) in 1993 are central to my concerns. Describing the
work of CAT as evolving out of British TIE, he nonetheless contends
that the writing process is 'most effective when a single dramatist
works with a director and an executive administrator'. This, he
maintains, 'creates a unified product that enables the educational
content to be illustrated and communicated by the particular
dynamics of theatre' (Jackson: 1993: 73). I am concerned that the
primacy given to the writer to 'communicate' via 'a product' is likely
to obscure the real educational value of TIE. In limiting the actors
to their acting alone he is happy to keep them away from 'creation'.
Though Mirrione sees the TIE play as needing to be bookended
within an initial workshop and a 'post-performance discussion', he
is in danger, I fear, of fragmenting the holistic framework present
in, for example, *When Sleeping Dogs Awake*. The first item in his

'pre-scripting' phase is to ask 'what is it that the playwright wants to impart to this student audience?' (Jackson: 1993: 74). The question should be, 'what learning area do I want to facilitate?'

This implicit one-way process is the road to dogma or, at least, closed thinking. Early on TIE evolved from agit-prop and Living Newspaper roots. Mirrione goes on to affirm that the writer must have 'a fundamental desire *to write about a pressing problem that will bring about a change of consciousness in an audience*' (Jackson: 1993: 81). I would argue that such a 'change of consciousness' (in Freire's phrase a 'conscientizing') needs the application of the ideas of Vygotsky or Giroux where the learning environment is framed within the ability to forensically examine rather than merely respond to a powerfully presented point of view. Unless the workshop bookends are particularly well honed to fit the overall unified concept of the programme, there would appear to be an exclusion of the children from the interpretative processes.

Contractual arrangements

It is probably already clear that contractual arrangements for the new actor/teachers were subject to huge variation emerging from local precedents. In the late 1960s and in the 1970s actors' pay was often at subsistence levels. Teachers were not much better off, though the existence of a pay structure related to training and experience offered a potential career structure. Most TIE companies thus sought to establish themselves on pay scales related to those of teachers. At Cockpit TIE and GYPT actor/teachers were employed on lecturers' salary scales though also expected to be Equity members. This was beneficial to the actor/teachers but made the commitment towards collective processes problematic when working alongside short-term employees or non-academic colleagues. The use of academic contracts was the most straightforward approach for those working in schools, but there was always potential for conflict when employees are attached to different pay scales. Administrators would be on Local Government Officers' rates and stage-managers on traditional theatre contracts. The actors' union, Equity, to which most actor/teachers wished to be associated, had no power to negotiate contracts of teachers. On the other hand, teacher contracts did not have the flexibility to deal with touring subsistence payments nor arrangements for working overtime or unsociable hours. Good will and commitment to the work meant that these problems rarely caused more than a local and passing sense of grievance, but they could puncture the collective idyll. Should directors be paid more than actors? What about writers, who are often required to attend the day's rehearsals and then go home to start their writing? What about the cleaner? Different roles might receive better remuneration than others as different trade unions achieved improved deals with government, national or local. Those companies who decided to pool their incomes and equalize pay had to deal with delicate issues around different roles' financial and legal accountabilities, and how to recognize the additional expenses of those with children or caring responsibilities. Action PIE was one company that developed a system of increments for those with children. At Lancaster, equal pay was limited to actor/teachers because of contractual restrictions. In trying to live the utopia, many such issues were sidelined. Such selective myopia would not in the end be enough and, when the funding environment changed so radically in the 1990s, these islands of socialist equality would largely become untenable. Jackson (interview: 24 June 2014) recalls that as soon as companies started to separate themselves from their main houses and needed to employ a range of skills to run a company, cooperative working and pay parity became, for some, problematic.

Equity did identify the contractual issues surrounding this new theatrical genre and during the 1970s, an official TIE contract came into being for use by actor/teachers, stage-managers and designers that simplified the situation, though administrative staff could not be included. Whilst many new companies moved to this contract, others preferred the teachers contracts which usually provided secure tenure for the individual (and by implication for the company). Indeed, another reason for thorough audition procedures was that company members on teacher contracts could potentially be employed indefinitely.

Training

How people gain the skills to become effective actor/teachers has been an underlying theme of much of what I have so far set down. Clearly an actor/teacher needs skills from both disciplines. As praxis developed, the tendency has been for acting to have primacy and for educational theory to come from training on the job, exposure to ideas in the rehearsal room, from sharing situations (such as those offered by SCYPT) and from theoretically astute directors. Warwick Dobson brought to the Dukes Playhouse TIE a background as a trained teacher and experience teaching in a Higher Education environment. He brought in ideas from Gavin Bolton and Vygotsky and was partly responsible for bringing the drama approaches of Heathcote and Bolton to the TIE movement. Also via SCYPT came introductions to political theory via such thinkers as Gillham and McEntegart. What was missing for many actor/teachers was formal academic training and the immersion in teaching and political theory was, for many, a real challenge to their assumptions about how theatre was created. At times since 1965 some institutions have endeavoured to offer training courses in Drama and/or Theatre in Education. Bretton Hall was one such that offered relevant option strands. Chris Vine reminds me of the crucial role played by Stuart Bennett in this respect, setting up the Community Arts Course at Rose Bruford College in 1976 which started to codify a range of training within TIE and community theatre.

Not all TIE training would boast such rigour and, though in time other universities started to include modules in Theatre in Education, these often only consisted of some thirty hours of tuition and frequently lacked theoretical underpinning of practical approaches, conflating TIE, DIE and Children's Theatre. The high levels of skills required in 'signing' and in facilitation were rarely given the attention required. This in turn led to later TIE projects falling into a genre of educational 'message' theatre. Additionally the motivations for working in TIE have shifted towards the need to 'boost the résumé' with many actors seeing any such work as treading water until some 'real' work comes along. For the actor/teachers of the 1960s, 1970s and 1980s such an attitude was rare. For them, to be an actor/teacher was a challenge, a nightmare, a dream and deeply rewarding artistically and politically. Much of the training was happening on the job. Formal training for TIE was resisted by conservatoire drama schools that undervalued the theatrical aesthetics of TIE and even created a prejudice against working in this area. As a result, many young actors entered the profession with low expectations of what would be required of them and were either pleasantly surprised by the artistic and theoretical demands or overwhelmed by them. From this eclectic intake were to emerge the actor/teachers of the day undertaking frenetic tours of perhaps ten schools a week, whilst others were driven back to the more traditional demands of auditions and the occasional excursion onto the proscenium stage.

Note

1 At this time Equity operated a 'closed shop' and for new entrants to the profession this often meant getting caught in a 'no card without a job and no job without a card' dilemma. Additionally, those wishing to work in West End theatres had to have completed a probationary period of membership.

CHAPTER NINE

International Perspectives and Influence

Britain was not alone in being the subject of the social, educational and political aspirations that led to the creation of TIE and, at a distance, we can see that the desire for a more positive future was present in war-decimated countries across Europe. Hopes for the future were shared by the global giants of the United States and the USSR though these were quickly soured by diverging ideologies, selfish ambitions and competitiveness (real and imagined) that immersed the world in the Cold War. It is perhaps not too idealistic to see performing artists raising themselves above the petty yet petrifying threats of nuclear annihilation and seeking to envision a better world. Alongside TIE there were other, more international, fruits of this season of human history. One of these was the growth of an international children's theatre organization, l'Association Internationale du Théâtre de l'Enfance et la Jeunesse (ASSITEJ).

The emergence of ASSITEJ

It cannot be argued that ASSITEJ was a 'fruit' of TIE, but it came from the same orchard and bears a remarkably similar developmental history. Nat Eek has documented the history and governance of ASSITEJ in three volumes from 2008 to 2014. He identifies the roots of ASSITEJ as being in the post-war mood of optimism and a broader awareness of other cultures (Eek: 2008: 33). He characterizes the post-War period as a time when cultural exchanges became popular, de-colonization led to a rediscovery of pre-colonial history (often with a socialistic bias) and there was comparative prosperity. In the political sphere this optimistic tendency was swiftly swept away by the Cold War, but either side of the East–West wall children's theatre was flourishing along parallel, separated, lines. In Britain the work of such practitioners as Brian Way and Caryl Jenner was raising the profile of children's theatre and influencing not only TIE but also professionalizing a specific genre of TfC. Behind the 'Iron Curtain', children's theatre was also being given a high profile and entrusted to highly trained practitioners.

The key driver in bringing these separate traditions into contact with each other was the newly formed UNESCO, which had set up the International Theatre Institute (ITI) in recognition of the important part that theatre could play in the reconciliation of nations through the arts. The focus of ITI was, however, very much on adult theatre. An initiative by France led to the setting up of l'Association du Théâtre pour l'Enfance et la Jeunesse (ATEJ) in 1967 with a view to creating an international organization for children's theatre. It was this organization that was eventually to become ASSITEJ. The key moment for the creation of ASSITEJ was an international conference and festival hosted by the British Children's Theatre Association in 1964. A Preparatory Committee drew up a constitution and in 1965, (the same year as Belgrade started touring schools with its TIE), ASSITEJ formally came into being. The theatrical, political and financial environment was the same for both strands of work for children, but whereas the TIE movement chose to develop its work in conjunction with educational philosophy, ASSITEJ was primarily concerned with the creation of theatrical work *for* (not with nor by) young people. From the very beginning, ASSITEJ was adamant that theatre for young people should be just that; its operational interests would not include amateur work by children or educational work involving children. Both approaches acknowledged the importance of theatre to the development of young people, but whereas TIE sought to use theatrical techniques to develop an understanding of humanity through personal engagement, the ASSITEJ approach was more traditionally grounded in the receiving of an aesthetic stimulus distanced by proscenium or other theatrical tradition.

The political context of ASSITEJ

In global institutions, power struggles are magnified and this was never more clearly seen than during the international tensions that developed within ASSITEJ. Eek documents descriptions of the squabbles over elections, voting rights, the constitution and official languages. He describes the political manoeuvrings within the executive committee and 'the Bureau' as well as financial disagreements (even irregularities at times) and the interference of governments through espionage. Such matters appear to have plagued the association throughout the early years in ways that make the ideological wrangling within SCYPT seem tame. At times Eek (Eek *et al.*: 2008 and 2011) cites personal ambition and manoeuvring by small cliques but there is an overwhelming sense in his record of interference by governments keen to use ASSITEJ as a vehicle for their own geo-political agendas. ASSITEJ's constitution was clear that the organization should be above politics, but it side-steps the question of whether theatre can ever be politically neutral. A non-political framework is easily fractured by the need for government financial support and governments do not finance organizations that they feel do not serve their interests. Eek reports how both the United States and Eastern Bloc countries placed agents within delegations and theatre companies crossing the Iron Curtain with occasionally humorous results, such as an under-rehearsed spy infiltrated as a dancer (Eek *et al.*: 2008: 70–1).

The optimism out of which ASSITEJ was born was unsettled by the faltering world financial situation that TIE in Britain was also facing in the mid-1970s. ASSITEJ centres in individual countries came and went in line with financial problems and/or local political circumstances and the only centres able to withstand these storms were either lucky enough to be part of strong economies or were backed by governments which prioritized the need for the influence and profile that they felt membership gave them. ASSITEJ remained a largely European organization but survived, despite a deepening Cold War and military dictatorships in Greece (until 1974), Spain (until Franco's death in 1975), as well as extreme right-wing governments in Portugal (until the revolution of 1974) and across a range of South American nations. Whatever governments' secondary motives, children's theatre was playing a role in keeping the world together.

This world changed in 1985 with the installation of Gorbachev as president in the USSR and the end of the Cold War in 1989. In 1988, the Solidarity Union was legalized in Poland (and Britons were treated to the paradox of their right-wing prime minister extolling the virtues of a trade union). In the same year, the Berlin Wall came down and Germany was reunified. Also during the same period, President Reagan bought short-term prosperity through a process of deregulation, borrowing and free-market economics. In South Africa, de Klerk began a dialogue on 'evolutionary change'. In China, thousands were trampled under government tanks in Tiananmen Square. The world was changing.

Eurocentricity

The politics of financial support and voting blocks were not the only bars to wider membership. ASSITEJ had been founded on western precepts of theatre that did not always reflect the theatre traditions of other cultures. In many emergent nations, the notion of the professional actor did not exist and the use of amateurs and children in performances excluded them from membership as they were unable to fulfil the constitution's criteria.

Language was another issue that militated against some developing nations. From the outset French and English were designated the official languages, to which Russian was swiftly added for political reasons and because it was the common language of the Eastern Bloc countries who subsidized advanced children's theatres. The former British and French colonies could cope satisfactorily with these arrangements, but most of South America was disenfranchised by the omission of Spanish as an official language and this was a constant source of discontent. Only the United States and European countries had the financial stability and theatrical infrastructure to remain at the centre of ASSITEJ. In 1987, the elections produced a European landslide with the only Asian country (Japan) being voted off the executive despite having been an enthusiastically active member (Eek *et al.*: 2011: 226). It was clear that for the foreseeable future ASSITEJ was to be a 'western club'.

In whose interests?

Even so, it is impossible not to recognize the huge contribution that ASSITEJ has made to the sharing, developing and professionalization of children's theatre. It has taken the need for a child-orientated theatre and pushed aesthetic boundaries, creating a genre that is vibrant and internationally respected. At the same time, at least until 1990, it remained an organization that was not only Eurocentric but also had a tendency to patronize its defined audience with a somewhat paternal vision of what children's theatre should contain. Themes were selected by adult directors who may, or may not, sympathize with the preoccupations of the young. We see in the lists of productions in Eek's volumes a preponderance of adult classics, myths and adaptations of children's stories that the adults feel the children ought to be exposed to. When, occasionally, political themes are present there is no opportunity for dialogic autopsy. Unlike TIE, children's theatre generally exists on a linear 'entertainment-information' axis. For example, in 1981 at the Congress in Lyon, it was noted by delegates that sex, violence and death were frequent themes and members longed for a happy ending (Eek *et al.*: 2011: 117). The point being overlooked is that such material can, in fact, be dealt with intelligently by theatre but it needs the interrogation offered by TIE techniques.

Early versions of the constitution of ASSITEJ wrestled not only with the place of amateurs but also the place of what was referred to as 'Creative Dramatics' (Eek: 2008: 40). ASSITEJ was in the hands of talented, well-meaning but usually 'old guard' theatre lovers whose experience of children's theatre emanated from the pre-war period. TIE was created by younger actors, directors and educators with a much more revolutionary view of how theatre could impact on young people's lives.

ASSITEJ and TIE

Superficially there are elements that inhabit the philosophies of both ASSITEJ and TIE (as exemplified by SCYPT). Both movements have concerned themselves with the need for specifically orientated writers and directors and for specialized forms of acting style.

Pedagogically, the ASSITEJ constitution acknowledges 'the role that theatre can play in the education of younger generations' (Eek *et al.*: 2008: 48) and at the 1968 Congress in The Hague the British representative, Gerald Tyler (speaking perhaps from the *zeitgeist* of student uprisings in Europe and the growing confidence of TIE back home) asked:

> Are we preparing the children for independent thought and action, or are we shaping him in our own image? (Congress minutes quoted by Eek: 2008: 86)

The Netherlands' delegate, Erik Vos, voiced similar concerns:

> The task of theatre is to raise questions, not give answers ... the Audience must feel that they participate in the creation .... The main aim is to allow the audience to handle reality. (Eek: 2008: 87)

Eek sums up this discussion at the General Assembly thus:

> Basically it was agreed that theatre can and should show the ugliness in the world, but the theatre must decide what and how much to show. (Eek: 2008: 87)

These comments present the essential difference in approach: ASSITEJ's children's theatre will feel bold enough to display ugliness but lacks the philosophical and theoretical underpinning that enables TIE's spectators to grapple with and process the stimulus meaningfully.

ASSITEJ was scrupulous in its avoidance of TIE and ideas emanating from the 'Creative Drama' camp. Such philosophies were regarded as amateur and aesthetically unsound. Even in the UK and with a common language, TIE companies were having to deal with multifarious misunderstandings of their work, so it is not altogether surprising that British delegates found it difficult to press the case for better understanding in a multi-national forum. At an executive meeting in Leipzig in 1972, both Tyler and Jenner asked that 'the place of creative drama in the world of children's theatre' be considered (Eek: 2008: 165). The British request was responded to in the international congress in Albany in 1972 that included a 'Creative Drama Day' at which Dorothy Heathcote ran a workshop.

Eek notes (2008: 214) that many European countries did not attend because of lack of interest in this work that, they felt, fell outside the constitution. The proposal to make Creative Drama part of ASSITEJ's remit was defeated by a margin of 2:1. This decision was ratified by the executive meeting in 1973. For ASSITEJ, as soon as the children left their seats and joined the actors the work became non-professional. It is perhaps symbolic that it was at this time that SCYPT began to emerge as an organization to codify and develop TIE praxis; clearly TIE was very different from children's theatre, and a key difference was that TIE was gaining a body of underpinning educational theory *in addition* to high aesthetic aspirations.

Tyler made another attempt and in 1975 persuaded the executive to set up a working party to look at Creative Drama within ASSITEJ and report back. This was openly opposed by Russia and Czechoslovakia who pointed out that the constitution 'did not seem to include' Creative Drama and that ASSITEJ had to 'guard its quality as an association' (Eek: 2008: 257). The next congress was held in the German Democratic Republic[1] sector of Berlin in 1975 and included a discussion of the role of professional children's theatre in general arts teaching in schools. Sats, the USSR delegate running this group, called for theatre to 'awaken the creative instinct in people, so that they not only followed but took the lead themselves' (Eek: 2008: 268). In another group the stalwart of UK children's theatre and DIE, Brian Way, led a discussion on 'the participation of audiences in professional children's theatre' which seems to be as close as anyone got to discussing TIE. However, TIE theory had moved beyond Way's drama experiments of the 1960s and the discussion seems to have run into the quicksand of terminology rather than progressing an appreciation of how participation can work within theatre. In 1976 it was suggested that those interested in Creative Drama should seek membership of the International Institute of Theatre Amateurs. This was endorsed by the executive in 1977 thus, according to Eek (2011: 76), putting 'an end to any further consideration of "creative drama" as a viable component of ASSITEJ'. Reading Eek's accounts, there is a sense that at this time the UK delegates really want to get to grips with these issues but that most other countries just don't 'get it':

At the time it seemed like a slap in the face to many members, but in the long run it strengthened the organization, gave it a stronger artistic focus, gave it credibility amongst its peers, and helped raise the level of performance in all countries. (Eek *et al.*: 2011: 77)

Although the battle for creative drama seemed lost after 1977, British delegates continued to push for consideration of TIE. Shaun Hennessey, in 1983, invited the Bureau of ASSITEJ to London to observe the work of Theatre Centre and the Unicorn Theatre. Eek notes that the Bureau attended the performance and then attended a reception (Eek *et al.*: 2011: 151). No other details are deemed worthy of recording. Not until halfway through Eek's second volume do we find mention of 'TIE'. Not that there is any sign that this was of concern to UK TIE companies who would not have seen themselves as part of the 'children's theatre' genre. What was regrettably lacking was respect for what TIE was achieving, though this could not be said of the British delegates who, by 1990, included Paul Harman, David Johnstone (in key financial positions in ASSITEJ), Vicky Ireland and Tony Gouveia: all practitioners with impressive TIE credentials. ASSITEJ was not a 'fruit' of TIE's success in the UK, but the TIE movement in Britain, through these prime movers, helped keep the needs of young people in focus and helped arrest the tendency for children's theatre to become solely a commodity prepared by one generation for another.

According to Harman (in Bennett: 2005), there was a major confrontation at the Stockholm Congress in 1990 in which, for the first time, an acknowledgement of participatory theatre held sway. This, he argues, led to a revitalizing of the Association through a doubling of membership and a concomitant move away from the Eurocentric model (Bennett: 2005: 55). In 2002 there was a move to streamline processes by making English the only official language. More UK companies became involved with ASSITEJ at this time, though as we will see, by the beginning of the twenty-first century most were in any case creating 'children's theatre' or 'educational theatre' rather than TIE.

The IDEA idea

The International Drama/Theatre and Education Association would seem a more natural home for TIE's international ambitions.

It was founded, paradoxically, in 1992 just as TIE was reeling from the effects of ERA. It is still in active existence with about ninety countries 'who are united in their commitment to making drama/ theater and education accessible, significant and present in the lives of children and the young everywhere'.[2] It sees itself as having a role in lobbying governments and agencies about the importance of drama and theatre for young people and supports research in this area. In Britain it has close links with National Drama and Patrice Baldwin is currently (2015) Chair of ND and former President of IDEA. Like ASSITEJ it has links to UNESCO and also to the International Amateur Theatre Association, which we have seen, is where ASSITEJ felt that TIE belonged. From 1992 IDEA effectively took over DIE work from IATA.

According to Gillham (1993: 14) the idea of IDEA arose from the National Association for the Teaching of Drama together with the Associação Portuguesa de Expressão Dramática in 1989 with the aim of creating an international organization to develop drama and TIE. This followed an NATD conference held in 1989 in the wake of ERA entitled 'The Fight for Drama – the Fight for Education' with keynote speeches from both Heathcote and Bond, which attracted over 400 delegates from twelve countries (Davis: 1998: 10–11). The first congress of IDEA was held in Porto with nearly five hundred delegates from forty countries. Western countries were well represented, but also many African, Asian, South American and Middle Eastern countries (including both Jordan and Israel). In 1992 Gillham was effusive about this achievement:

> There are very few organisations which one can truly say are WORLD organisations. That such an organisation and such a conference has been brought into being almost entirely by the efforts of those concerned is a **wonderful** (not in its debased usage) achievement. (Gillham: 1993: 14)

After the setbacks of ERA it is clear that TIE in the UK was making an impact with its approaches across the world and the conception of IDEA was certainly one of the fruits of TIE in the early 1990s and 'precious beyond the value that its participants extracted from the conference' (Gillham: 1993: 15).

Divisions emerge in IDEA

By the time of the third Congress in Kisumu, Kenya, some of the same issues that were plaguing ASSITEJ seemed to be appearing. The lack of non-European delegates present perhaps reflected a systemic Eurocentricism. There were arguments amongst delegates about proxy votes and about the majority needed to change the constitution and some concerns were also raised about accountancy procedures following the previous Brisbane Congress (O'Sullivan: 1999). The focal point of the Congress was, however, a theme close to the heart of TIE practitioners: 'What can be the role of drama/ theatre in education in a rapidly changing world entering a new millennium?'. Sub-themes emphasized the cultural aspects of this question and O'Sullivan reports positively about the nature of the informal discussion that took place.

This naturally close relationship between SCYPT companies, NATD and IDEA was not to last and Davis, in his bitter article in *Broadsheet* in 1998 felt that the dream of 1992 had been shattered and that, in IDEA, the '**appearance** of serving young people ... is appearance only'. The reason for this disillusionment was what Davis saw as the divergence that had emerged between making IDEA an organization which could pro-actively support young people through drama and TIE, deciding on priorities and supporting initiatives to support key needs, and allowing IDEA to become a means of internationally showcasing work and facilitating networking (Davis: 1998: 12–13). For Davis the tension between constitutional aims and actual practice was in danger of pulling IDEA apart with more and more power being absorbed by the Executive to the detriment of democracy and fiscal security within the organization.

Davis recalls that at Brisbane, Gillham, as SCYPT representative, had canvassed to get more African delegates to stand for the Executive and this had been objected to. Gillham had formal charges brought against him and the attack on SCYPT somehow became extended to an attack on a gay SCYPT member who had supported the rights of a gay Kenyan theatre worker (Davis: 1998: 13–14). Another casualty of this sad saga was Tony Grady, Secretary of IDEA (and incidentally a member of NATD) who, because of his reluctance to action anything that might be libellous was removed from his post. It later came to light that votes had been miscounted, but the General Council ignored advice from their lawyers to re-run the vote. It was indeed a dark period of IDEA's history.

In the following issue of *Broadsheet* (Vol. 15, Issue 1) the President of IDEA responded to Davis' claims, rejecting the notion that there were 'two tendencies' within IDEA, arguing instead that variations were the result of varying democratic decisions (O'Farrell: 1999: 58). He goes on to reject the claims of financial mismanagement and he also vigorously defends the mechanisms by which Tony O'Grady was suspended and removed from post (O'Farrell: 1999: 60). In the same edition of *Broadsheet* the Journal Committee of NATD responds to O'Farrell's arguments claiming that he has ignored the accusations of homophobia within IDEA, failed to respond to the questions surrounding the legality of the vote and that IDEA was in breach of its own constitution which forbids discrimination on the grounds of sexual orientation. It is surprising that following this bitter exchange NATD remained a member of IDEA until 2001.

IDEA continues today with a brief covering both techniques of working with drama in the classroom and also theatre presentation itself as part of the world of child drama. The arguments about the relationship between drama and theatre performance in schools have exercised commentators and practitioners for years and have little place here, except inasmuch as they affect the nature of TIE. It seems though that performance has become more important to IDEA's philosophy, though Neelands in his keynote speech at the Canada Congress, maintained that 'since its beginnings ... IDEA has worked to provide a cultural platform for different performances from all around the world' (Neelands: 2004: 33). Neelands sees IDEA's mission as a forum for 'social and economic differences to be ... negotiated' (2004: 33), 'to gather together to participate in making ... theatre for social rather than purely entertaining reasons' and to encourage solidarity and empathy with those who 'are different from ourselves' (2004: 35). Most of today's TIE companies would feel quite comfortable working in this environment alongside drama teachers, but for others the treatment of SCYPT members who worked so enthusiastically to set up IDEA left a sense of betrayal. It is a fruit of SCYPT and TIE of the 1990s (with others) and its original aims and objectives are something of which the TIE movement can be proud.

Further fruits

SCYPT remains a legal entity though is in abeyance. In the following chapter, I will examine in more detail the tendency in the 1990s for companies to eschew educational theory and try to operate within the demands of the National Curriculum. As theory became less central, SCYPT became less relevant and membership fell away. The last SCYPT conference was in 1997 and the last Journal appeared in 1998. The core companies of SCYPT agreed a new approach to training in 1995 and the following year set up the SCYPT Co-operative that toured a new Gillham TIE play, *Bone Cage*. Also set up in 1996 was the International Centre for TIE (ICTIE) that focussed on SCYPT's role in theoretical training.[3] Classic conceptual TIE was falling out of favour and ironically it is overseas, separate from IDEA, that new opportunities were emerging. ICTIE set up an international conference in 2000 in Jordan attended by a multitude of foreign delegates including representation from the former Yugoslavian countries, Iraq, Iran, Syria, Egypt, Palestine, Lebanon, Vietnam, Sweden, the United States, the UK and Australia. (In 2015 that seems an impossible combination.) It was funded by the British Council and the Noor-Al-Hussein Foundation thus extending Jordan's reputation for encouraging TIE. (See Attel in Jackson & Vine (eds): 2013: 259–62 and for a full description of the conference see Bazely *et al.* in *NATD Vol. 17 No. 1*.) Once again, Geoff Gillham had been a prime mover in creating these SCYPT initiatives. He was to die the following year (2001) at which point the project foundered, depending as it had done, on relationships he had fostered. Gillham had been a highly controversial player in TIE and many still blame him for the fracturing of the 'TIE movement'. His certainty and inability to compromise were often irritating but came from his enthusiasm and conviction of the power of theatre and TIE to enable people to change the world. He underestimated the capitalist system's resilience and his frequent prophecies of a socialist dawn many found wearisome, especially when played out in an eternal turf war between the Workers' Revolutionary Party and the Socialist Workers' Party. His faith in the young and in theatre was though, unshakeable. Prior to the Amman Conference Gillham had been involved in using TIE and DIE methodologies in the context of Bosnia and Herzegovina in the Pax Project (1997) that aimed to offer a new approach to peace building and reconciliation. These liaisons with Bosnia and Jordan continue today with NATD's projects.[4] The Pax Project and ICTIE were small but important fruits of TIE as the new millennium dawned.

Despite these disparities between SCYPT TIE companies, ASSITEJ and IDEA, TIE in Britain was not insular. Rather, TIE was very protective of its roots and hypersensitive to any dilution of its belief in young people and the humanizing effect of its pedagogy. ASSITEJ had only a marginal overlap with these aims and though originally there was concomitance between TIE and IDEA, this was not to survive. The 1990s was a period of decline for classic TIE companies as ERA took hold, and whereas IDEA adapted to these changes, the remaining classic TIE companies became estranged from those organizations following the new hegemony.

Further afield the development of TIE in Britain was reflected in other parts of the world, notably the United States, Australia and Canada. The 1990s was also to see experiments in the developing world with issue-based projects that came to be known as 'Theatre for Development' and which used many of the approaches of Theatre in Health Education that also emerged at this time. These are the subject of subsequent chapters but can be seen as constituents of the rich harvest of fruits that TIE brought to the table by the early 1990s. First we will consider the effects of ERA on the delivery and content of TIE in Britain during the 1990s.

Notes

1   GDR – East Germany – was a Russian satellite state at this time.
2   http://www.idea-org.net/en/articles/Welcome_to_the_global_drama_of_ IDEA%21/) [accessed 11 February 2015].
3   I am indebted to Ian Yeoman for this information about the SCYPT Co-operative and the ICTIE.
4   See www.natd.eu.

Afterword

Chris Vine

I will attempt two tasks here: to widen the focus and, in collegial spirit, to question some of the author's perceptions.

The two case studies successfully highlight important characteristics of mature TIE. *Careless Talk* resonates as a fine example of holistic, participatory work. The debt to DIE practices is plain to see. The use of the facilitator to stop the action and change frames, so that the audience can be challenged to think critically *on the outside* as well as think and feel *on the inside*, is a simple yet profoundly important strategy, easily taken for granted but not always understood. This moving in and out, is not designed to provide the opportunity for the company to explain or reinforce its message. On the contrary, it provides essential aesthetic distance and creative gaps (Jackson: 2007: 6, 179–81) to allow the young people to make their own meanings.

There is, however, one crucial element missing. Throughout the book, Wooster repeatedly quotes Freire. He also underlines a central tenet of TIE: to teach young people *how* to think, not tell them *what* to think. This connects directly to Freire's critical pedagogy and his concept of conscientização: 'learning to perceive social, political, and economic contradictions, and to take action against the oppressive elements of reality' (Freire: 2000: 35). Conscientization is more than consciousness-raising. The key word here is *action*. The opportunity for action, albeit in a fictional context, is what TIE provides above all other theatre forms. It is an opportunity that *Careless Talk* fails to offer. The young people voice their opinions, explain their views, develop arguments and offer advice, but essentially they do this on behalf of the characters. The drama swirls around them but is not happening *to* them, and although implicated, they are not the ones 'making it happen' (Bolton: 1979: 53). Contrast this with *School*

On The Green (GYPT: 1984). It employed many of the same drama conventions and strategies: the influences of Bolton and Heathcote were strong. Here too the young people were positioned to look in from the *outside*, to witness history unfolding, in 1914 rural England, and to identify with other children from this distant past. As in *Careless Talk*, they were invited to step into role, becoming their classmates and experiencing their world on the *inside*. Later they switched roles. They stepped into the shoes of the parents, farm labourers, at the bottom of the social order. As they moved between worlds, they were challenged to explain what was happening – and why. The crucial difference is that they were also confronted with dilemmas that required them to *take action*, and then experienced the consequences of those actions, often in conflict with the characters, each other – and the law. The drama was happening to them but they were also 'making it happen' (Bolton: 1979: 53). They were required to feel, to think, to act and to reflect. They were the *subjects*; they experienced TIE praxis.[1]

Writing of *When Sleeping Dogs Awake*, Wooster conjures a compelling picture. I can imagine the young audience poised on the edge of their seats, enthralled by the 'strange' (in the Brechtian sense) characters, engrossed by the inciting tale of murder, and gradually 'awakening' to the impending threat. *Sleeping Dogs* offers a contrasting model of TIE practice: the well made play followed by a workshop. It also raises some important questions.

Before addressing these, I will challenge an underlying assumption that frames the study: the suggestion that above a certain age (9 or 10) full participation, as exemplified in *Careless Talk*, is problematic, and the traditional audience-actor relationship necessary. In my experience, some of the most effective and affective immersive programmes have been implemented with older secondary school students: for example, *Race against Time* (GYPT: 1978), *Land Fit For Heroes* (GYPT: 1982 and 1984), and *Conflict* (Perspectives: 1974). In these programmes, students were required to be in-role, in a 'living-through' (Bolton: 1979: 52) experience. Recently, I have witnessed similar engagement in the US in TIE work for teenagers and adults. This in no way invalidates the Belgrade's choice, but I reject the idea that full on, in-role participation is not appropriate with older audiences.

The style of *Sleeping Dogs* raises an interesting pedagogical question. Wooster stresses its use of metaphor. The play creates a metaphorical world, reminiscent of Orwell's *Animal Farm*. The central metaphor proceeds from the basic simile that, in this fictional world, the dogs are *like* the exploited and oppressed of the world and the humans are the oppressors. This simile is used as the foundation for creating a complex metaphor that can be interpreted to contain class conflict, the ownership of capital, colonialism, slavery, even genocide. The key word here is 'interpreted'. Metaphor goes beyond simple comparison. However, within this metaphorical world we see explanatory enactments that are not themselves metaphors but analogies: the treatment of the Shortlander dogs *parallels* the experiences of colonized peoples and demonstrates how they give rise to immigration, racist ideology and actions. The analogy has an objective meaning. The audience needs to understand this correspondence if the stated goals of the programme are to be achieved. Varied personal *interpretations* of the overall metaphor will not suffice. (Wooster cites passages that therefore explicate the metaphor.) There is an implicit if not explicit agenda here.

Elsewhere, Wooster quotes Freire to point out that education cannot be neutral, and I would not expect *Sleeping Dogs* to be so, but its intentions highlight the pedagogical dilemmas of working in an art form – and style – that begs subjective responses. When Wooster asserts 'it is clear that the stray dogs are a metaphor for all those with a common class interest', or again, 'we ... can see the ideological truth to which Precious is blind', I have to ask, 'is it clear?' and 'can we?' More pertinently, could the young people? Here we encounter the tension between didacticism, a desire to see *our* meaning understood, and a constructivist theatre pedagogy that invites audiences to make their *own* meanings, *which may not coincide with ours*. We cannot have it both ways. Did the subsequent workshop help to resolve this contradiction? We hear it was integral: an impression is given, but frustratingly the details are unclear. This said the programme may be applauded for its aesthetic ambition and the trust invested in the intelligence of the young people.

In Chapter Eight Wooster examines the evolution of company structures and working practices. It is worth underlining that the struggle to develop democratic working practices, perhaps seen as an indulgence today, was not incidental. It was a fundamental expression of the values that infused the work. These live on in progressive, contemporary applied theatre practices that display 'classical' TIE approaches.

The role of SCYPT as a conduit for artistic, educational and political ideas is another theme that re-emerges later in this chapter. SCYPT was important, but there is more to the story. Take, for example, the influence of DIE. It reached companies from multiple sources. Perspectives' founders were introduced to the work while studying at Bretton Hall. Greenwich had access to the ILEA Drama Advisory Team containing DIE practitioners such as Cecily O'Neill and Alan Lambert. The influences of Bolton and Heathcote were demonstrable and helped shape the participatory emphasis in GYPT's work.

The political analysis of the likes of Bennett, Pammenter and Romy Baskerville also pre-dated SCYPT. Their socialism infused the goals, content, working methods, company structures and aspirations that Wooster interrogates so fully. Arguably, they made SCYPT possible.

Later, sister companies such as Gay Sweatshop, Women's Theatre Group and Graeae offered analyses that had roots in more personal identity politics. These were not SCYPT companies, but their influences found their way into the TIE lexicon. Theatre Centre, which was a SCYPT member, also exerted considerable influence on the movement, championing the cause of diversity, providing stages for marginalized voices, and offering training workshops at its base.

These alternative perspectives, attacked by some as 'bourgeois diversions', were an important counter-balance to the doctrinaire class politics of other factions. Quietly but insistently, new questions were asked about our politics, art, education and *representation*.[2] These influences, owing more to an inclusive Freirean perspective than a narrow class-based analysis, continue to be influential today.

Wooster posits that most training was given 'on the job' by companies and SCYPT. Bretton Hall is also mentioned, but the Rose Bruford Community Theatre Arts Course (CTA), brainchild of Stuart Bennett, was of central significance. This Course trained a new generation of young TIE artists and introduced other engaged, community practices. Its breadth of vision offered an inspired early model for later applied theatre training.

These are but a few of the unrecognized influences. We do a disservice to the work if we compress our complex – often hidden – histories into a single cohesive narrative dominated by a few individual voices, and overlook the contradictory cross-currents that helped forge the rich diversity of theories and practices that have helped TIE survive, as I believe it has.

This brings me to my final points. To suggest TIE and Applied Theatre are opposing genres is to create a false binary. Applied Theatre reaches far beyond TiHE. It embraces a range of progressive theatre practices, *including TIE*. The New York MA Course, rooted in Freirean pedagogy, positions DIE/TIE practices as indispensable requirements for the applied theatre practitioner. TIE may never flourish again in its iconic early forms, but it continues to exert influence worldwide. We should nourish the fruits but also look to different spaces and places to cultivate new shoots beyond the institutions and funding frameworks that are so antithetical to progressive practices. There are many forums where its best traditions are being kept alive. Perhaps now is the time for a renewed radicalism.

Notes

1 The term 'praxis' is used here in the sense that Freire uses it to describe the cycle of 'reflection and action upon the world in order to transform it' (2000: 51).
2 It may tell the discerning reader something about TIE's early history that the four 'elders' writing in this book are all white men!

PART THREE
Shoots?

CHAPTER TEN

The Legacy of ERA: Funding and Programme Content

Reaction to the Thatcher years

It may be thought strange that what I have identified as the most fruitful period of TIE occurred at the moment that it was most under attack from the philosophical changes in education introduced by Thatcher's government. Thatcher's first target on gaining office had been the trade unions – their 'unreasonable' demands and restrictive working practices. That battle won (as exemplified by the defeat of the miners in 1985), full attention was turned onto the failures, as the Tories saw it, of teachers and the education system. There had been meddling with schools' policy from the early 1980s and this culminated, as we have seen, in ERA. It was during this same period, and in response to it, that TIE and especially the SCYPT affiliated companies, were faced with the hardest choices. It became even more important to defend genuine dialogic educational approaches whilst at the same time developing such praxis would widen the gulf between government policy and TIE's philosophy. Edward Bond, addressing nearly 400 delegates at the NATD conference in 1989, having given an astute analysis of the government's intentions with its education policy, spoke to DIE and TIE practitioners thus:

We are cultural products and we take our humanity from our culture, either through assent, either by questioning, either by accepting a universal order or by creating an opposition …. if I have stated a time of problems … it is a time, not of pessimism: I've never felt more useful as a creative artist than I feel now … I've never felt the ability to speak, the *need* to speak … greater than now …. I'm absolutely certain that y*ou* are part and a very important part of the answer. (Bond: 1989: 17)

This was the spirit that produced some of the iconic TIE work of late 1980s. The battle to save education was underway. The unions may have been defeated but left-sympathizing sensibilities within education, including TIE, could not be left unbowed. Antagonism increasingly festered against all aspects of heuristic education.

Like many workers on the left of politics, actor/teachers took an active role in resistance to Thatcher's industrial and educational policies. TIE companies also had a series of intermediaries to deal with: the purse-holders, the Local Authorities and the Arts Councils. As we have seen, the Local Authorities' Education departments would be effectively neutered by ERA as all key decisions were devolved down to schools or, in curriculum matters, transferred up to central government. Even should they wish to do so, LEAs would increasingly find it hard to offer financial support to peripatetic actor/teachers.

Funding policy changes

The second funding steam, from the Arts Councils, came under more surreptitious attack. It has been noted how the ACGB and its locally devolved sister organizations, the Welsh and Scottish Arts Councils, had taken an increasing interest in TIE work. In Wales, the policy developed to have a TIE group in each of its eight counties.[1] This positive regard was rarely founded in a profound understanding of the work but it was recognized that TIE introduced children to theatre and was reaching social and geographical strata that much mainstream theatre was unwilling or unable to do. The concept of an 'Arts Council' is to maintain a firewall between the ultimate funders (the tax-payers via the government) and the recipients of the financial support. This protective barrier is always vulnerable to strain but, in the 1980s, distinct fractures appeared. The prevailing mood of the day was shifting towards a conservative hegemony of 'excellence' and cultural value. Experimental approaches were being forced out of fashion and replaced by functionalism and utilitarianism, something which, in 1989 the Gulbenkian Foundation (a long-time patron of TIE) saw fit to raise as a major concern (Calouste Gulbenkian Foundation: 1989). The theatre to be lauded was that which either reflected the classical canon or was financially self-supporting. In a supreme myopia, London-based policymakers assumed that 'theatre' was what the West End offered and, as it survived without subsidy, why should other regions not manage in the same way? Subsidy was under pressure and choices would be justified in terms of preserving the culture and encouraging entrepreneurship during a time of economic hardship. It is the manipulation of government funding and the 'there is no alternative' approach that Thatcher espoused that created the environment in which the Arts Council reviewed its own funding policies in *The Glory of the Garden* (1984). As will be deduced from the title, the focus was on concentrating financial investment on those companies that were the flowers of England's cultural garden (Wales had its own, suspiciously similar set of policies). TIE and young people's theatre would be under threat if they could not demonstrate their credentials to be part of this baroque garden.

For SCYPT companies, this seemed not merely an incidental effect of government policy but a deliberate attempt to silence them. A conference held in Warwick in July 1984 discussed the *Garden* proposals to which all relevant parties were invited, including TIE companies. They gave a good account of themselves:

> What happened at the conference, in no small measure due to the powerful but careful intervention of the SCYPT companies, was that ACGB's own policy was totally rejected in favour of retaining the independence (and funding) of YPT/TIE and other small-scale companies. (Editorial: *SCYPT Journal*: 1984: 3)

The editorial lauds the conference contributions made by many of the leading TIE companies of the day which influenced many delegates. The editorial maintains that those with open minds were won over and those who 'were ready to pick up the stick of "low artistic standards" or "political indoctrination"' were silenced. As the editorial itself concedes, despite the argument being won, if the government was intent on getting rid of conceptually based TIE, then it would. For some, the attack on TIE was a deliberate political act and for others, TIE was just collateral damage in the battle for the soul of education.

Can TIE be apolitical?

For Thatcher and her acolytes, education was a hotbed of socialism and needed to be brought under control. Indeed, the teachers of the 1980s had been the children of the 1950s and had grown up in the spirit of optimism described in Chapter One. It has become a cliché, but all theatre is political in that it either implicitly challenges or implicitly supports the status quo:

> [Education] will always be in the service of either the 'domestication' of men or of their liberation .... Neutral education cannot, in fact, exist. It is fundamental for us to know that when we work on the educational curriculum ... we are engaged in political acts which imply an ideological choice. (Freire: 1972b: 174).

Later in the article, Freire goes on to point out that this 'domesticating education' requires the 'de-dialectization' of thought (Freire: 1972b: 176); thus TIE with its educational aim of encouraging dialogic thought and forensic social analysis was bound to come into conflict with the establishment:

> Education must be conceived as aiding young humans in learning to use the tools of meaning making and reality construction, to better adapt to the world in which they find themselves and to help in the process of changing it as required. (Bruner: 1996: 19–20)

Bruner's analysis is key here, for he acknowledges the need for children to 'adapt' to the world but also to 'change it as required'. The argument is not, as those on the right fear, that authentic education will place children outside their real world but for them to understand the 'real' world and, 'if required', to change it and not merely to accept that the world is immutable. Giroux's approach is similar and he notes that any attempt to encourage critical engagement with the world is portrayed by the establishment as either irrelevant or unprofessional (2000: 4). By the late eighties TIE's response was to hone the work and to facilitate this approach to learning. The more effective it threatens to be, however, the more necessary it becomes to neuter it. Some companies very quickly came under scrutiny and for others the slow withering effect of ERA was allowed to take its gradual toll.

First to feel the effects were those companies who led the opposition to government and Arts Council policies. Gillham reports (*SCYPT Journal 20*: 1990) that some teachers pulled out of the *When Sleeping Dogs Awake* programme fearing it would be 'unsuitable' for their children. He asks 'what *is* suitable?' and this, in turn brings us back to the purposes of education. Teachers are often subject to the whim of the 'cop in the head' (to use Boal's term) when dealing with any contentious issues (politics, death, sex, racism, mental health and so on). The political climate of the late 1980s and 1990s was not conducive to taking risks in these matters, and yet they are the very stuff of which our lives are made, 'fundamentally universal categories of human experience' (*SCYPT Journal 20*: 1990: 20) and thus should be central to our education:

Children are capable of dealing with 'difficult' and complex human experience because they are living in this world, not some other, 'world of the child'. (*SCYPT Journal 20*: 1990: 21)

Again, we can turn to Freire for guidance:

It is only through an education which does not separate action from reflection, theory from practice, consciousness from the world, that it is possible to develop a dialectic form of thinking which contributes to the insertion of men as subjects in their historical reality. (Freire: 1972b: 181)

The problem arises when it has been decided that this is not the outcome that government seeks from education. It becomes unsuitable for children. Upon these rocks of 'suitability', several key companies quickly foundered. As early as 1985, Action PIE, in Cardiff, had lost their funding as a result of an 'unsuitable' project entitled *Questions Arising in 1985 from a Mutiny in 1789* that revisited the Mutiny on the Bounty (ironically the subject of

Action PIE's first project in the 1970s) in the context of the Miners' Strike. It was one of several projects that this increasingly abrasive company had offered to schools and they were one of the first to lose funding as a result. Nicholson (2009: 33) cites this project as one where the use of Brecht's *Lehrstücke*, with its use of direct address, opened the company to accusations of manipulating opinion and in those febrile days, it was certainly high risk to compare the mutiny with the actions of the miners. Another victim was Cockpit's 1983 programme *The Pitcher Plant* that addressed issues of sexuality and was banned by a nervous ILEA.

As an actor/teacher working through this period, I recall the tensions that existed between believing that a particular approach to education was crucial and at the same time realizing the effect that such pursuance might have on the company's existence. Do you retreat to fight another day or throw oneself into the firing line? Action PIE and others chose the latter but many companies in the next decade attempted to survive through mutation – though it is moot as to whether they remained true to the TIE genus. By the turn of the century, many familiar names in TIE had disappeared altogether including, for a time, even Belgrade (1996), though today programmes exist as part of a community and education wing of the main house theatre, producing occasional theme-based TIE projects and work that elides TIE with youth theatre.

SCYPT, which we have seen, was virtually to disappear by the end of the decade, was the focal point for the defence of TIE. By 1992, the new curriculum was in place (though under constant revision). A National TIE Crisis Campaign was held in 1993 calling (hopelessly) for a financial bailout to assist companies that had lost their financial support and requesting an inquiry to look into future funding. The campaign next sought to engage the wider arts world with an Arts Forum in 1994, 'The Future is at Risk', but it 'did not attract the numbers that had been hoped for' (*SCYPT*: 1995: 30) largely due to the lack of support from Equity, the actors' union, key members of which seemed reluctant to ally themselves to TIE radicals. It was just one of many bureaucracies, including Labour run councils, that, in the 1990s failed to resist the attack on arts and education which in turn created the hegemonic approach of 'delivery-of-outcomes' education and the general undervaluing of theatre arts in Britain. Bond was clear about the situation:

You've got to be stopped .... I don't have conspiracy theories ... I have conspiracy *facts*. There are people sitting round tables who will say things like that .... Apart from being naff and stupid and a waste of time, money and energy ... it is also the cause of social deviance. It disrupts people, it makes them unhappy and stops them learning 'proper things'. (Bond: 1989: 19)

Giving up the fight?

For some at least the fight for education had become too draining and there was a growing sense of weary submission. Thatcher had convinced the country that 'there was no alternative'. The constant scrutiny from a political panopticon was a debilitating experience for companies at this time, as they tried to demonstrate adherence to the National Curriculum whilst seeking to make authentic educational programmes. There was also the constant fight for funding and the shape-shifting nature of the criteria for this funding. After ERA, even if companies successfully fulfilled both artistic and educational requirements, then judgements about fiscal governance and 'value for money' would be brought to the fore. Yeoman (1994) tells of one such incident when Lancaster TIE (at the Dukes Theatre) came under such scrutiny. Concerns about artistic and educational value having been rebutted, it was left to accountants to search for financial weakness or, as Yeoman puts it, to judge the company's 'leanness and fitness for the market-place fray' in a world where the government seeks 'to commodify every aspect of our human existence' (Yeoman: 1994: 47). SCYPT and NATD journals of the era frequently have articles calling for support, mounting campaigns and announcing closures of TIE companies that had been at the forefront of innovative work in schools since the 1960s and 1970s.

In short, the demise of 'classic' TIE during the 1990s was political rather than artistic or educational. The perceived politics of the companies, what O'Toole has called 'the volatile mix of progressivism and constructivist educational philosophies' (O'Toole: 2009: 482), had had their genesis in the more radical and optimistic post-War years. What had really changed was the political world in which companies found themselves after 1979. Consumerism and the worship of market forces created an incredibly hostile environment that still exists today. Giroux noted in 2000 that public education faced 'an unprecedented attack from proponents of market ideology' (Giroux: 2000: 84). He was writing of the United States but the situation in the UK was identical. What threatened 'classic' TIE at this time was not the politics within, but the politics without. Giroux's interpretation of Freire is useful here, for he argues (Giroux: 2000: 150–2) that the role of the teacher is not to impose views nor to just offer multiple points of view but rather to develop critical teaching practices based in existing reality, encouraging 'rigorous engagement' with ideas. The doctrine of market forces cannot coexist with such an educational approach. Once Thatcher had nailed the new doctrine of market forces to the door, there would be no going back.

This potential for political conflict was always there, as Pammenter noted in Jackson's 1993 edition of *Learning Through Theatre*:

> If TIE is really to do with freedom for development of the child; if it is to attempt to base its approach in child-centred education, then its practitioners must be aware that they are swimming against the tide. (Pammenter in Jackson: 1993: 58)

That tide has since become a tsunami in terms of educational developments in Britain as government invests fully in Freire's 'banking model'. Pammenter points out that TIE is bound to be political, dealing as it does with 'every emotional and material condition of our lives' and he makes the case for dialectical learning which 'can only exist if real positions are taken' (Jackson: 1993: 62). He rightly points out that any bias must be conscious and present only to encourage dialogic processes; 'dogma is unacceptable'. In the 'reformation' politics of the era, the definitions of what was dialogism and what was dogmatism were subject to increasingly reactionary definitions, from all shades of mainstream political thought. So whilst O'Toole is correct to say that 'TIE ... has been intensely and explicitly political since the late 1960s' (1992: 46), I would contend that this for the most part was the benign politics of the child learning to understand the world and themselves within the world. It is in the interests of those who control the educational policies of our children to keep things as they are or to make more efficient and productive the systems that benefit the status quo. Any schooling that seeks to envisage another way of being will be seen as a threat. Schools are not to be valued for teaching the 'skills of democracy' but are to be measured against the need to reproduce 'values, social practices and skills needed for the dominant corporate order' (Giroux: 1997: 119).

Mutate or die

It is perhaps necessary to emphasize once again that the ideas of Bruner (and Vygotsky) were not always common currency amongst actor/teachers in the way that Heathcote, Bolton and Boal had become. Less so the analyses offered by Giroux that only appeared in the 1980s. Such theoretical awareness tended to reside with the TIE directors and sympathetic academics who took a keen interest into how TIE praxis was fulfilling the needs of education. Even teachers, had they been exposed to such ideas in their training, were given little freedom to engage with such concepts and, after ERA, none at all. If there were those in government think-tanks who knew of this Marxist-derived radicalism, they would not have been sympathetic to it. Education was to serve the economy, to provide the workers to fill the jobs that needed to be done. Where, if anywhere, was theatre to fit into the curriculum?

Ofsted (the body responsible for the inspection of public educational establishments in England) issued a report in 1998, nearly a decade after the introduction of the National Curriculum, which considered the place of theatre and drama in schools. The role of drama it saw as being in the delivery of Attainment Targets in English whilst also contributing to a pupil's 'personal, social, moral and spiritual development' (Ofsted: 1998: 45). Drama also offered opportunities for children to develop writing skills, confidence, listening and evaluation skills (Ofsted: 1998: 50). This emphasis on measurable outcomes necessitated a major change in the relationship between TIE and schools (see Readman in Jackson: 1993: 267). Not only had TIE companies been increasingly accustomed to a conceptual analysis around what was now called the PSHE[2] curriculum, but the amount of curriculum planning required was 'in advance of timescales operated by many TIE companies' (Jackson: 1993: 272). In order to survive, TIE companies would have to change their theoretical/political approach, their working methodology and their teacher support structures.

Programme content would firstly have to be able to defend itself from accusations of political content. This, as we have seen, is paralogistic though some companies developed ingenious ways of encouraging intellectual analysis whilst dealing with classical (examination) texts and introducing universal moral questions as part of workshops. (Participatory pieces became increasingly rare as the time allotted for programmes was reduced from a day to perhaps one or two hours.) The second and immediate effect was that TIE programmes now had to make themselves relevant in terms of National Curriculum criteria. Projects would be accompanied by detailed mapping of where content matched Learning Objectives at the appropriate Key Skills level. A typical programme might well have links within English, geography, history, art as well as the PSHE curriculum. Ironically, as the humanistic value of drama and theatre was being marginalized in schools, it was found that whole areas of emotional education were becoming neglected. Drama and TIE often managed to survive by tapping in to this 'market' where teachers felt unconfident. Sex and moral education, health education and 'citizenship' became important subject areas for TIE, for the educational reforms had failed to identify the part that was played in developing rounded human beings by drama and theatre; the well-adjusted 'baby' had been thrown out with the mucky political bathwater. Of course, through liaison with teachers and through the provision of teaching materials, TIE had long since attempted to guide teachers through the potential of the stimuli they brought to the classroom. The pressures on teachers were now such that previews and consultation proved ever more difficult to arrange and support was boiled down to those elements that could be mapped on paper. Teachers would feel that they had enough to cope with without taking on follow-up work. It was increasingly difficult for them to conceive of cross-curricula work that the National Curriculum seemed specifically to discourage. Once again, TIE might well become in these circumstances a theatre 'treat' for the children and a moment's downtime for the teachers.

The decline of public investment from Local Authorities and arts organizations was the third element of this vicious triangle that compounded the problems for TIE. As the funding streams of the last twenty-five years dried up, other sources were sought. We have already seen the effect this would have on company stability and how the lack of annual funding would mean that companies could not plan, could not maintain consistent teams and thus could not develop praxis coherently. Increasingly the term 'actor/teacher' was to disappear as work in schools became just one of the possible employment sources for young jobbing actors with marginal knowledge of any of the tropes of TIE (see Wooster: 2007). The alternative to these traditional funding sources were 'project grants' from traditional education or arts funders but also from such disparate bodies as health education organizations, social services, the police, anti-drug charities, and others. I will consider this work more fully in the next chapter, but the nature of TIE was under extreme pressure to change. Notions of scaffolding learning to empower children to engage with the world were proscribed. What children needed was prescribed by the Learning Objectives on which they were tested on a regular basis. A mass-testing regime can, of course, be very labour intensive, and thus the system evolved that would only test that which could be easily accumulated and assessed. Measuring 'humanness' does not fall easily into such a regime.

It is unlikely that TIE was the direct target of government policy, despite Bond's words at the NATD conference quoted above – if only it had been regarded as so dangerously influential! But TIE was certainly collateral damage in the urgent battle to get educators under control. Schools had to survive, as did teachers, though in a new relationship with government. TIE did not have this basic security and the various effects of ERA marked the beginning of the end for this way of teaching and this conception of what education should be.

The survivors

By the end of the 1990s there were few, but some, companies that had survived intact and, through the continuing support of their Local Authorities and/or their appropriate Arts Council, continued to work within the paradigms of the 1970s and 1980s. In Wales, the Wales Arts Council (from 1994 the Arts Council of Wales) continued to support eight companies well into the first decade of the twenty-first century. After 1990, however, few offered TIE in a way that would have been recognized in the 1980s. Programmes became performance-based, often without any relevant workshop, content to lose any connection with educational theory. Some (such as Theatr Clwyd and Theatr Iolo) happily moved into children's theatre (albeit of high quality) and, with others, became merely perfunctory in their provision of educational context. An exception was Theatr Powys that, under Louise Osborn and later Ian Yeoman, continued to develop praxis. Theatr Powys, as previously mentioned, was fortunate in having its Local Authority funding moved to a non-education budget thus protecting it from LMS. Secure funding became increasingly elusive and even in a company like Theatr Powys, contracts became short-term and disaggregated from the security that previous actor/teachers had enjoyed. Though there was a sustained attempt to re-employ the same practitioners in order to maintain continuity, there was more employee turnover than previously and expertise resided in fewer and fewer permanent company members.

In England similar events were occurring but also new companies were emerging that had adapted to the new conditions. GYPT mutated into GLYPT (Greenwich and Lewisham Young People's Theatre) by 2005 and still offers YPT shows and interactive projects. Leeds TIE (closed but then quickly re-established in 1993) became dependent upon project grants and targeted work beyond conventional educational venues. In fact, Leeds can boast three TIE companies as it also hosts Blah Blah Blah (set up in 1995) who have managed to develop TIE praxis using both workshop and participatory approaches whilst serving schools' creativity agendas and Alive and Kicking who produce work more related to children's theatre. Recent work by Blah Blah Blah and Leeds forms part of case-studies in Chapter Thirteen. The other English survivor that will be considered alongside 'the Blahs' and Leeds is Big Brum, based in Birmingham since 1982 and with a legacy from many of the key progenitors of TIE. Chris Cooper (director 1999–2015) came into TIE under the influence of Geoff Gillham, Warwick Dobson and Ian Yeoman. Edward Bond, one of the most important playwrights in Europe in the last fifty years, has collaborated with the company on ten separate TIE programmes in recent years.

Such survivors are extremely rare. Already Theatr Powys has been cut. When, in 2010, the ACW announced its list of clients, Theatr Powys (after nearly forty years) was excluded as it no longer fitted the Arts Council Wales' agenda. The Local Authority, anxious to find budgetary savings, used this as an opportunity to withdraw its partnership funding and the company closed in 2011. The new priorities of ACW had been set by a little-known committee (The Arts Strategy Board 2007) made up of Arts Council members, politicians and business development organizations. The investments of the ACW were thus determined by the political considerations of the Welsh Assembly Government; the 'firewall' protecting the arts from politics had been removed. The Welsh Assembly Government required that spending maximized 'the cultural value of the arts spend by linking with wider social economic and cultural objectives'. Arts spending had to develop the international profile of Wales; target health priorities; fuel the 'creative economy'; encourage 'cultural tourism'; and generally assist in regeneration.[3] A company offering a high quality educational and artistic experience to rural schools found it hard to meet these criteria (though in most respects they had done so) and there remain suspicions of political disenchantment behind the decision to curtail funding. Theatr Powys, Theatr Gwent and Spectacle Theatre were all cut in 2011 and only Spectacle now exists attracting project grants to create programmes in response to the educational, artistic and training needs of local communities, including the learning and business communities.

The old model of TIE was being made unfit for purpose. Companies, if they wished to survive, would have to find ways of accommodating the new purposes of education as outlined in the Curriculum. TIE would have to adapt and put out new shoots.

Notes

1 I have written about the particular nature of TIE in Wales in *Contemporary Theatre in Education* (2007).
2 Personal, Social and Health Education which later became Personal, Social, Health and Citizenship Education.
3 Minutes of the ASB can be found at http://Wales.gov.uk/topics/cultureandsport/arts/strategyboard/meetings. I have written about this in the context of funding decisions in Wales elsewhere (Wooster: 2012).

CHAPTER ELEVEN

Adapting to Survive

Whilst classic TIE has been in decline since the mid-1990s, the number of companies describing their work as TIE has continued to increase. Students emerging from drama, Applied Drama and Applied Theatre courses, are often passionate about using the emollient effects of theatre to achieve social change. In this they share the fervency of early TIE workers. Whilst much of this work fails to live up to TIE's originating precepts, it can be regarded as the genre struggling to adapt to survive. Much had been learned about engaging pupils through theatre, though the educational environment became increasingly less conducive to the development of critical thinking and the consequential lack of a sound pedagogical underpinning at times offered a bland approach to learning. The devastating financial and educational effects of ERA eradicated much of the innovative pedagogy surrounding TIE as it had developed. The new shoots that emerged from this devastation had to survive in a world of educational targets and measurable outcomes.

This new TIE now has a significant influence in a wide range of contexts in UK schools, promoting Health Education and Citizenship, combating anti-social behaviour and prejudice, and generally dealing with problematic PSHE areas. There are also companies using TIE on behalf of agencies to combat domestic or child abuse or to assist in the rehabilitation of offenders inside and outside prisons. TIE is seen as a palliative for a range of difficult areas even including sexual orientation. (See, for example, the Department of Education and Skills Research Brief RB594.) TIE derived methodologies have also found their way into legal and medical training, in recruitment processes and corporate training. Across the globe, approaches from TIE have been applied to emerging nations' development strategies and health programmes. The influence of TIE seems to be enormous, but not all this work is built upon coherent pedagogy. In adapting to survive the aims of TIE companies' programmes are frequently those of behaviour modification, message transmission and moral propaganda, though the more astute companies make valiant attempts to place issues within dialogic contexts.

Theatre in Health Education (TiHE)

Contemporary use of the phrase 'theatre-in-education' is synonymous in the minds of teachers, funders and even actors with TiHE. The number of TiHE companies continues to proliferate and not all are long-lived. Some are formed for the sole purpose of responding to a project grant being offered, whilst others, such as the now defunct Cragrats, develop franchise-like approaches to the work through which they can offer material across the UK. The company 'Tip of the Iceberg' offers the 'complete' PSHE package:

> 2 Performances (now and the future), workshops, classroom activities, Q and A sessions and a teacher's pack all addressing issues around sex, drugs, self esteem, control and decision making, supporting sex education. A years [*sic*] PSHCE in a day! http://www.tipoftheiceberg.biz/education/education.html [accessed 11 February 2015]

This 'TIE' is about gathering large numbers together and staging messages followed by a Q&A sessions. We are a long way from classic TIE.

For Prendergast and Saxton (2009), TiHE, Theatre for Development (TfD), Prison Theatre and Museum Theatre all fall under the heading of Applied Theatre. Whilst many of these 'new shoots' offer valuable interventions, I wish to differentiate them from the TIE model described in previous chapters. Indeed the pedagogies of classic TIE have rarely been understood by those working in formal education and this is now compounded by the fact that most of them are too young to have had any contact with it. The 'message' model (which fits neatly into the Applied Theatre approach) has become the default, whilst contextual programmes are overlooked. Prendergast and Saxton list Ball's seven commonalities with TIE (Prendergast & Saxton: 2009: 88) but what is missing from the list is that TiHE will *know* that it has a message and TIE will allow learning to be discovered. TiHE is 'about raising awareness and changing behaviour' (Prendergast & Saxton: 2009: 89) and this, I propose, is a 'banking model' of knowledge acquisition. This elision of TIE with Applied Theatre, especially TiHE, occurred during the 1990s when, as we have seen, TIE came under educational pressure to adapt and the key source of income switched from LEAs to parcels of project funding. In order to survive, companies began to accept project grants to teach 'about' specific issues determined by the purse-holder. Intervention was the *raison d'être* of TiHE and liaisons with respected funders could demonstrate a company's credentials as part of the fabric of the new education hegemony. These 'one-off' projects decimated previous ways of working and led to a proliferation of short-term companies, short-term contracts and little continuity of staffing, theory, practice or schools' liaison. Teachers would now be asked to accept this 'product' as they would any other resource from an outside agency. Market forces and consumerist structures dominate the education system. The argument would run something like this: the children have to be taught about the dangers of drugs; the teachers do not feel equipped to do it; therefore, pay a TiHE company to come into school and give the message in a dramatic way for as small a cost as possible. The school has done its duty and can tick the box – drug education delivered.

One cannot argue against the good intentions of these projects. Self-evidently young people need to know that smoking/excessive drinking/drug use are bad for you; that gun/knife crime is bad; that domestic violence/child abuse is unacceptable; that racism/sexism/homophobia/Islamaphobia/bullying is despicable; or that our sexual lives are important and need to be guided by principles, respect and care for our health and that of those we love. We need to know these things. Indeed, most of the young people trouping into a TiHE performance *will* know these things before they cross the threshold of the school hall. What will the TiHE programme be able additionally to offer?

Well, this is theatre; so it will be able to offer them examples of these negative behaviours. It will enable us to see more than one perspective and to view hidden consequences; the bullied contemplating suicide; the object of racism forced into stereotype; and the 'flash forward' to a smoker dying of cancer or emphysema. For some students, there might be a workshop allowing individuals to challenge the behaviour of characters and suggest alternative scenarios and outcomes. At the back of the hall, there may be a representative of the funders who will be noting responses in order to write up their reports on the outcomes of their investment. Teachers too will be ticking boxes on the PSHCE curriculum. At the end of the project the pupils will return to normal classes having learned what they already knew – that smoking is bad and that bullying hurts.

I am being unnecessarily harsh in order to make the point; many children may well have their awareness raised and strategies presented to them. But, knowing something is hurtful or harmful does not stop you from doing it. Knowing is not the same as learning. This in itself presents a problem for the funders, for they require results. They have bought a commodity and will expect immediate outcomes (measurable behaviour change) as a result of the TiHE programme: the bullies and bullied will cheerfully leave the hall together arm-in-arm. As Jackson (2007) points out, 'the meaning has to be made and experienced within the drama', else it is just sweetening a message or illustrating a pre-determined reality. This is not how authentic teaching works but it is the approach to teaching that the new TIE finds itself driven to employ.

Warwick Dobson regrets the demise of the old model of TIE and fears that the TiHE-centred model is 'always in danger of doing the opposite of what it intends to do' (interview: 8 October 2014). In his current work with students, he avoids the notion of 'message' and regrets the lack of quality TIE. Prendergast and Saxton (2009: 43) give an example of what these 'dangers' might be. They report that following a drugs awareness project one child fed-back that 'now I would feel safer taking drugs as I know more about them and their effects'. This disturbing outcome reflects perhaps the lack of proper training of actors (the term 'actor/teacher' has fallen into disuse) and the lack of pedagogical theory. When using Forum, for example, few actors will have fully absorbed Boal's concept of *metaxis*; the interplay between the world of the play and the world of the spectator; and will oversimplify the skills of the 'Joker' or facilitator.

Greer (2011) expresses similar concerns in his critique of TIE programmes dealing with homophobia. He notes that despite the desirability of challenging normative expectations:

> any possible advocacy of coming out within anti-homophobia TIE work is tempered with a recognition of the circumstances and potential consequences of such disclosure, and also recognises ... the possibility of a rational closet in the name of self-preservation. (Greer: 2011: 56)

More simply, in demonstrating the inequities of homophobia, it would be possible to instil fear into an adolescent about any notions of coming out. This danger would be exacerbated if funders and teachers were expecting immediate changes in behaviour. Prejudice unfortunately is not logical, else rational argument would be sufficient to dispel it. Perhaps the most that should be sought is the beginning of a change in attitudes. For the young person struggling with their sexuality, the programme should perhaps reassure, offer strategies for hope and certainly legitimize but not offer false confidence. Only programmes that treat prejudice through dialectical analysis can truly begin the process of a change of understanding. The alternative is to consider homophobia within a 'liberalising agenda of tolerance and inclusion ... bordered by historically heterosexist cultural values' (Greer: 2011: 63). Implicitly, the message to those suffering prejudice can be 'you are different from us but we are liberal enough to pretend that you are the same as us'.

Classic TIE, based on theoretical approaches, recognized that real learning requires a dialogic approach, working from where the children are and scaffolding them to a more profound understanding. In the case of smoking education, for example, alongside the strategies for resisting peer pressure and presentation of graphic health warnings, it might be appropriate to identify the wider interrelationships between consumerism, hedonism and addiction and how these are exploited for profit. With personal prejudice too, there are deeper issues than are usually covered by a TiHE programme, such as where do we learn such behaviour and what is it about the human psyche that draws us to such counterproductive expressions of power? My criticism of much TiHE and Applied Theatre work is that it is not offering a holistic approach but a band-aid that allows the hegemonic body politic to continue its life unquestioned. Prentki and Pammenter have set out the problem thus:

> The value of the Applied Theatre process resides in its ability to turn the participants into useful members of society. Therefore the outcomes are measured in terms of social benefit: how many prisoners ceased to reoffend? How many participants gave up their habits of substance abuse? How many children stopped truanting from school?... The system is never to blame and so the system is never challenged, still less changed. (Prentki & Pammenter: 2014: 10)

Freire argues that education must be about decoding reality and problematizing the surface structure. Only then can one understand 'the dialectic that exists between the categories presented in the surface structure, as well as the unity between the surface and deep structures' (Freire: 1985: 52). This is what the new TIE, in its guise as TiHE, generally fails to do and instead imposes a reality and closes down conscientization.

Theatre for development

Theatre for Development is clearly another shoot that has adapted from TIE largely mediated through TiHE memes. Indeed, health issues (especially HIV/AIDS) have been a recurring topic of TfD programmes in emerging nations (see Carklin in Prendergast & Saxton: 2009: 39–40). In the same volume however, Prendergast and Saxton describe a diverse range of TfD projects concerning women's rights, political process and human trafficking. TIE is only one influence on TfD. The nature of these projects often reflect local theatre traditions and these may differ fundamentally from Western-based forms in their use of non-professional performers; the use of storytelling techniques; the interpretation of role-play; and in the theoretical underpinning of the learning process (see Mosse in Cooke & Kathari: 2001; Chinyowa: 2008; Prendergast & Saxton: 2008). In place of heuristic practice:

TfD was soon appropriated for message transmission, largely in the service of non-governmental organizations (NGOs) that had outcome-led agendas designed to meet utilitarian objectives. (Pammenter in Jackson & Vine (eds): 2013: 93)

Pammenter posits an alternative approach, closer to classic TIE, in which local cultural tropes are used to address the question 'what do we want to say to our audience? Why and how?' (Jackson & Vine (eds): 2013: 94). This is not a search for a 'message' but for an interpretation and a seeking after insights. Chinyowa has a similar question:

Whose interests are being served by the workshop? Are the workshops being framed *by* the people and *with* the people? (Chinyowa: 2008: 6)

Mosse proposed that in TfD knowledge must be looked at 'relationally', as 'a product of social relationships and not as a fixed commodity' (in Cooke & Kothari: 2001: 17). In the same volume Cleaver criticizes the use of the word 'empowerment' which is connected, in her view, to the loss of a 'radical, challenging and transformatory edge' in TfD projects (Cooke & Kothari: 2001: 37). Nicholas Hildyard (Cooke & Kothari: 2001: 60) makes an observation that takes us to the heart of the problem:

'Telling people what to do' does not always bring the desired effects.

Pammenter's work in TfD has taken an approach that allows the audience to become performers and facilitators of their own learning, 'making meaning in pursuit of changing their own lives'. This dialectical approach to problems may not always endear participants to their governments or even the intermediary NGO sponsors. There are several examples of pedagogically sound TfD projects in Jackson & Vine (eds) (2013). As well as those offered by Pammenter, Adams (Jackson & Vine (eds): 2013: 294ff) describes an HIV/AIDS project that seeks to encourage a re-examination of cultural attitudes towards women but through a process of empowering the participants to engage in a critical pedagogy. McDougall (in Gallagher & Booth: 2003: 173ff) lauds the use of popular community theatre forms in TfD to bolster political reform and 'to tilt at the failures of social and economic development' (Jackson & Vine (eds): 2013: 174). When she praises the use of popular theatre 'to entice audience interest and effect positive behavioural change' (Jackson & Vine (eds): 2013), one has to consider who is setting the agenda. Chinyowa points out that the 'process of raising awareness requires the active participation of the community who are the subject and the object of development' (Chinyowa: 2008: 5). Freire and Boal set the tone here, rather than wider TIE theory; Freire's work with Brazilian workers and the work going on in emerging nations is about whether the banking model of education is to be accepted or whether an ownership of knowledge is required for true education and liberation. Pammenter, at the end of his chapter (Jackson & Vine (eds): 2013: 101) makes an impassioned plea for TfD to adopt the best practice of TIE in order to avoid betraying the young and to raise with them the question of 'what is to be done?' rather than 'you need to do this'. Both TiHE and TfD are susceptible to political influence. Hailey observes that the challenge for TfD is to meld the radical and anti-establishment ideas of Illich and Freire with 'the operational priorities of donors and their concerns for effectiveness and value for money' (in Cooke & Kothari: 2001: 99).

Prison theatre

Prison Theatre is perhaps more related to theatre-making and as such the links with TIE are more tenuous. Clearly there is an educational goal, that of rehabilitation and the reduction of recidivism. Indeed, such projects may implicitly seek to socialize rather than conscientize, though the best work will be seeking to enable the participants to objectify their situations and be empowered to alter their lives and social contexts. It would seem axiomatic that 'change' needs even more fully to come from within the individual. It is also necessary to consider whether the traditional aims of Theatre of the Oppressed, and TIE more generally, fit easily within this context, for we may feel that an offender's situation has its roots in political structures that need to be challenged. Prendergast and Saxton relate some interesting case studies that debate many of these issues (Prendergast & Saxton: 2008: 119ff).

Perhaps the best-known company in the UK working in this area is Geese Theatre whose work derives from the original Geese Theatre in the United States. They have grounded their theoretical approach in Social Learning Theory and Cognitive-Behavioural Theory, using interactive performance and workshops to help participants develop life skills:

> One of the main aims of our drama-based work … is to help create a gap between the participant's beliefs and his behaviour. Playing the role of a victim of crime, for example, will often challenge the participant's belief that nobody got hurt as a consequence of his offending and that it was 'just a laugh.' http:// www.geese.co.uk/why-geese [accessed 20 October 2014]

Geese Theatre makes extensive use of masks as a way of offering a different perspective in order to facilitate personal change. This technique also protects the participants into interacting with the characters very much as a participatory role might do with younger children or a group frame might do in a secondary school project. Their work has been extensively described elsewhere (see Jackson: 2007) but for the purposes of my argument, I wish to draw attention to this approach of offering protection into analysis, which is related to TIE methodology.

'Playing for Time' theatre, based at Winchester University, offers the opportunity for students on Applied Drama courses to work alongside prisoners. Here, the emphasis is on the creation of theatre (rather than the presenting of a performance followed by workshops) but clearly the value is seen to be in the journey rather than the destination. Annie McKean cites the influence of Heathcote, Bolton and Boal in the approaches taken, using these theorists to workshop ideas using processual drama, Forum Theatre, hotseating, Image Theatre and 'Role on the Wall' approaches (see also McKean: 2006).

Prison theatre clearly has the aim of enabling prisoners to rejoin mainstream society and is therefore inherently problematic as it evades the necessity to facilitate challenge of that society. It takes two to integrate. It can be argued that the processes at work are those of socialization rather than conscientization.

Heritage theatre

Companies offering 'heritage projects' have also proliferated since the 1990s, taking their inspiration from TIE methodologies from previous decades. Jackson (2007) offers us an analysis of this genre of work and here I will merely try to identify the TIE legacy. TIE regularly used historical contexts as jumping-off points for contextual investigations and several programmes have been exampled in previous chapters. There is no reason why this could not have continued after the National Curriculum but it was assumed that history should be delivered 'straight' with no, potentially political, contextualization. The opportunity to learn *from* history rather than *about* history has, as a result, become marginalized. This anodyne view of history has found a home in much heritage and museum theatre as part of the nostalgia industry. In *Careless Talk*, children had talked to their grandparents about their wartime experiences in preparation for the exploration of universal themes. Heritage theatre, I would suggest, tends to soft-focus events, curtailing authentic learning. Children are likely to learn, not about hardship and innate exploitation but rather that butter-making by hand was fun and that writing on slates, learning by rote and the threat of physical punishment in schools was a laugh:

> I think the past should still be going on. It[']s GREAT. (Response of a child to a heritage project, quoted by Prendergast & Saxton: 2008: 158)

Universal issues about the ambivalence of change/industrialization/ unemployment and the question of whose interests are served are generally left untouched. Some projects take a more analytical approach and Prendergast and Saxton describe a project where an attempt was made to dramatize a slave auction (Prendergast & Saxton: 2008: 159ff) and received criticism for giving a negative portrayal of African Americans. I would suggest that classic TIE has the theoretical techniques to deal with such an issue more holistically and am reminded of the 1984 Pit Prop piece, *Brand of Freedom*, which began with a slave auction before engaging the children in a much wider exploration of human rights.

Many of the quiddities of TIE are missing from this form of educational theatre. Whilst there may be a limit on group sizes and teachers may have been provided with contextualizing materials, the focus will be on what 'really' happened and 'bringing history to life' rather than mining the conceptual learning inherent in events. Children (and indeed, adults) are fed a fictionalized view of the past that may trivialize and ignore the inherent universal lessons. If this happens, then projects serve only to entrench hegemony and filter out political analysis. Jackson points out that several techniques from TIE are to be found here, from Forum and hotseating to strong performance and storytelling techniques. He cites the use of historic characters that place the spectators in role within the historical context (2007: 237). The educational value of this would, once again, be dependent upon the quality of the facilitating techniques of the actor. Opportunities for 'dialogic encounters' (2007: 242) are present but are rarely exploited.

All the new 'shoots' of TIE mentioned above would arguably not have existed without the developments in TIE and DIE underpinning them. Inasmuch as they assist young people to comes to terms with themselves in a contradictory world, they are to be welcomed and valued. But there is a concern to be expressed when critical analysis is sidelined or tramlined around the difficult need to question and challenge accepted definitions and solutions. The new shoots of TIE all too often serve the hegemony rather than offer it up for forensic examination.

Drama therapies

The web of drama and theatre-based behavioural interactivities has become very tangled during the twentieth century (which in itself is testament to the importance of creative play to human well-being). Finally, I want to acknowledge the relationship with drama therapies. The origins of such therapies have developed independently (from psychologists such as Moreno) but have also drawn extensively on theoretical approaches of drama practitioners. As such, the link for drama therapies is directly to those practitioners rather than via the intermediary influence of TIE.

It is in the use of role-play and the associated learning processes of participation that the commonalities are most clear. Slade and Way defined a clear faith in the power of drama to change behaviour and both eschewed drama as primarily performance. Heathcote too believed that partaking in a 'what if' situation is not the same as acting and that it is the journey not the destination that should have precedence. Cattanach, as a dramatherapist, echoes Heathcote's belief in the centrality of the child and regards play as 'the way that children make sense of the world' (Cattanach: 1996: 157) and that through play we can be 'appropriately distanced from the consequences of such symbolic choices' (Cattanach: 1996: 158). Chesner seems drama processes in the same way, permitting an 'oblique look at the issues of power within a group' and to 'help clients 'rehearse' for political changes in a wider context' (Chesner: 1995: 131). Emunah uses the term 'acting for real' in her dramatherapy and describes how clients are not acting to entertain, escape or mislead'. Rather 'it is acting for release, discovery and renewal' (Emunah: 1994: 302).

The relationship between psychodrama and the work of Boal presents a further concordance of influences. Increasingly in his work, Boal moved from the deconstruction of political oppression (Boal: 1979, 1993) to that of personal and familial oppressions (1995). In both the political and personal spheres, Boal is operating in the same way as the therapist: identify, analyse and then confront in order to achieve change. Whilst Boal sought to induce a political analysis, the psychoanalyst is seeking to illuminate a 'positive, pivotal point' (Holmes & Karp: 1991: xv) so that drama becomes a 'rehearsal for the future' (Holmes & Karp: 1991: 89).

The nature of participation in TIE offers further concomitance with therapeutic practice. The emotional engagement of children in participatory role allows them a framework in which to develop an analysis of events. Cattanach sees dramatherapy in the same way, allowing an understanding 'of the relationship between our internal and external worlds' (1996: 302). And:

> In both dramatherapy and psychodrama the physicality of the experience brings the emotions and the unconscious onto the stage. (Chesner in Jennings: 1998: 115)

It is thus clear that what drama-based therapies have in common with TIE practice is the implementation of distancing and objectivity that facilitates learning processes in what Heathcote has called a 'prismatic illumination' (Heathcote & Bolton: 1995: 112). Jennings talks of clients working in 'liminal time' and uses the same metaphor of illumination 'where there is the possibility of discovering what we did not know we knew' (Jennings: 1987: 15).

Government policy

UK governments had never understood the nature of TIE except perhaps to be aware that it tended to raise awkward political questions. The 2008 McMaster report, *Supporting Excellence in the Arts: From Measurement to Judgement*, acknowledges the role of theatre in offering life-changing experiences whilst avoiding the political implications of this. It clearly carries the baggage of a market-driven approach to the arts that parallels that imposed on education. At times this report offers support for artists, requiring funders to act as defenders of artists' freedoms (1:3) and requires management boards to contain at least two practitioners (1:5) but also suggests a 'Knowledge Bank' which could be used to 'feed into and support the appointment process and to advise on potential candidates' (1:5). This sound like vetting. Additionally all funding bodies should 'have and take up the right to be involved in the appointment processes' (1:5). This tight funding grip is a long way from the governance of TIE in the 1970s that should still be relevant today:

> It is difficult to imagine artistic autonomy achieved and safeguarded without institutional autonomy. (Klaic: 2012: 163)

As Jackson points out (2013: 35ff), the Arts Councils' response to such ideas was to devise a system of decision making through the designation of 'National Portfolio Organizations' (NPOs) prioritizing funding for companies meeting the subjective criteria of excellence, diversity and international links.

Though necessary, whenever assessment criteria are applied there is the danger of abuse. Having 'measurable outcomes' can easily become the excuse to cut companies whose work does not 'fit' politically or artistically. It will then be to the assessment criteria that funders turn for vindication. The move, within TIE, from contextual work to thematic work makes this process easier.

An unambiguous target for a piece of work enables it to be judged on 'measurable' outcomes. Klaic perceives potential for malice in such decisions:

> In the United Kingdom, there are several reasons to believe that the recession is just an excuse to implement long-held ideological convictions about shrinking government and rendering the market predominant in the realm of cultural production as elsewhere. (Klaic: 2012: 158–9)

Assessing success

Allen *et al.* (1999) give an account of the complexities of assessment procedures that emerged in the 1990s. Their article describes a project about auto-crime funded by Plymouth Community Safety Strategy Group. It was overseen by a multi-agency group who wanted to know if it was getting value for money and used the university's social sciences department to measure this. Immediately, it became clear that the different agencies expected different things. All agreed that TIE was a good way of dealing with something that was difficult for teachers, but Health Promotion wanted to measure children's change in attitude; the LA wanted to assess how teachers were assisted in delivering the PSHE curriculum; and the Safety Strategy group wanted to see immediate behavioural change (Allen *et al.*: 1999: 22–3). This potage of desirable outcomes reflects the mess that can result when learning is subsumed to message. The need to judge the project is framing the project. The curriculum demands that learning objectives are demonstrably attained whereas what should actually be required is that the *understanding* of the learners undergoes a critical shift. Rather than inputs from offenders, from police and probation officers (which were part of the programme and designed to instil fear), I would suggest that what was required was consideration of the pressures on young people to be thrill-seeking hedonistic consumers. The project needed to work in a ZPD where their own knowledge of the world could extend them to an understanding of the societal pressures at work. Or, in Freire's terms, it needed to conscientize their learning rather than just having their consciousness of an issue raised. The children knew when they entered the room that 'joy-riding' was wrong. In fact, for those not involved, there was a danger of glamorizing the activity. The project was followed by workshops using Forum, hot-seating and tableaux creation with the aim of showing the children 'that people are responsible for their own actions' (Allen *et al.*: 1999: 24).

The researchers followed-up the project seven months later with interesting results (Allen *et al.*: 1999: 26ff). Most children remembered the play in detail and one child reported that he would be 'too scared to joyride' as a result. Also the play 'explained things' and was 'less boring' than just being told. Many remembered finding the joy-riding scenes exciting (which is concerning) and some children talked enthusiastically to the researchers about their own experiences of joyriding rather than those depicted in the play. Finally, the researchers make the sanguine point that nothing was learnt that could not have been learnt in other ways (Allen *et al.*: 1999: 28). This is the danger – that TIE praxis has become debased by its separation from theory and in many cases has become a sugar-coated way of taking a 'message pill' that could be as easily delivered by formal teaching or video. The researchers recognize this. Drawing on Best (1992), they point out that emotional and rational feelings cannot be separated and that feeling requires understanding of the objective situation.

The implicit moral education being undertaken by a project such as this runs the danger of socialization. The researchers here note that 'moral development in the classroom tends to focus on the child's ability to make moral judgements based on sound reasoning' (Best: 1992: 31). Whilst not claiming that there is any moral ambiguity about the wrongs of joyriding, this approach does presume that moral education consists of children absorbing and accepting the hegemonic values presented. These researchers ask, 'who ultimately decides on the legitimacy of 'personal values?'' (Best: 1992). The question is even more strongly placed by Giannouli and Pammenter:

> Creative learning does not start with somebody else's 'shoulds' and ' oughts'. It does not start with somebody else's decisions and interpretations of the world which they insist that we should understand and live by. These views and opinions exist only as the starting point of a dialogical construction of meaning for those growing into their own world. (2009: 46–7)

The researchers for the promoting agencies felt that though much of value was learned from the programme they felt unable to guarantee that it had offered value for money based on quantitative measures. Even the best TIE is not going to offer Damascene illumination but rather a possibility for change. If you offer TiHE as a cure, however, you must take care that you are not offering snake-oil.

TIE has had to mutate to survive the post-ERA world. The TIE that has emerged in this time has the power to adapt to the changing needs and priorities of a utilitarian education system. Some of these mutations are to be treated with a good deal of suspicion – not because the perpetrators set out to abuse TIE technique but because the socio-political environment demands certain approaches from them and companies lack the theoretical confidence to find more legitimate ways of pursuing a vision of a better world. There is a need to have regard to what fruits these new shoots might put forth.

Henry Giroux

If the likes of Freire, Bruner and Vygotsky were correct in their analysis of what education should be doing, their ideas should be at the forefront of TIE theory, but this is no longer the case. Since these practitioners, others, like Giroux, have emerged to stress the need for education to be a conduit of liberation but it is increasingly difficult to see any application of these approaches. Discussing the teaching of history and the tendency in recent decades to reduce it to a list of events, of 'facts', he notes that:

> If critical consciousness represents an ability to reflect then ignoring history means a loss of its ability to emancipate. (Giroux: 1997: 9)

His attack on the 'culture of positivism' that suppresses historical consciousness chimes with early TIE approaches but is distant from contemporary 'heritage' projects. Giroux attacks the paucity of education that excludes interpretative processes, something that has been a quintessence of educational developments in the UK and the United States in recent decades. The assumption is that 'facts' are value-neutral whereas the most crucial fact is that knowledge is socially constructed. This is apparent in the structure of educational curricula where to facilitate fair and objective grading, only those matters which can be designated true or false are admitted into assessment. In terms of human existence, it leaves unquestioned the issues that matter most: 'those economic, political and social structures that shape our daily lives' (Giroux: 1997: 13) and leads to a world where both oppressors and oppressed can see no alternative. What is required, maintains Giroux, is the means to confront 'the assumptions embedded in a given educational paradigm' (Giroux: 1997: 17). The participatory TIE approach offered this opportunity, and we must be wary of 'TIE' that in fact only places before audiences an interpretatively closed view of social reality. Giroux would be sympathetic to the TIE approach that offers rigorous interrogation of knowledge. Indeed, whilst seeking to take the moral high ground, the positivist is actually denying the notions of ethics, for there are no moral choices to be made; it is true or false:

> Critical thinking as a mode of reasoning appears to be in eclipse in both wider society and the sphere of public school[1] education. (Giroux: 1997: 26)

The danger is that 'facts' are seen as absolute rather than part of a dialectical process. For classic TIE, theatre is the catalyst for critical analysis. Without such an approach, says Giroux, human freedom is under threat; critical thinking 'must be seen as a fundamental, political act' (Giroux: 1997: 26).

Training

Given that TIE has spawned or influenced so many approaches to educational, social and community theatre, it is of no surprise that the early training in TIE at drama schools and on drama degrees has largely been supplanted by courses in Applied Drama and Applied Theatre. These courses draw heavily on Heathcote, Bolton, Boal and Neelands (amongst others). Educational theory will only occur through the intermediation of these drama theorists which otherwise resides in the Education Departments of the same institutions. Courses have to be generic to cover the breadth of situations in which the theatre might be applied. We should remember that formal training was non-existent during TIE's early years. TIE lacked the coherence of academic training and such courses as developed followed the praxis rather than created it. As previously outlined, little of the education theory that emerged from 1970–1990 was formally studied by actor/teachers but rather was gleaned through SCYPT and from motivated directors or other company members.

Existing companies have had to adapt to survive and emergent companies have moulded themselves in the image of the new approach to education. Training has followed, trying to create the specialists that the wide pattern of DIE, TfD, TiHE, Prison Theatre, Heritage Theatre and so forth require. Whilst courses include the study of DIE and TIE, most will also prioritize an understanding of the demands of the National Curriculum with the (correct) implication that, to offer career possibilities, it is to this that attention must be paid.

Currently many universities offer Applied Drama or Applied Theatre courses that contain a TIE module of some twenty or thirty hours teaching (often with an additional practical project). Courses contacted report that the emphasis is on practical approaches to performance, workshop and facilitation skills. Many mention work undertaken in schools, targeting curriculum areas such as the environment, history and literacy or in response to LA commissions to produce TiHE work.[2] That much of the practical work has a tendency towards TiHE should not surprise us. Classic TIE companies would work for, perhaps, six full weeks researching, devising and rehearsing performance and workshops. For students working within a twenty or thirty credit module, a TiHE approach is going to be far more feasible.

One respondent (Sue Mayo at Goldsmith's University) noted that 'a lot of international students are attracted to the UK because of TIE and the place of drama in schools, 'only to find both rather in decline' (email: 6 October 2014). Dobson makes a similar point in interview, noting that his students (in Victoria, Canada) get 'really fired up' when exposed to classic TIE but the situations in which they will be working will not permit them the luxury of such an approach. Like many students, they will tend to produce TiHE-related work that is easier to fund, research and present. Neither the training infrastructure nor the funding and curriculum environment are conducive to classic TIE and the new TIE exhibits a more pragmatic approach to its objectives. In seeking the 'shoots' of fresh TIE in the classic tradition, it seems we may have to look elsewhere.

Notes

1 British readers should note that 'public school' refers to the schools in the US state system, not to private schools.
2 These general comments are based on replies received from a circulated appeal to university drama departments in September 2014 about the nature of their TIE-related courses.

CHAPTER TWELVE

Some Contemporary International TIE Programmes

I do not intend to replicate the wide-ranging and profound work that Jackson and Vine (2013) have undertaken in describing TIE-related projects across the globe. As they and others have demonstrated (and as has been explored in the previous chapter), TIE tropes have been adapted and applied in a wide range of contexts from health and heritage to emergent nation development and prisoner recidivism by companies internationally. The applications of TIE-derived methods have found fertile ground in which to thrive in locations across all continents. I will mention some of these in passing where those locally involved in TIE work have offered useful insights and will also examine a few programmes in some detail in order to identify where the influences of British TIE can be found. Some of this influence will be found to come from the pragmatic shoots of the new TIE, but in other work we will discern derivations from the 'classic' tradition.

The United States

In North America, one of the most notable educational arts organizations is the Creative Arts Team in New York. In the 1993 edition of Jackson's *Learning Through Theatre*, Riherd and Hardwick state that the work of CAT was 'firmly rooted in the British Theatre in Education movement' (205). They also describe the importance of conflict resolution through drama using Forum-like techniques. Chris Vine is now the Academic Program Director for the MA in Applied Theatre at The City University of New York (CUNY), School of Professional Studies. In an interview (21 September 2014), he notes that when he became Artistic and Education Director at CAT in 1993, the company had a passing acquaintance with Boal's work that he helped to develop within the context of Freirean pedagogy which remains central to current work. Students undertaking the CUNY MA programme study Vygotsky, Piaget and Bruner as well as Gardner's theory of Multiple Intelligences, bringing together the cognitive and affective to create the programmes of work. The work of key drama theorists is also fundamental and Vine cites the work of Bolton, Heathcote, O'Neill, Dobson and Neelands amongst others. He points out that there has never been a funding regime comparable to that once offered by the Arts Councils and LEAs in Britain and this has shaped the development of TIE in the United States. In addition to the familiar problems of a restrictive timetable, it is unusual to even have access to studio space in which to work; the choice will be between classroom or a fixed-seat theatre environment. Despite these limitations, CAT has continued to disseminate TIE methodology in a range of curriculum and health project initiatives. Following a successful TIE conference in 1996, it was instrumental in creating a TIE network within the American Alliance for Theatre and Education which became the Applied Theatre Network but retaining 'its recognition of, and connections to, TIE practices' (Chris Vine: interview 21 September 2014).

A range of examples of CAT's educational theatre work are to be found in Jackson and Vine (2013: Chapter 13). Much of this work is clearly in the range of TiHE and Applied Theatre work as previously described. Like most companies all the work has to be securely grounded in the curriculum and projects are often funded by sponsors with clear agendas on what learning should be 'delivered' and how this is to be measured:

It has shifted the balance of the work from the broad humanistic goals of changing perspectives and deepening understanding, through the aesthetic experience, to a more instrumentalist approach to building specific capacities, improving skills and changing targeted behaviours. (Wheelock in Jackson & Vine (eds): 2013: 246)

Helen Wheelock's work with CAT reflects this approach with much emphasis on creativity, literacy and storytelling both with children and in the training of teachers. When funding permits the work is closer to TIE on the DIE-TIE axis with teams of two actor/teachers engaging the children in a drama that will demand decision-making (see Jackson & Vine (eds): 2013: 231). But the performance work in these projects does not always involve a theatrical structure. Generally the methodologies at work are processual drama and role-play rather than fully-formed TIE. The intentions of the work are clear. There are projects to develop literacy and creativity or to combat bullying or inform about HIV/AIDS. It is often necessary to follow the grant-aid to deal with whatever is the educational 'hot-topic' of the day. For Wheelock the key function of her work is to support teachers who are 'stressed beyond belief' by the burden of assessment and to disseminate the drama skills that can help them achieve pedagogical goals (interview: 7 December 2014). As is currently the case in Britain, we see here a version of TIE that aims to ameliorate the burden placed upon teachers not only to deliver a utilitarian curriculum but also to offer social band-aid. For TIE companies that is the route to finding official support and funding.

Heavily influenced by the approaches of CAT, and especially Boal, is Theatre Espresso led by Artistic Director Wendy Lement. Espresso's project, *Justice at War*, demonstrates the nature of TIE-related work currently available in the United States. *Justice at War* has as its declared aims the exploration of the meaning of democracy and the learning of tolerance. It also aims to allow students to vocalize feelings about injustice and specifically to consider prejudice against Japanese-Americans during the Second World War.

Justice at War

Justice at War (first toured in 2005) begins with a short performance piece that quickly sets the context for what follows. The joyful, carefree dancing of two young people is interrupted by the sound of a bombing raid. A newspaper seller announces the Japanese attack on Pearl Harbour. Extracts of the report are read and a contemporary radio report is played. We see citizens become concerned about the number of their neighbours who are of

FIGURE 12.1 Justice at War *(Theatre Espresso 2005). Mitsuye Endo is interviewed by a government attorney. Photo courtesy of the company.*

Japanese extraction. The order for all such Japanese-Americans to report to 'relocation camps' is announced. A Japanese-US woman, reading the newspaper, appears concerned. We are four minutes into the project.

Immediately the audience are placed in the frame of 'Justices of the Supreme Court' in 1944 and set the task of considering the case of a Japanese-American internee, Mitsuye Endo. They are reminded of their duty to uphold the law and not be swayed by emotion. They have to decide whether, under the law, the US government has the right to intern her. In the formal setting of the court the case is presented by an attorney for the government and by the military. Their key (and somewhat disingenuous) argument is the need to protect this ethnic group from racist attack. Counter-arguments are offered by the internee and her advocate, based principally on the fifth amendment of the US constitution. In the course of the evidence, a great deal is revealed including the attitudes of the authorities towards this group of citizens.

> The final section of the programme offers the 'justices' an opportunity to ask questions of the attorneys and witnesses prior to reaching a decision about the policy of internment. The decision is a personal one and is demonstrated by a show of hands. A justice is selected to relay the decision to the court and to Mitsuye Endo.

This project clearly has a relationship to TIE in its use of frame and in the creation of space for the spectators to engage with the material from a distanced perspective. Lement reports that the structure of *Justice at War* has become a standard approach for the company, offering as it does performance elements and an opportunity for analysis. The company is made up of a core group of actors who have developed an ensemble approach though they also undertake work outside Espresso. When recruiting they seek actors who share their values, have the ability to play a variety of roles and, crucially, display an educational instinct which will enable them to take on the role of 'joker'/facilitator. Clearly the work has been influenced by Boal, but Lement also cites the work of the historian Howard Zinn as being of central importance to Espresso's work (interview: 13 October 2014).

Where the work diverges from TIE is in its containment within the particular moment of history. This may be related to the fact that in an hour's project, there is no time to allow broader contextualization but there are rich possibilities here to examine the related contexts of racial profiling, Guantanamo and Islamaphobia and, indeed, the universally contentious issue of dealing with 'otherness'. The Study Guide that accompanies the programme offers suggestions for further study of the Pearl Harbour attack and offers ways in which the situation of Mitsuye Endo could be empathetically examined. A further exercise invites students to consider whether reparations should be due to Japanese-Americans who suffered as the result of government policy. It is also suggested that this discussion be extended to a consideration of the rights of Native Americans. Such particular investigations could take a more universal perspective but were this to happen, the accusation of political bias would no doubt soon follow. It is increasingly difficult for TIE programmes to offer opportunity to critically examine historical events in terms of the socio-political context. By restricting discussion to parametered curriculum areas, dangerous political territory can be avoided.

It is not my intention to denigrate this work, however. It is the product of the particular environment that we are living through and strives within the boundaries set to offer creative contexts in which the minds of children can be opened to possibilities. There is a limit, however, to how much can be achieved when bounded by the straightjacket of a positivist curriculum, an unbending timetable and the watchful eye of those fearing political dogma.

Canada

In Canada are further examples of educational work being created for schools though not, Dobson points out, demonstrating the quality that those exposed to the classic model would recognize. He cites (interview: 8 October 2014) the Carousel Players as a company that produces very well-respected work for young people in schools but which is 'message' orientated. Recent projects have dealt with learning disorders, friendship, peer pressure, bullying and self-esteem and project work on the themes of imagination, creative play, teamwork, character development and kindness (www.carouselplayers.com accessed 25 November 2014). These programmes are not offered as 'TIE' but share the same concerns and approaches of much of the contemporary TIE work discussed in the previous chapter. They are clearly educational programmes but within that narrow definition of 'education' which concerns itself with the transference, rather than the creation, of knowledge.

Australia

Despite a strong commitment to Applied Drama and Theatre in recent years, the same paucity of TIE exists in the antipodes. In Australia, 'TIE' is used to describe 'delivering pre-packaged plays to school audiences' (Hunter in Jackson & Vine (eds): 2013: 171). Her description of these pieces is all too familiar:

> Precisely clocked shows with minimum set-up and pack-up: perky adults playing children characters: and relevant didacticism

based on bullying, Australian history or adaptations of [children's books]. (Hunter in Jackson & Vine (eds): 2013: 171)

Hunter's analysis is that, though the form of classic TIE has been lost, the 'intent' of the progressive approaches to education underpinning it have survived in other ways. The Belgrade model, she argues, was destined to fail in Australia where geography, education policy and the nature of professional theatre itself all conspired to provide an arid environment for it to take root. She further describes attempts to conjoin the political intent of British TIE with the provision of theatrical outreach for main house productions. As in 1960s Britain this was found to be unsatisfactory by both partners.

What we see in Australia is an attempt in the 1970s and 1980s to import and transplant notions of TIE as they were developing in the UK, and often with ex-pat Brits as the key protagonists. In Australia, the notion of educational theatre was forced to develop in a different direction in order to survive. British TIE could not be the model and instead there has been a tendency 'to pursue a much more performance-only tradition with high production values, maybe with pre/post discussion and workshop' (O'Toole: email: 21 September 2014). Interestingly, this description would fit much of the work that sails under the banner of TIE in the UK today. In the same correspondence, O'Toole notes the extensive use of Boalian approaches in tackling social issues, though even this is of 'varying quality'.

Writing in the 1993 version of *Learning Through Theatre*, O'Toole and Bundy also identified a growing sense of Australian self-confidence and, whilst the left-wing, participatory ideas were attractive, workers in this area also sought cultural independence (Jackson: 1993: 136). They report that, as early as 1981, the participatory model was being dismissed by Australian companies. This abandonment may have been because few people had seen it done well or, possibly, that 'to do this well was often just too hard' (Jackson: 1993: 136). In this respect, educational work that has developed in schools in Australia since the 1980s is now being reflected by the new TIE in the UK.

As with ERA in the UK, Australia had its own educational reform in 1993 that presented some of the same problems to those wishing to work in schools. The curriculum became highly centralized within each state or territory and the administrative structures became more hierarchical and mechanistic. Educational innovation was not encouraged and using theatrical approaches with small groups became impossible. The overall effect was to create a genre of educational theatre centred on the writer. Hunter reports that a dialogic approach to learning through theatre lost out to a didactic approach (in Jackson & Vine (eds): 2013: 177) and, by the mid-1990s traditional TIE had disappeared or become youth theatre (Jackson & Vine (eds): 2013: 182). As in the UK, the new approach tended to emphasize learning about creative processes alongside personal and political development. Initiatives such as artists-in-residency schemes and drama programmes, she maintains, 'foreground young people's central role as co-agents of meaning making in the arts'. (Jackson & Vine (eds): 2013: 185).

New Zealand

In New Zealand the situation is comparable though O'Toole notes that the company Applied Theatre Consultants uses devising processes 'straight out of the classic TIE mould' (email: 21 September: 2013) in creating the *Everyday Theatre* project dealing with domestic abuse. I give this example to demonstrate how current applications of TIE-derived influence show the same TiHE concerns around social issues that is to be observed in the new TIE in the UK. It is also a useful example of how traditional approaches of role and frame are being developed to respond to the new media cultures of young people.

Everyday Theatre

*E*veryday Theatre begins with a twenty-minute performance piece for over a hundred children from impoverished backgrounds about family relationships in which the threat of violence is always close. The programme, sponsored by the Department of Children, Youth and Family, is framed within the artifice of a video game. Familiar approaches such as Forum Theatre, the trying out of alternative courses of action, viewing flashbacks, hotseating characters and using the 'thought button function' are facilitated by this game structure. Pupils are offered the opportunity for the decisions within the game to be made harder in order that they might become 'gamesmasters'. The metaphor is that 'life is a game' (O'Toole: 2009: 486) which they can practice in order to win. O'Toole points out that care was taken to avoid stereotypes (for example, by casting a female as a perpetrator of violence) and problematizing the familial and friendship relationships portrayed to create complex situations involving poverty, culture and class. Easy solutions are avoided and care is taken, through the 'game' motif, to protect the pupils into dealing with these highly personal areas.

In the workshop section the events are reviewed, slowed down and replayed. The children are split into groups and they are involved in processual drama, hotseating and Boalian workshops to try and help the family in their role as 'trainee gamesmasters'. In the workshops, the story is retold in different ways and the children find out about the characters' backgrounds. A second workshop uses depiction and writing in role. Possible outcomes are explored and presented to the rest of the class and the characters. Finally children are invited to create a video of the future fortunes of the characters and they advise a 'Commission' on how to help families in these situations. The 'finale' is for the characters to watch the children's 'video'.

O'Toole accepts that this programme differs from 'classic' TIE in many respects (O'Toole: 2009: 497). He notes that the sponsors of the project are from outside education and the content is not a curriculum requirement. Thus the work is disengaged from the routine life of the school. Areas of similarity he identifies as being that the work is created for a specific age group, takes place over an entire school day and deals with an area of a child's concern. Certainly some methodological tropes of TIE are evident in this programme. Peter O'Connor, of Applied Theatre Consultants, maintains that the project does not seek to take a set of messages into schools but rather to offer a process which enables the discovery of those messages (www.youtube.com/watch?v=Gx8r-gPa6tA). That a 'message' is there to be 'discovered' should alert us to the fact that this is a step away from classic TIE. O'Connor insists though, that because the situations are so real to the children they are keen to find real solutions. This company uses the term Applied Theatre rather than 'TIE' which, according to O'Toole, has long been out of favour in the antipodes though this is less true in South East Asia.

Hong Kong

The Chung Ying Theatre Company was set up by the British Council in 1979 and developed a range of TIE and DIE work in Hong Kong. Estella Wong worked as their head of TIE department from 2001 to 2006 and describes the work of the group at that time as 'moral or value education' as well as encouraging the 'understanding of theatre art form, creativity etc.' (questionnaire: 29 November 2014). The company seek to foster drama education 'in keeping with the mission of modern education: enhancing youth's multi-dimensional thinking, stimulating creativity and promoting language ability' whilst promoting 'theatrical arts, exploring cultural exchanges and enriching cultural life' (www.unescohkied.org/chung-ying accessed 30 November 2014). Wong reports that the main aims of the TIE projects of Chung Ying were to use participation to explore decision-making and understanding; to enjoy creative activities; and to appreciate theatre arts (questionnaire: 29 November 2014). As with Applied Theatre Consultants in New Zealand, it is clear that there is an inheritance from the TIE legacy. Primacy is given to an exploration of how and why the world is as it is; one should be seeking creative solutions to identified problems, not merely learning 'creativity' per se, though in some political environments this may not be possible. Even in the 'liberal' western democracies, we have seen how TIE companies that championed critical thinking and offered a vision of change have been peremptorily cut, slowly financially suffocated or gently marginalized educationally. We should be heartened by all such attempts to offer flourishing authentic teaching when the environment is so unconducive.

Now at the Hong Kong Academy for Performing Arts, Wong is keen to develop TIE and other participatory approaches with her students and regards the involvement of teachers in the TIE programmes as central. The key theorists that she draws on with students (and in her previous work directing TIE) include the names one would expect – Boal, Heathcote, Bolton, Davis, O'Toole and the work of Big Brum and Bond. Their practice emerges in the range of participatory approaches adopted including process drama, reflection and Forum. The way in which this work has moved outside the classic TIE model is in the use of theatre games, theatre making, improvising and in the creation of performances to demonstrate a crystallized understanding of the children's thoughts at the end of the programme.

Thus TIE is facing similar pressures to adapt to narrow pedagogical priorities in many parts of the world. As a result, much contemporary TIE, whilst owing a great debt to classic TIE, is coming up with the same solutions – to become the servant of curricula preoccupied with the transference of hegemonic knowledge. I conclude this whistle-stop tour in search of classically influenced TIE, however, in Eastern Europe where a different focus in the work is apparent and the shoots are more clearly grafted upon classic TIE stock.

Hungary

> Round Table Theatre in Education Company's mission is to give children and young people the opportunity to explore and understand the most relevant questions of our time through artistic work [and to produce] high quality participatory theatre in education programmes… aimed at specific age groups, with strictly one class participating at a time.[1]

Established in 1992 the company works in a legacy clearly derived from early British TIE.[2] Atilla Farkas, of Round Table, cites Big Brum and Edward Bond amongst its primary influences. He also acknowledges the continuing impact of O'Neill, Gillham, Vygotsky and Bruner (questionnaire: 21 November 2014). By limiting group sizes they are able to use participatory techniques 'in which theatrical and pedagogical goals are evenly fulfilled'. Generally the participation is through distancing role in which participants can safely offer ideas and opinions about 'how democracy works and how they can affect the world'. The current season (2014–15) includes a collaboration with Cecily O'Neill for 8–9 year olds and Bond's *Broken Bowl* for 10–11 year olds, directed by Chris Cooper, then director of Big Brum. Recurring themes include how and when authority should be resisted and how fear impedes our ability to analyse the social construction of reality.

Hungary can boast a second company with a direct TIE legacy. Káva Drama/Theatre in Education Association has existed since 1996. Their work centres on 'the world of the school, the topic of social disadvantages, and the topic of democratic citizenship' (Takács: questionnaire: 18 November 2014). As with Round Table, whilst many personal issues are touched upon, they are set within wider considerations of power relationships: coping with the power of others; the power of money; and coping with tyranny – the treatment of Romas. The company has the intention of dealing with personal, family and social relationships and considers these within the context of wider social structures.

For Takács, TIE from Káva offers young people an experience outside the usual theatrical forms to which they react enthusiastically. He notes ruefully that the Hungarian education system does not encourage open questioning and reports the experience of every TIE practitioner that teachers are always surprised at the response of children not known for their quality of classroom contribution. Káva has a very similar list of influences to that of Round Table and again works closely with Big Brum. A consideration of two of their projects will demonstrate the close relationship with classic British TIE.

Bábok (Puppets)

Bábok (Puppets) 2008 is a sophisticated piece of participatory theatre for young adults. A young prince is refusing to get prepared for a press conference at which, we later learn, he will be named as the new ruler. He is accompanied by two servants whose job it is to persuade him but who, in the final analysis, have no power over him. The prince is questioning his role in life, his identity. Even though this first section is a performance, the servants move among the informally seated spectators involving them in the task that has to be completed. The prince himself is scornful of his position and the expectations of him. The servants turn to the young people to glean their understanding of the situation and they respond, not from any frame but from the experience of being adolescents. The servants try to explain that 'we all have to learn rules and learn to obey them'. The prince joins in – 'why do we have to adapt to the world?' He criticizes the

FIGURE 12.2 Bábok/Puppets *(Káva 2008). The servants seek advice on how to persuade the prince. Photo courtesy of the company.*

servants for their inability to find their own way in life and their insistence on fitting in and doing their job. He gathers a group of pupils to discuss his concerns. The servants vent their anger at the prince with a second group who try to explain the prince's behaviour to them. Even if they empathize with the prince, the servants have to serve the king. The prince remains adamant in rejecting the suit (and all it represents), the press conference and the wishes of his father. A confrontation between father and son takes place in which members of the class role-play the prince for him, explaining his actions to the king.

This project allows the pupils to explore, in a 'no-penalty zone', questions of socialization versus responsibility to family and society. Interestingly Káva does not find it necessary here to place the spectators in a particular frame. Despite their 16 year-old sophistication, they are enabled to 'play' the game with the actors and take their part very seriously. They voice their own concerns about the world by talking to and about the prince. At the end of the piece, the prince acknowledges that there are so many possibilities but that he now knows what he is going to do. The piece ends at that moment and the question is left hanging for later analysis in or out of school.

The way in which spectators are involved in the programmes without the immediate protection of a role or frame is an interesting development from previous secondary school projects mentioned, such as Actions PIE's *Crossing* or Theatr Powys' *The Apothecary's Story*. It is a salutary reminder that the ability to not only 'suspend disbelief' but also to play a game with intense belief is not lost to teenagers. Another Káva example, which there is not space to explore here, is *Apalabirintus* (*Fatherlabyrinth*) in which conflicts within family and working situations are explored with three different actor-drama/teachers[3] playing the father with slightly differing approaches to the problems they meet at work and at home. In this project, the spectators sit on (not at) the edge of the playing space and, in the final section, are seated such that the living room becomes a traverse catwalk between the young people who are fully involved in the conflict analysis and resolution. As with their advice to the prince in *Bábok*, they are talking about themselves whilst talking about a safe 'other', discovering what they didn't know that they knew.

Work with younger children similarly shows links with classic TIE.

Gubanc (Tuffy)

In *Gubanc* (*Tuffy*) (2011), the 8 year olds are introduced to Tibike and his dog Tuffy. Both realistic and fairy-tale structures are used. Tibike has been left in the care of his aunt in the real world, but this adult has many of the aspects of a fairy-tale villain, making unreasonable demands on Tibike and being cruel to his dog whilst outwardly seeming charming and friendly. She takes the dog for 'a walk' in order to abandon him, having left Tibike to make cookies, something he's never done before. For the children there is a strong element of humour in the tale as Tibike, and we, can understand the dog whilst the aunt hears only barking. Whilst the aunt is walking the dog, the role of being friends to Tibike is assumed and he asks them about what he should do. They suggest calling his mother and the aunt returns as he is doing so. She takes over the call explaining that Tuffy has run off and can't be found. We hear her lie about the search she has made and the good relationship she has built with Tibike. Afterwards, she accuses the boy of stealing and says that as she is an adult his parents will believe her not him. He believes that they will stand by him. He is sent to his room and prepares to leave the house to search for Tuffy.

In the second part of the story, in the forest, we move into a different, magic world, deepening the sense of alienation and archetypal danger that fairy tales contain. A storytelling mode is used by the actor-drama/teacher to develop a narrative and contract the children to help find Tuffy. A child offers a secret code word and they practice using this as a method of signalling to each other. They find Tuffy imprisoned in a strange house in the forest owned by a woman who clearly is the magic forest equivalent of the aunt. She refuses to give back the dog maintaining that she has control over the world of the forest. Tuffy appears, gagged and distraught. She offers (in true fairy-tale style) to return the dog if three (totally unreasonable) tasks are completed. With the children's help, the tasks are accomplished. The 'witch' is only finally defeated however when the children, signalling with their secret word, surround her in an unbroken circle and Tuffy removes the ring which is the source of her power.

FIGURE 12.3 Gubanc/Tuffy *(Káva 2011). Children, in role as Tibike's parents, confront the aunt. Photo courtesy the company.*

Finally the story returns to the flat and to the 'real' world where the children take on their final role as the parents of Tibike. This gives them emotional distance through which to process their reactions and a confidence to speak which they have seen denied to Tibike by his overbearing aunt. They are now empowered in the real world as they had been in the fantasy world. Individual children take this role but also the group face the aunt together. In their responses and questions, the children are exploring their own feelings of injustice in the child's world. The children are considering what can be done when the vulnerable are faced with oppressive, dictatorial power.

Albania

My final destination is Albania where, at the end of 2012, a small company was set up by Shkëlzen Berisha, previously an actor/ teacher with Theatr Powys. Of all the 'shoots', his company, Qendra e Hulumtimit Progresiv (which he translates as the 'Progressive Exploring Centre') is perhaps the frailest of the examples given. It currently exists as an NGO dependent upon project grants but regular, reliable finance remains elusive despite the enthusiastic support of the current Minister of Culture. The Ministry of Education is less able to find funds, even though teacher response to the company's first project *Fjonge e Argjendtë* (*Ribbon of Silver*) was overwhelmingly effusive.

The company's situation resembles that of the early practitioners of TIE. Whilst the work is lauded by educational and theatre officials, there are as yet no financial structures to secure the work in the long term. There is occasional talk of placing the work within the remit of the National Theatre. Supportive agencies are keen that the company should work at a greater distance from Tirana and with a repertoire of projects, seemingly unaware of the financial and contractual implications of this. In my visit to the company,[4] it was clear that its existence was heavily reliant on the good will of company members and that even enthusiastic supporters were unable to appreciate notions of research, rehearsals, production, touring and subsistence. All they could see was the easy confidence with which the company encouraged the children to look afresh at the world around them, without noticing that the company had not even proper transport or a working base.

Fjonge e Argjendtë (Ribbon of Silver)

The project I viewed was inspired by a previous Theatr Powys programme, *Ribbon of Silver*.[5] The programme, for classes of about twenty five 8–11 year olds, empowers children to find their voice in a situation of injustice. The story begins in the classroom when one of the actor/teachers becomes Georgie and we see brief scenes from his itinerant life. It's supposed to be his first day at school, but he doesn't want to go. The opinions of the class about the importance of school are sought and the children's responses validated by the facilitator. They agree to be the children in the story and when Georgie comes into the class they are helpful and supportive. He is very withdrawn however, refusing to respond. The class gently examine a banner or ribbon that Georgie carries with him and which is decorated with seemingly unconnected words: 'harmonica', 'clothes peg', 'caravan', 'music' and 'breathing'. When pushed to explain, Georgie takes fright and runs off. The children decide to follow and help him.

In the hall they are sat, as audience, in a semi-circle. The set represents the door to a traditional Romani caravan. In this performance section we learn a lot about Georgie, his dog (another talking dog!), his mother and the history of his family and their travels. We watch as Georgie muses and daydreams. Significant objects appear in the stories as he recalls events from his life. We even see him holding himself as a baby. The structure of this section is mesmerizing, drawing the children in with highly complex motifs. There is a sense of strong cultural tradition, of isolation and independence. The import of the words on the banner becomes clearer.

The story is regularly stopped so that the children can share, interpret and consider how to support Georgie. A moment of hiatus comes when a character that the children call 'the Big Boy' orders Georgie and his mother off the land. The children immediately accept that this actor/teacher, who has been energetic dog and friendly facilitator can now be this cruel threat. Towards the end

FIGURE 12.4 Fjonge e Argjendtë/Ribbon of Silver *(Qendra e Hulumtimit Progresiv 2014). The children explain the meaning of the images that they have arranged. Photo courtesy of the company.*

of the piece, the children are invited to consider the ribbon and all the objects afresh and to lay them out sculpturally to explain their importance. They start by posing Georgie in the picture and then arranging the objects in relation to him, explaining their decisions as they go. This approach gives voice to the less vocal. Finally, the children discuss their picture and the plight of Georgie and his mother.

Older groups are given an opportunity to confront the Big Boy after a session in which they agree what arguments to use with him. Through a carefully moderated twilight hotseating session, the children are encouraged to find their voice in the face of injustice and misapprehension. Issues of relocation of populations are currently a controversial topic in Albania but the children's assertions that 'you should help them', 'there's room for all' or 'let them stay' are only one level of analysis shown; another child asserts that story-objects are his culture and culture is memory.

FIGURE 12.5 Fjonge e Argjendtë/Ribbon of Silver *(Qendra e Hulumtimit Progresiv 2014). The children confront 'the Big Boy'. Photo courtesy of the company.*

'The ribbon keeps the memories alive.' Another child angrily tells the Big Boy: 'you differ in your wealth but you don't differ in your humanity'. What more is there to say?

This project was a salutary reminder of just what children can achieve when facilitated by trained and caring actor/teachers. Many of the TIE tropes are here, from Heathcote's questioning approaches to an application of Vygotsky's ZPD. The small team of actor/teachers create a theatrical scaffold in which the children can take what they know about friendship, justice, respect, culture and loyalty and apply it to the situation, thus developing their notions of responsibility, citizenship, human rights, tolerance and communication.

The shoots of TIE continue to grow and develop. We can see, however, that similar political and social pressures are impacting on approaches to education. Lacking sufficient philosophic nutrient, many of these new TIE shoots lack the pedagogic credibility of classic TIE but they are evidence of a drive to use theatre to help heal the world. It remains to be seen whether, in acquiescing to the new reality, the fruits of this work will be of benefit to theatre or to education. The work coming out of Eastern Europe has a closer lineage to classic TIE, largely through its links with DIE and companies like Big Brum, and these shoots promise a more authentic approach to the need to empower the young. That this work should be thriving in such countries as Hungary and Albania is perhaps surprising and admiration must be tempered by the knowledge that here too the environment could change very quickly and, as in Britain, companies may be forced to use their skills to bolster educational approaches of questionable value.

Notes

1   www.kerekasztalszinhaz.hu [accessed 30 November 2014].
2   Adam Bethlenfalvy, an original member of the company, wrote an article for *NATD Volume 24: Issue 2* in 2008 describing the formation of the company and its first production, *Bone-Cage* by Geoff Gillham.
3   Káva uses the term 'actor-drama/teacher' to describe their practitioners.
4   November 2014.
5   The original Theatr Powys' version is described more fully by Ian Yeoman in *The Journal for Drama in Education*, Vol. 26, No.1.

CHAPTER THIRTEEN

Some Survivors

The conditions which led to the abiogenesis of TIE no longer exist and it has had to evolve. For many companies this has meant cherry-picking certain techniques and methods to create an educational theatre appropriate to positivist contemporary educational philosophies. These are the main shoots of TIE within the broader Applied Theatre portfolio. A few companies remain committed to a utilization and development of theatrical tropes that will provide a framework for genuine education to take place. I have given some examples of such work in Eastern Europe, but there are also survivors in the UK.

The city of Leeds seems to be a remarkable example with at least three TIE companies. Leeds TIE Company, founded in 1970, is now joined by Theatre Company Blah Blah Blah and Alive & Kicking. Alive & Kicking give themselves a wide brief, producing children's theatre and pantomime as well as creating 'epic narrative journeys that explore complex moral and social issues and offer a cross-curricular and community focus'.[1] The work has a clear bias towards theatre arts, with an emphasis on performance and storytelling to 'promote drama and literacy' and to act as 'a springboard for work across the curriculum'.[2]

The second Leeds-based company is Blah Blah Blah, set up in 1985 with a particular brief to help develop creativity. There is an emphasis on enhancing the creative possibilities within the curriculum but also the company continues to engage with and develop the TIE methodologies that were current when it was formed. The company has accepted the necessity to work within the National Curriculum strictures, supporting teachers and sharing drama and theatre skills.

The Raft of the Medusa

The company first toured *The Raft of the Medusa*, inspired by Gericault's painting (see www.louvre.fr/en/oeuvre-notices/raft-medusa accessed 11 May 2015), in 2008. Aimed at 14–16 year olds, the project placed them in role as assistants to the artist trying to create the painting. The project was remarkable in that it enabled this somewhat sophisticatedly self-conscious age group to physically recreate the painting, unpicking the implications of the images and the social and moral climate in which it was painted. (Briefly, the picture shows the conditions on board a raft that had been abandoned by other survivors of the wrecking of the Medusa. There are clear implications from the painting, and from contemporary accounts, of cases of murder, cannibalism and other inhuman acts by the occupants of the raft.) The participants in the drama learned the story in a feeling way, having to consider exactly what one would do to survive and the nature of humanity.

FIGURE 13.1 The Raft of the Medusa *(Theatre Company Blah Blah Blah 2008). Pupils at Don Valley School help recreate the image for the artist. Photo courtesy of the company.*

The piece combines elements of DIE, role-play and TIE, with the artist and his assistant acting as facilitators, feeding-in information and enabling discussion about what the painting shows, or implies, about human ethical behaviour. The teaching pack that accompanies the project signposts learning for many curriculum examination requirements but points out that 'it does not link specifically to any assessment units' (*Teaching Pack*: 2013: 1). There is a possibility for the political causes of the raft incident to be considered both within the project and as part of the follow-up where, it is suggested for example, that a comparison might be made between the attitudes of the authorities to the survivors of the Medusa and those of the New Orleans floods in 2005.

Raft presents us with a significant example of the legacy of TIE methodology and its adaptation to meet the requirements of current educational policy. It manages to remain a valuable and meaningful experience for the· young people, enabling them to conscientize experience whilst navigating safely within current educational expectations. A more recent project by 'the Blahs' examples an interesting experiment in form.

Messerschmitt vs. Spitfire – a love story

The autumn of 2014 saw the culmination of a collaboration between 'the Blahs' and the Theaterhaus Ensemble of Frankfurt: *Messerschmitt vs. Spitfire – a love story*. There is not a strong TIE tradition in Germany, though Haddon reports that 'there is a growing expectation from schools in Germany that shows should be accompanied by a workshop' (Haddon: 2014: 13). The piece thus had a straightforward structure of performance followed by workshop and there was some direct address and occasional participatory involvement. The play toured in both the UK and Germany. In the play an artist is coming to England to present an exhibition, 'Families, Art and War', based on the experience of childhood in the Second World War.[3] The premise of the play is that she wants to talk to young people in England about this exhibition. In particular, she is concerned about including the disturbing images of the firestorms and the young people in school are framed as this advisory group.

The play is performed bilingually and our engagement with the characters forces us to challenge preconceptions of the War. The company hopes that 'it kicks off a search for the past that is relevant for young people' (*Teacher Pack*: 2014: 2). Central to unravelling the themes are the characters of two cousins, one born and brought up in Leeds and the other in Frankfurt. They are grandchildren of two German sisters and, in the context of the unexploded bomb have to negotiated their own ideas of identity against the ironic discovery of a British bomb that threatens them all. The participation, however, is of a different order from that which one would expect to see in a fully fledged TIE project. Information and opinion is frequently sought from the audience and, at one point, they are brought onto the set to consider what their first thoughts would be when faced with the prospect of an evacuation due to the discovery of an unexploded bomb (a frequent occurrence in several German towns). The key point of involvement, however, comes in a post-performance workshop where, after some warm-up games using depictions, the task is set to create a statue based on the *Angel of History* (inspired by Walter Benjamin's *Thesis on History*) – an image that has featured in the play. The 'statue' is to be placed in the school to convey whatever the young people want to say having seen the play. *The Angel of History* sculpture has been central to the 'exhibition' around which the performance is framed, and now the young people are invited to respond to the sculpture using their own bodies to extend the themes.

The programme, though drawing on a range of TIE techniques, works more in terms of a creativity workshop than a classic piece of TIE. Having been exposed to a complex performance which questions the nature of war and places such difficult considerations within the context of personal relationships, the workshop actually invites the young people to turn away from these universal issues and back to the personal issues surrounding their own lives in school.

FIGURE 13.2 Messerschmitt vs. Spitfire *(Theatre Company Blah Blah Blah 2014). The artist creates a sculpture of 'The Angel of History'. Photo: Lizzie Coombes for the company.*

'The Blahs' have successfully found a niche in which much of the traditional methodology of TIE continues to be exploited, though orientated towards the creativity agenda of the accepted curriculum. Many of its approaches are innovative and they can be seen as experimenting with developing the form in ways that will permit key quiddities to survive. Notions of renegotiating social reality are less pre-eminent.

The third Leeds company has a direct link back to early TIE through Paul Swift who has worked with several companies since the 1970s. He regards the current incarnation of Leeds TIE as being one that still adheres to the original TIE objectives of 'theatre that looked critically at society, that challenged received perceptions to increase understanding and facilitate change' (email: 31 October 2014). He believes that this radicalism has been the reason that there has been a concerted effort to close TIE down. Swift's email continues:

> TIE has always been beleaguered. When I joined the Belgrade TIE in 1975 the company was under threat of closure.... The original Theatre Clwyd Outreach Company I was part of was closed down after 2 years essentially for doing a play about Northern Ireland. In the 80s and early 90s Leeds TIE were stalked by the Daily Mail who were trying to frame TIE as a group of dangerous revolutionary communists.... TIE always had enemies within the establishment. To survive it had to keep a low profile, which means that now there is scant visible evidence of what it really was and what it achieved.

The emergence of the current Leeds TIE may bear some explication. Like all TIE teams, the effects of ERA impacted on the company's ability to work effectively. There were moves in 1993 to absorb the work within that of the Playhouse Theatre, using it to market main house productions and appropriate the TIE funding. The intervention of Equity prevented outright redundancies and the actors were guaranteed employment in the main theatre. In the summer of 1993, during the summer holiday break, the TIE company was closed. The actor/teachers had no interest in joining the main company and decided to try and keep going without this patronage. Half the previous company, thanks to fortuitous project funding from the Wellcome Foundation, was able to continue working and toured to secondary schools and hospitals with a programme about the genome project. In this way, Leeds TIE was following the route that many TIE companies were being forced down by the new funding regimes. The monies garnered from this tour would be used to finance the next, though the company would be working at subsistence levels and with little security.

Many companies working in this way ultimately failed. Others became part of the TiHE merry-go-round previously examined. Somehow, Leeds TIE has managed to subsist on such project grants whilst maintaining its commitment to being a theatre for social change. It has developed a policy of identifying groups of *any* age and, with the backing of selected funders, creating TIE projects that will both satisfy the purse-holder and the political outlook of the company. Whilst being a regular recipient of Arts Council project funds since 2001, the company determinedly keeps a distance from any notion of 'message' theatre whilst dealing with complex socio-political issues.

Bad Mummy

The 2011 programme, *Bad Mummy*, will serve as an example. The programme was developed in collaboration with the Welsh company Spectacle Theatre Ltd., where it toured as *Bad Mammy*. It is a half-day project dealing with mental illness and its impact on the wider family. The piece is presented to secondary school children placed in the frame of 'social workers' who have been called in to decide on the fate of the children in this dysfunctional household. The mother has been admitted to hospital and in the play we see the estranged husband at the house trying to sort out what will happen to the two children, only one of which is his natural child. The central drive of the play is the gradual unveiling of the progress of the mother's illness. Slowly the events of the past months and days are revealed through an ingenious theatrical device that gives emotional and critical distance not only to the characters in the play but also to the 'social workers' viewing the story. All are protected into an understanding through the use of the little girl's toys. It is a technique reminiscent of that used with children suffering trauma and involves using dolls and other toys to tell the story. Just as puppets or masks can protect us into seeing the world objectively, so the little girl indicates what has happened using her toys. The father and, eventually, his intensely alienated son, are brought into the story which the children are both desperate to tell and fearful of revealing.

Through this device the father is forced to empathize with the mother (not so much put in her shoes but put in her dressing gown), and the children are able to reveal to the audience of social workers and to the father what has been happening. Their interpretation of events is trapped in the child-world view, but the audience can read the situation with more sophistication. The effect is simultaneously

FIGURE 13.3 Bad Mummy/Bad Mammy *by Paul Swift (Leeds TIE and Spectacle Theatre Ltd. 2011). The father is forced to play the role of the child's mother. Photo courtesy Mark Johnson (mojoffoto. com) and Spectacle Theatre Ltd.*

humorous and disturbing, working in the same way as does the metaphor of the stray dogs in *When Sleeping Dogs Awake*. A variety of themes become apparent including family break-up, inter-personal relationships, alcohol abuse, domestic abuse, sibling rivalry and even, a final indication of incestuous child abuse. Outside the home, there is a friendship between the boy and a young member of a neighbouring family who are seeking asylum. The attitude of the father and, we find out, the mother, towards this family is a major cause of the boy's delicate state of mind. He has tried to help his friend by printing family pictures for him. The mother has destroyed both the prints and the original disc – destroying the friend's link with his family, past and culture. The father's attitudes are framed by his being in the army, which had led to the marriage break-up and also given him his own demons to deal with despite his sympathetic veneer.

The play thus offers, in an hour, a toxic mix of compacted social and personal issues. Thus far the spectators have been little more than audience, occasionally being asked for reassurance and agreement, but without close participation. More detailed engagement with the issues is facilitated through the workshop. Its aim is to explore the young people's attitudes to the issues in the play. Questions are decided for each of the characters that are then presented to them, though the company does not intimate that they have the answers. Thought-tracking is often used, including for the absent mother. The old standby, hotseating, is given a new twist in that the spectators are invited to be the characters to answer the questions from their peers. This neatly avoids the frequent tendency in hotseating sessions for the questioners to merely extract motives out of the characters. Instead, the young people have to demonstrate their understanding of the people in the play and their situations. Additionally, Steve Davis reports that Spectacle's workshop allowed pupils to interview characters not in the play but who might have insights into the situation. It is at this stage that they may be required to speculate on the characters' situations in the future by creating scenes with still or moving images. As social workers, the final plenary session invited ideas for how the story might end – to find ways forward for the family. For both companies, the aim was to engage the young people empathetically in issues of which they will be aware in their own lives. They will be enabled to break through barriers of isolation and find confidence in reflecting upon complex social situations.

Swift feels that the company's approach is more than just the standard investigation of social problems (interview: 29 November 2014). No answers are given except those coming from the young people. They have to decide what is going on and why. He believes this approach promotes and enables change by exposing the hegemonic ideology that disempowers. Here we see the influence of Gramsci, Vygotsky and Bruner, as well as the drama influences of Heathcote *et al*. Leeds TIE seeks to take its work beyond the traditional educational environment, offering its work to adult community groups, children and young people in and out of a school setting.

One of the most innovative aspects of this work is that of its being taken out of the education institutions thus avoiding the inherent curriculum and political limitations. There will be less financial security and access to the work will not be as universal, but there will also be fewer strictures placed upon the critical thinking that the company seeks to engender. This aspect of the work can be seen as a positive mutation, widening the concept of where and when education can and should take place. This is also an approach being taken by the Drawn to Stars company, based in London and Wales. In *Science in the Sky* the company worked with elderly participants and 'vulnerable students' from a rural Welsh secondary school in an intergenerational project which addressed issues of climate change through an imaginative exploration of 'what it is to be at home in the world'. Aimee Corbett (who worked at both Big Brum and Theatr Powys) and Vanessa Hammick describe the project as 'an exploration with no right or wrong answer or message' (email: 11 February 2015). It is perhaps only outside the increasingly restrictive education system that such shoots can emerge and such questions be posited.

TIE in the twenty-first century cannot be the TIE of the 1960s. Swift recognizes that early TIE believed that it would be enough to expose injustice and untruth and change would follow. We are now subject to international value systems of culture, finance and politics in which we are all implicated. The drive towards measurable outcomes seems unstoppable and the outcomes are of questionable value. Freire points out that 'if we don't transcend the idea of education as pure transference of knowledge', we risk political illiteracy (Freire: 1985: 104). Such illiteracy may serve the interests of the establishment but there seems to be actual collusion by the oppressed in this oppression. The question remains: why do human beings act against their own interest? It is a question that the playwright Edward Bond has wrestled with for sixty years.

The company Big Brum has existed since 1982 and was built on the theoretical educational philosophies of the time. Even today, teachers' packs contextualize the company's work within the analysis of Vygotsky. The influence of Bruner, as well as Heathcote, is also a clear feature of the methodologies that they employ in working with young people. The company has also become a powerhouse for sharing (evangelizing even) the tropes and memes of both TIE and DIE across the world. We have seen how companies in Hungary, Albania and Hong Kong have been influenced by its work. Chris Cooper, director of the company from 1999–2015, works with emerging DIE and TIE practitioners through Drama Rainbow in China where the government is increasingly concerned that their education system excludes the nurturing of creativity that they recognize will be essential to China's future. This at a time when Big Brum has recently lost the security of being within the Arts Council's 'National Portfolio' and has to depend on specific project funding for the foreseeable future.

As with all the companies mentioned in this section, educational changes have forced new ways of working. It is virtually unheard of to offer full-day projects, and the pressure is always there to increase 'audience' numbers despite the undermining effect on workshop approaches. Big Brum's resource packs contain detailed information for teachers to help them relate the programmes to a range of curriculum targets. There is also a noticeable effect on the creation of the material. *Touched* (2013) by Chris Cooper had a cast of three. Bond's latest play for the company, *The Angry Roads*, has only two. Not that is an issue in itself, but it is clearly a restraining factor when formulating the workshop elements of the programme.

The Angry Roads

The Angry Roads (2014) is a performance piece for 13 year olds and above, enveloped within a workshop framework. The young people are not required to accept a frame and their participation is as spectators and as themselves. Bond has been very specific about the set. It is barely furnished though with each item of furniture and props carefully selected. This is the first task for the spectators. The facilitator welcomes the group and emphasizes that there are no right answers to the question the play will pose: 'what is it to be human?'. He reassures them that, better than him, they *understand* the world even though they might not be able to *explain* it. He invites the spectators to really *look* at the room and its contents and then to speculate upon the people who live there. Immediately they are being engaged with an event in a way that TV, social media and film do not require of them; they are learning to read signs, learning to be spectators.

FIGURE 13.4 The Angry Roads *by Edward Bond (Big Brum TIE 2014). The actors prepare the children to decode the play. Photo courtesy of the company.*

An actor, Norman the son, takes his place on the set. He is sorting the toys of his childhood with the intent of keeping, selling or disposing of them. There is little else other than these toys in the room: two non-matching dining chairs and a well-worn table. The sense is of impoverishment and alienation, though it is only when the father arrives that we see just how impoverished is the relationship between father and son and how deep their emotional isolation.

The play is a challenging one. The father is an elective mute and 'communicates' with his son through hitting the table, which inexplicably, the son appears to have learned to interpret. The process of the play involves the gradual extraction by the son of the story behind this emotional paucity. That this happens at this point in time is related to the boy's intellectual development and maturity, his frustration and the catalyst of a significant anniversary that is about to take place: the anniversary of an accident in which his father, then a night taxi driver, killed a woman by running over her. This happened before Norman was born. That he cannot know and yet *has* to know is the relentless driver behind the son's insistent questioning and guessing and his father's non-verbal responses. Slowly he chips away at this voluble silence until he guesses the whole truth: that his father was in a relationship with the women he killed and that they were arguing that night about the child he had fathered. He had run down the woman, extracted the child from where it had become trapped in the windscreen wipers, placed it tenderly in the mother's arms and then run over them both again, pressing them into one corpse. He never spoke again.

The young people are left with many questions that the workshop allows them to clarify; to muse upon the reasons for the characters' behaviours, the mutism, the sorting of the toys, the method of communication and the motivations for past and present actions. In the second act of the play, the father returns injured from an industrial accident and, as the son gets closer to the truth, he binds his own mouth with the material of the sling supporting his arm, reinforcing his determination to avoid communicating. This (and all the characters' actions), the young people are empowered to interpret as a result of the initial 'sign-reading' process. At the end of the play, the son leaves the house with his bag packed, his last thought that 'they didn't tell me I had a brother'.

In one version of the final workshop the young people are invited to recreate the moment of the accident in order to understand it and to speculate on the father's last spoken words, the nature of which has pre-occupied Norman throughout the play. The description of the accident as described in the play is slowly repeated, read over the action: the taking of the baby from the windshield, the placing of it with its mother, the covering with a shawl. What is it that the father whispers? Another version of the workshop is described by Sorrel Oates in the *NATD Journal* (Vol. 31. No. 1: 2015: 28). Here, the pupils deconstruct the moment in which the father looks at his son for the first time. Was this the first time in the play – or in his life? The students play out versions with and for each other. Oates reports a moving sequence in which the young people intuit that the father perhaps sees his own self reflected in the son's face.

FIGURE 13.5 The Angry Roads *by Edward Bond (Big Brum TIE 2014). The father binds himself as the son realizes the truth. Photo courtesy of the company.*

This is not TIE of the 1970s and 1980s. The programme is a neoteric evolution infused with the intentions of TIE and using methods that have been adapted from the past to serve the present. I have made the case earlier that the 'theatre' in Theatre in Education offers the invented structure of an imagined reality that enables young people to safely examine the emotional and political content. Richard Holmes, playing the father, describes the mechanism thus:

> We needed just to tell the story of a man and a son who spend all their time together. Actually what we are exploring is a man that doesn't speak but says a lot, using his son's voice, and a son prevented from talking about his own story. (Holmes interviewed in 2015: *NATD Journal 31.1*: 15)

It is a play about disaffection and the dissociation of young people from a world over which they have been taught they have no control. It is a construct at the edges of naturalism and thus enables them to relate their own lives and their existential disengagement from the world to the theatrical metaphor presented. By considering the lives of the characters in the play and their actions, they can safely unpick the dissociation that they observe in the world where 'reality has lost its voice' (Holmes interviewed in 2015: *NATD Journal 31.1*: 16). When the son leaves with his suitcase at the end of the play, 'he's taking his experience with him out into the world and we don't know what he does do, where he's going to go or what he's going to become, but we do know what he is taking with him':

> So that is a worry. It is a concern. It's a responsibility and I think that is what Edward is proposing to the young people and to us in that final moment. (Danny O'Grady: *NATD Journal 31.1*: 18)

Bond describes the son as 'a living question'. Like the play's spectators, he must 'either ask that question or substitute an inappropriate answer'. Bond maintains that questions about the human situation must be addressed or life becomes 'a hobby or they become fanatics' (Bond: 2014: *The Angry Roads* teaching notes).

The copious teacher support material for this programme contains detailed expositions by the company and by Bond himself of the ideas behind the play. The company had also offered sophisticated support for teachers through CPD events and the notes further offer numerous ways in which teachers can use the play to approach the PSHCE curriculum.

Much contemporary TIE hangs onto the methods but has sacrificed the educational soul of the genre. Work such as that of Big Brum and the other companies featured in this chapter have hung onto the educational imperatives and have attempted to evolve the methodology to serve the new reality. Young people in 2015 live in a different world from those of the 1980s. For Big Brum, young people are constantly being burdened with the guilt for a world they have not created. I have quoted Heathcote's maxim that through drama, children get to know what they didn't know that they knew, but this play is 'about what we know, what we don't want to know and how we avoid knowing what we don't want to know' (*The Angry Roads*: Teacher's Resource Pack: 2014). Today there is perhaps, even before young people can want to change the world, a necessity to face the dysfunctionality of the world as it is:

It's a cliché... when people say stand back and get a better look. But that's intellectual, not moral – it's when you go further into the situation, when the situation drags you into it, that you see more clearly. (Bond: *The Angry Roads*: Rehearsal notes: 2014)

There are no doubt other UK companies worthy of mention. My purpose has been to use examples to identify where the DNA of TIE clearly exists and where the absence of it may lead to questionable outcomes. I hope that TIE workers who feel their programmes also offer authentic teaching will not be offended by their omission from these necessarily brief examples. These few have served to help me identify an approach to the work that is attempting truly to fuse the aesthetics of theatre and the essential function of education, creating an environment in which change can be envisaged and pursued. My chosen examples have sought to differentiate TIE from the exploitative inclinations of theatre that seek only to transmit hegemonic messages.

Notes

1 www.aliveandkickingtheatrecompany.co.uk [accessed 11 February 2015].
2 Ibid.
3 Anthony Haddon describes the development of the project in *Drama: 20:2*.

Afterword

Anthony Jackson

One theme in particular runs through this section of Wooster's study that I'd like to pick up and reflect on. That is, the polarization that Wooster sees – in TIE and in education generally – between, on the one hand, 'message transmission' (or Freire's 'banking' model, characterized by a tightly prescriptive set of National Curriculum targets) and, on the other, the more dialogic approach that fosters debate, analysis and discovery – the rounded education that places the learner at the heart of the teaching and learning process. Wooster is right to point out the negative impact that ERA has had in so many respects, not least in its undermining of the role of local education authorities and in the tightening and narrowing of the curriculum. However, just as the *principle* of a National Curriculum is not in itself one to be shunned, we would presumably not wish to shun the value of imparting knowledge or indeed of conveying messages. What matters is how it's done and whether or not the 'delivery vehicle' opens up or closes down genuine opportunities for exploration, creative engagement and expression.

Creativity within the curriculum has recently become a particular bone of contention. While government advice on the revised (2014) National Curriculum is that there continues to be space for the arts and for creativity, the rise of the target-driven culture in education (as elsewhere) has certainly privileged the readily measurable subjects such as science and maths above the 'soft' subjects of drama, music and art. But at least the noise about the need for creativity in the curriculum and for an established place for the arts in delivering that broad and balanced curriculum the government claims to want has been growing – and from industry leaders as well as educationists and the arts councils.[1] ACE may not value TIE *per se* but, within its diminishing budget, it has arguably tried to fund on a strategic basis theatre for and with young people, theatre that reaches out to young and diverse audiences, and theatre for the very young. The Theatre Company Blah Blah Blah (Leeds), Travelling Light (Bristol), M6 Theatre (Greater Manchester) and Big Brum (Birmingham) are all examples of companies drawing on TIE and related participatory approaches all of whom are/have been supported with NPO three-year (renewable) funding. The McMaster report for the ACE on artistic excellence (2008) also set down some helpful markers by defining excellence as that practice which can engender change in people's lives.

From the point of view of artists working in schools, such movement of opinion is vital in keeping alive the opportunities for creative, investigative and challenging projects *including* those funded through message-driven social amelioration programmes. Nonetheless, Arts Council cuts across the UK have undoubtedly seen a progressive fragmentation of the artistic and educational base from which new initiatives flow and the withdrawal of NPO status from some innovative companies (including Big Brum as already noted). Training opportunities for future 'actor-teachers' or 'teaching artists' have likewise severely diminished.

So, even within these constraints and threats, *can project-funded, message-driven work still offer genuinely educational, dialogic theatre?* I share Wooster's concern about the loss of 'classic TIE' from the school landscape. But let's acknowledge that ingenious and compelling practice can take place in the least propitious circumstances and beneath the surface of goal-driven short-term projects. The glass is at least a quarter full! In an adverse climate, TIE or TIE-related work still goes on and can still contribute much to young people's education, often in less visible ways than in the past. Various forms of 'applied theatre', often drawing on classic TIE practice, can reach young people and other sectors of the population that other forms cannot. Let's not underestimate the value of practice such as that of Geese Theatre that works to serve the rehabilitation goals of the prison service yet is capable of combining striking theatrical imagery and intensity of action with participatory structures and of thereby engaging offender participants in ways that other programmes cannot. Two brief examples[2] will I hope suggest the kind and variety of TIE-type work that can evidently reached its target audience, keeping close to values espoused by 'classic TIE' practitioners in the past while operating in an antipathetic educational environment.

Forever (M6 Theatre, 2000–2002) was a TIE programme for 14–16 year olds that dealt with teenage pregnancy and parenting issues, funded by a charitable trust keen to promote educational best practice in tackling these issues in schools. Having to meet a specific set of goals and learning outcomes, the company drew on its already existing track record of close collaborative work with schools and young people to translate those goals into ones that would work in theatrical terms. The approach was not to find ways of sweetening the messages about responsibility, forging respectful relationships, thinking ahead and taking precautions, but of making the piece work as a persuasive and compelling theatrical whole that young audiences would be drawn into without feeling patronized. It had to be effective aesthetically, in its own terms, not function as a mere illustration of a pre-existing and overt message. It succeeded on many levels, as three different evaluation and research studies testified. Interestingly, evaluators learnt as much about evaluating theatrical impact as they did about the signs of genuine attitudinal change that many young people exhibited. The play used humour, naturalistic acting style and inventive stylized theatrical devices, with which teenagers readily engaged; it ended on a note of crisis in one teenager's life; and the subsequent workshop with opportunities to 'hot-seat' characters from the play, although following a familiar TIE format, proved invariably lively and provocative. No answers were given; the only answers sought were those articulated by the student participants when they confronted the key characters. Implications for the students' own lives were for them to infer, not imposed from without. The level of student engagement, often intense, ensured matters would not be dropped.

This Accursed Thing (Ashmore & Associates, 2007–2008) was an example of what Wooster has categorized as 'heritage theatre' – a term that is as insufficient as the oft-used 'museum theatre', suggesting theatre that does no more than illustrate bygone lives and times, taking us, perhaps nostalgically, back to worlds far removed from our own. Such limited forms can be found of course across the museum sector but, at its best (a qualifying phrase that I find, like Wooster, essential to include in any generalized discussion of the work), such theatre can offer powerful, engaging and provocative insights into aspects of our past that still shape the present. This professionally produced, project-funded, interactive performance piece was designed to be part of one museum's commemoration of the Abolition of the Slave Trade Act in the British House of Commons in 1807. The 'message' was all too clear but its impact and multi-levelled processes were complex. It utilized many techniques common to classic TIE (including audience participation) but took place in and through the museum spaces and was therefore shaped by the physical conditions and educational goals of the institution. Two performers took on a variety of roles and the whole was framed by an out-of-role introduction and 'de-brief'. It was performed both for 'casual' adult and family audiences and, on specific days and with appropriate adjustments, for organized school groups. Above all, it tackled head-on, and quite uncomfortably, the arguments made at the time both for and against the trade ('this accursed thing') and challenged audiences to confront the prejudices and economic 'necessities' of the time, and to make connections with the present. Often the debates that occurred in the final de-brief were as much about the legacy slavery has left us, about modern slavery and about the mechanics of change as about events of the past. Longitudinal evaluation confirmed the unsettling power and long term impact the piece had for many audience members, young and old. The downside was that, although the museum found money to revive the piece twice, budget constraints brought the productive relationship between museum and company to an end.

The larger question of how such work can be funded on a continuing basis in the current climate is fraught and unresolved – but while practitioners in partnership with educationists continue to practice and to innovate and audiences continue to experience and value such work, even if sporadically, there is every reason to hope that, in its various guises and against all the odds, TIE and TIE-related work will not just survive but continue to inspire and enrich the lives of young audiences. It is up to those of us who work in, observe, research and teach this field to ensure it does. Noise must continue to be made, *alongside* those who campaign more broadly for a central place for the arts in the curriculum.

Notes

1 On the arguments for more creativity and less 'exam factory' approaches to the curriculum, see, for example, Dominic Wyse (2014); also www.independent.co.uk/commercial/wise/a-more-creative-approach-to-education-9799386.html; and www.culturallearningalliance.org.uk/news.aspx?id=155 [accessed 25 January 2015].
2 For further details see Jackson (2007: 219–21; 223–7, 2011: 13–24).

Conclusion: The Last Fifty Years of TIE

The title of this conclusion is deliberately ambiguous. In setting out on this journey, I was concerned to record the rise of TIE as a unique educational tool and to show how its influence persists despite its current parlous state in the UK. On the way I have discovered that the 'shoots' of new growth that I have searched for are increasingly distant from 'classic' TIE. I have found myself using that term 'classic TIE' more frequently in later chapters in order to distinguish it from the multitude of practice that now goes under the TIE banner. It has felt uncomfortable to do this – as if I am relinquishing a point of principle and admitting TIE's historicism. As with the phrase 'classic cars', there is an implied acquiescence that they were great in their time: quirky, fun, with idiosyncratic design features and state of the art engineering but no longer suitable to the economic, environmental or business world of today. Is this also true of classic TIE?

I argued in the first section of this book that the abiogenesis of TIE came about as the result of very specific conditions. These conditions provided the means by which TIE first occurred and then quickly mutated into a highly complex educational and arts organism – and this despite frequent hostile attacks. The determined optimism of the post-War years was one of these conditions, the others being the economic background, new approaches to education and attempts to democratize theatre. Few of these conditions pertain today and, indeed, the whole cultural landscape for young people has changed in the face of the revolution in technology and social media.

The economic and social context

It will be apparent to those who have lived through the second half of the twentieth century that a major shift has occurred. The notion of the state offering health, advancement and employment to all its citizens has gently been edged aside in more recent decades. The NHS is increasingly, by overt and covert means, undergoing a move into the private sector. Mental health issues, which have increased exponentially in our dysfunctional society, are still regarded as of secondary importance. Support for those unable to work is being eroded and those needing social support are increasingly demonized. Financial markets react positively to redundancies because they are the obverse side of increased profits; unemployment is good for business. In Britain, and across Europe, parties on the extreme right are gaining support and much of the press joins in the vilification of 'economic migrants' and 'asylum seekers', both of which terms one would expect to invite sympathy. Todd (2014: 356–7) quotes a study showing that 60 per cent of UK citizens regarded themselves as working class in 2013. But this is not the working class of the 1930s and 1940s. They have learned to take on debt to attain the aspirations of their forebears, and their Labour Party has encouraged this class ascendancy. The optimism of the 1950s has been fulfilled on credit and tied people into an economic system that cannot be questioned.

The financial crisis of 2008 might, in another time, have caused a serious questioning of financial and political structures. In 2015 it is clear that the 'solution' is to strip away the Welfare State and the 'quality of life' agenda (of which theatre was a part) whilst the financial markets try to get back to 'normal'. The salaries and benefits of working people have been depressed, causing more debt and destitution whilst the salaries of the richest have become further inflated and protected. According to a *Guardian* article (15 May 2014) an Office for National Statistics Report posits that since the 1970s there has been a rapid accumulation of wealth by the richest and that, currently the richest 1 per cent own as much as the poorest 55 per cent. Membership of trade unions never recovered from the closure of Britain's heavy industries in the 1980s and many of today's 'working class', employed in the care and service industries, are too fearful of victimization to risk joining a union. In any case, the reform of industrial legislation in the 1980s undermined the ability to take collective action. The Labour Party is losing working-class and middle-class support to the 'fascist-lite' parties of the new right-wing whilst in most respects the policies of all parties differ only in nuance.

In the late twentieth century the British public had become accustomed to a level of public service that included theatres, libraries, recreational facilities, day centres, parks, adult learning opportunities, and even access to legal aid. Charitable groups supporting victims of domestic abuse or those with drug dependency might hope for financial assistance in carrying out their work. Much of this social infrastructure has been under pressure for several decades. Britain, it seems, can no longer afford these 'frills' that, if people want them, they need to pay for. This is the culmination of the market forces approach that has become the hegemony. We are individuals who may make choices about our lives and our economic priorities. Thatcher famously said in 1987 that 'there is no such thing as society. There are individual men and women, and there are families'. If it was not true then, it has become truer in the intervening years.

What hope then for a theatre company asking for money to take projects into schools that offer empathy, solidarity and the ability to identify the possibility of change? Even if the need for such values is admitted there must surely be a cheaper way to teach them?

The educational context

As has been seen, ERA changed fundamentally the relationship between schools and their communities, and between schools and central government. The National Curriculum has been constantly refined but the underlying principles have remained the same, tending to consolidate the notion of school as a utilitarian process of preparation for today's (not even tomorrow's) business needs. This is most vividly demonstrated by the growth of Academy, Free and Faith schools in recent years. Academy Schools are funded directly by central government often with financial input from industry. The 'academization' (as it is known) of schools has been promoted by all the main political parties. 'Free' schools are a type of Academy that can be set up by parents, educational charities and religious groups. The UK has always had a tradition of faith schools but these too have grown in number and now include many Muslim schools. Faith schools are required to follow the National Curriculum except in the delivery of religious education where they may follow their own teachings.

What is most surprising is that, despite the determined pursuance since the late 1980s of a rigorous curriculum encompassing the educational needs of all children, Academies are not required to follow the National Curriculum, but only to offer a 'broad and balanced' curriculum that includes Maths, English and Science. Free Schools don't have to follow the National Curriculum at all. The need identified in 1988 for fixed Learning Objectives in every subject is seemingly no longer an issue. It is tempting to welcome this loosening of the National Curriculum strictures but in fact the need for previous rigour has been replaced by examination syllabi and the 'league tables' on which school success will be measured. For the private schools the National Curriculum was never a requirement and they continue to offer a broad education, small class sizes and high levels of resource. They will then gain access to the most prestigious universities and be rewarded by precedence in attaining public office or in the City. State schools are meanwhile chasing good examination results by teaching to the test. The 'banking model' of learning takes precedence with pupils being fed what they need to pass examinations. Freire points out that 'the educator's role is to propose problems about the codified existential situations in order to help the learners arrive at a more and more critical view of their reality' (Freire: 1985: 55). There is little sign of this in accepted educational policy.

There are, of course, school subjects that do not easily fit this agenda of measurable outcomes and one of these is drama. Drama, along with the other Arts and the study of Media, are now referred to by government as 'soft' subjects and a process is underway to make the examinations of these subjects more academic and to discourage universities regarding good results in these subjects as evidence of ability. Ministers actively encourage children away from the arts and towards sciences which 'keep young people's options open' (Education Secretary Nicky Morgan quoted in *The Independent*, 7 February 2015). It is as if Gardner's work on Multiple Intelligences had never made an appearance. Chamberlain, who is both a freelance drama facilitator and a member of Tie Dye Drama, picks up on this point:

> Constructivist learning through the use of drama engages multiple intelligences and enhances skills integral to all industries. (Chamberlain: 2015: 34)

We should note however, that she implicitly finds it necessary to justify drama by its service to industry. This is the trap of which we must be wary, for above all, as the education system becomes more commodified (and thus measurable) it becomes more remote from the possibility of expanding the aspirations of young people to change their worlds. Young people are being prepared for a world that will not exist. The only really valuable education that can be offered them is one based on creativity, questioning and the tangential seeking after positive change. In parts of the world that we traditionally associate with rote learning and factual knowledge, we see an increasing interest in the need to encourage creativity for no other reason than the fact that future economic success depends on it. In Britain the government holds that creativity is a frill unless linked to economic progress. Policymakers neglect what they most seek because the system we have invested in is immutable. But even the CBI, in its 2014 report *The Creative Nation*, stresses the importance of creativity as part of Britain's industrial future. The head of the CBI warned in an article in *The Times* that schools were producing 'pupils who were "exam robots"' (20 November 2013). Industry it seems recognizes the need for creativity though they would probably be less sanguine about the need for critical thinking.

What hope for a theatre company who offers to come in and offer creativity, dialogic thought and alternative ways of seeing the world? The teachers may sympathize in their hearts, but there is a curriculum to be covered and a league table to climb.

Theatre and young people

Young people seem increasingly fascinated by performance and less and less inclined to attend theatre. One of the changes that has accelerated in the last fifty years is the rise of the celebritocracy with its attendant attractions of fame, glamour and wealth. Teachers of drama and theatre, at school and in higher education, will no doubt have noticed that increasingly young people are totally (and often confidently) focussed on stardom. Youth theatre thrives (though less so as a result of recent cuts in funding) but attendance at professional performance seems less attractive. Today's young will turn to television, cinema and streamed media for their entertainment. The common factor of these media is, even when 'interactive' they do not allow reciprocity of engagement. The communication is one-directional. Even in an 'interactive' video game any variable of change, any possibility of effecting outcomes, is already programmed within the parametered choices of the menu.

It is tempting to hope that, in due course, media-based entertainment and education programmes might be able to offer the educational experience alluded to by Bruner, Vygotsky, Giroux, *et al.*, but this is hard to envisage. The structure and outcomes of all such media are in the hands of their creators and there seems to be no possibility of them offering a dialectic engagement with ideas in the hope of fashioning an egalitarian society of the future. Indeed, why would they want to?

What hope is there for a TIE company to gain access to these young minds and to allow them to explore what it is to be a human being? They would first have to be allowed into schools where, increasingly, they would find children at desks, computer tablets in hand, looking for all the world as if they were holding Victorian slates as they tried to memorize facts.

A future for theatre in education?

At its best TIE was a profoundly successful way of offering an authentic learning experience; one which transcended 'the idea of education as pure transference of a knowledge that merely describes reality' (Freire: 1985: 104). All the best notions of children's developmental and educational theory can be found enfolded within TIE. It offers a safe, fictive, context in which the complexities of social reality can be addressed, analysed and challenged. Young people can be invited to question the ways things are and dialogically consider the status quo. It encourages citizenship and understanding, alongside creative thought and a determination to make a better world. But this is not the function of contemporary education. Schools find that the strictures of curricula, examinations and timetables preclude TIE approaches. Arts Councils have fallen out of love with TIE and to them 'participation' has become a synonym for 'performance' in youth theatre. Local Authorities no longer have the funds for any enhancement activities. The only monies available for work in schools will come, as we have seen, from sponsors with specific agendas who want a message delivered, not forensically examined.

In the aftermath of ERA Bond warned the TIE movement that the establishment would not permit the encouragement of the 'radical innocence' of the young:

> That is why they want to *stop* you and they *do* want to stop you... It is *necessary that you are stopped*. (Bond: 1989: 16)

Not all will agree with Bond's statement and you may disagree that the fear of TIE was as overt as he implies, but it rings true in the context of how recent governments have sought to mould education in a way that eradicates the possibility of challenge. In whose interest is political illiteracy? Despite the increasingly dire economic situation there is little sign of any resistance to the hegemony of banking education and the last 'classically' based TIE companies face death by a thousand cuts. Shades of this pessimism are to be found amongst many of the early practitioners. Paul Swift (interview: 29 October 2014), of Leeds TIE, continues to try and attract monies to work using authentic TIE approaches. He feels that The Arts Council and the Education Authorities adopted a policy of cutting funding to TIE and encouraging repertory theatres to replace TIE companies with freelance actors. For Swift though, the motivation was largely responding to the need to make cuts and TIE was a convenient target. He does agree with Bond though that the choice to cut established TIE companies, in spite of their much valued, high quality arts and education provision, was also motivated, in some quarters, by an aversion to TIE's radical philosophy. It is a precarious situation. Jackson (interview: 24 June 2014) is slightly less pessimistic, resisting Bond's overly dire warnings, believing that the formats still work 'when you get them right' but feeling that the structure of companies working on 'shoestring' budgets and the concomitant lack of liaison with teachers make close dialogue with schools difficult if not impossible. Colin Hicks notes that, despite the virtual demise of TIE, a lot of the practitioners from the early days are still around and 'still trying to make things happen' (interview: 18 June 2014). For Tag McEntegart (aside from the work of Big Brum which continues to develop the legacy and spirit of TIE's theoretical and practical approaches) the most coherent legacy within the formal education system is to be found in the Mantle of the Expert work which, she argues, uses 'the same pedagogy and understanding but without the theatre performance elements' (interview: 23 June 2014).

In the end though, McEntegart's analysis is not hopeful. She does not think that TIE can or will return in its old form. In her interview she goes on to question the future shape of TIE:

> It belonged to a particular time the building blocks of which no longer exist. To name only two: a state-subsidized regional repertory theatre system across the UK and enough political will and money in local authority education budgets to support peripatetic groups of trained artist-educators whose job it was to provide, *as a free service* additional curriculum and educational support to teachers in schools in their endeavours to educate young people.

TIE, for all its quiddities, is expensive and to be made available to all schools and all age-groups (as was once envisaged) would involve significant investment and a placing of drama at the centre of the curriculum. This is unthinkable in the foreseeable future. Current funding arrangements mean that there can be no stability for companies wishing to develop coherent theory and a relationship with teachers. 'Hit-and-run' projects for those in social need seem to be the future for theatre within education. Even outside education, the theatre that is deemed successful is that which needs no subsidy and is rewarded by market forces.

On a more positive note, we have seen that there are shoots: companies trying to develop work using the DNA of classic TIE in different parts of the world. The attempts in Albania and Hungary are especially interesting in this respect. Others are more inclined to adopt and adapt the band-aid model of TiHE – shoots of perhaps a lesser order. Another very welcome aspect of current training is the number of young people who aspire to use a fusion of education and performance in order to challenge the social problems that increasingly predominate in society. This optimism is to be found within the many Applied Drama and Applied Theatre courses and in the use of drama approaches in all manner of social, developmental and therapeutic situations. And these approaches are much needed. As the human condition becomes more existential and as human beings become more prone to associated mental health issues, taking comfort from whatever social or chemical opiate is available, the need for intervention becomes stronger. There is a tacit recognition that the deficiency can be made up by creativity – in drama, music and art. Thus, whilst denigrating these subjects in schools, society is increasingly turning to them for emotional and social first aid.

They can only be first aid, however. These applications of drama and theatre, in promising cures, may find in due course that they are expected to justify their existence with measurable outcomes. Whenever arts funding is under pressure it tends to stress its value to society by talking of 'job creation' or 'quality of life' or tourism. But what happens when a government decides that these things are not measurable in terms that it will accept and, on balance, it would rather spend the money on improved ways of assessing children's examination performance (or whatever is the priority of the day)?[1]

Humans are social beings who learn through play. This spirit of creativity is what makes us human and has given us the power to shape our world. If play is excluded from our learning processes then a dystopian brave new world awaits. In a keynote speech to NATD in September 2014 Bond pointed out the importance of 'knowing oneself' and that it is the lack of self-knowledge that brings down all the great tragic figures of theatre. When children are engaged in TIE they are enabled to think: 'we are making it happen *and* it is happening to us at the same time' (Bond: NATD keynote: 2014). Life itself, of course, can be described in these same words. Many applications of drama, and much self-styled 'TIE', offer (often questionable) momentary solutions but do not have the power to ask the question, 'what is it that makes us human?'. And if the question remains unasked it will remain unanswered.

However unlikely it seems, we must hope the future has a space for TIE. But from where will the political change come that recognizes the need for authentic education and the part that TIE can play in delivering it? In *Theatres of the Left*, Samuel *et al* note that there are many examples, in early twentieth century political theatre, where 'the stage might be seen as anticipating politics rather than reflecting it' (1985: xvi). It is a fearful possibility that much contemporary 'TIE', serving the 'banking model' of education, is itself anticipating the future inflexibility of education and politics:

We are… living in dark times, in most parts of the globe: the over-riding question remains, what are we, as educationalists, going to do about it? (Giannouli & Pammenter: 2009: 35)

Note

1   A highly detailed but accessible statistical analysis of the value of drama and theatre in education I would recommend the *The DICE has been cast* (2008), also available on-line at http://www.dramanetwork. eu/educational_drama.html

CHRONOLOGY

	Politics and Society	TIE, Education and Theatre
1911		Finlay-Johnson publishes *The Dramatic Method of Teaching*
1912	Suffragette movement becomes more militant	[Growing influence of Naturalism in theatre
		Growing influence of psychoanalysis]
1914–18	Great War Women employed in factories	
1916		*The Montessori Method* published
1917	Russian Revolution	Caldwell Cook publishes *The Play Way*
1918	Suffrage extended to property-owning women over thirty	
1921		Ministry of Education Report on use of drama in schools
1924	Labour Government elected but fails to push through social reform	[Growth of political agit-prop theatre in non-theatre settings designed to unionize, politicize and offer visions of change by 'x-raying' the mechanics of social structures.]
1926	Deteriorating economic situation leads to General Strike	
1928	Suffrage for all women over 21	

(*Continued*)

1929	Labour Government re-elected but unable to introduce reforms	
	Wall Street Crash	
1930s	Unemployment rises to over 20%	
1934		MacColl and Littlewood set up *Theatre of Action*. Changes name to *Theatre Union* in 1935
1936		School leaving age raised to 15
1938		Dewey's *Experience and Education* published
1939–45	Second World War	
1942	Beveridge Report produces 'cradle to the grave' vision of social welfare system	
1944	Education Reform Act	Education Reform Act sets up Tripartite system of education, free to all children 11–15 years old
1945	War comes to an end	Brian Way sets up *West of England Children's Theatre Company*
	Labour elected with landslide under Clement Atlee Expectations are high for social change	
	Programme of nationalizing key industries instituted 1945–7	
1947	Notional beginning of the 'Cold War' between the eastern bloc and the West	
	Indian independence and Partition	

(Continued)

1948	US support for European reconstruction through the 'Marshall Plan'	
	National Health Service established	
	State of Israel created	
1949	NATO established Republic of Ireland established ending all British influence in Eire's affairs	Ministry of Education publishes *The Story of a School* noting social benefits of drama
1950	General Election – Labour majority reduced to thirteen	
	Korean War begins	
1951	Labour loses election and Winston Churchill (Tory) becomes prime minister. The Conservatives will remain in power for the next thirteen years	Heathcote appointed tutor at Durham Institute. Over the next sixty years she develops a series of remarkable approaches to using drama as a learning medium
1952	Iron and Steel industries de-nationalized	
1953	Korean War ceasefire declared	Brian Way sets up Theatre Centre
1954	Anthony Eden becomes prime minister	Peter Slade publishes *Child Drama*
	Food rationing ends Korean War ceasefire declared	
1955	Commercial Television begins in UK	First visit of Brecht's Berliner Ensemble to London
1956		*Look Back in Anger* first performed
1957	Suez Crisis leads to resignation of Eden. Harold Macmillan becomes prime minister	
	European Economic Community established	

(Continued)

	Britain tests nuclear bomb	
	Campaign for Nuclear Disarmament formed	
1959	Macmillan campaigns under the slogan 'you've never had it so good' and is re-elected	
1960		Pinter's *Birthday Party* receives first production
1961	The contraceptive pill introduced to Britain	
1962	Voucher system for immigration adopted Competing youth cultures, 'Mods and Rockers', fight it out at seaside towns 1962–4	Vallins and Harman, at the Belgrade Theatre, develop a scheme of outreach work for schools in Coventry
1963	Alec Douglas-Home becomes prime minister National Service abolished Kennedy assassinated	Newsom Report, *Half Our Future*, analysed the education of less academic children Fear of 'Brain Drain' leads to building of additional universities (7 new H.E. institutions were built by 1966)
1964	Harold Wilson (Labour) becomes prime minister Resale Price Maintenance abolished leading to expansion of supermarkets and the decline of small enterprises US Civil Rights Act	Introduction of General Certificate of Education, the first qualification for Secondary Modern School pupils
1965	Abolition of the death penalty	Belgrade's First Theatre in Education Project Holt publishes *How Children Fail*

(*Continued*)

		l'Association Internationale du Théâtre de l'Enfance et la Jeunesse (ASSITEJ) set up to support and develop children's theatre internationally
		Bond's *Saved* first performed amidst huge controversy
1966	Sterling Crisis. Investment restricted and tourists banned from taking more than £50 out of the country. Pound devalued in the following year Child Poverty Action Group set up	John McGrath *7:84* company touring with politically committed projects aimed at working classes Arts Council recommends that TYP and TIE should come within the scope of their support
1967	Homosexuality decriminalized Abortion Act passed	*Plowden Report* on Primary Education, praises child-centred approaches Ministry report on drama in schools mentioning TIE for the first time Brian Way publishes *Development Through Drama* TIE companies set up in major cities across Britain Theatre censorship abolished
1968	Paris riots involving a coalition of left-wing groups and students. Student demonstrations and occupations occur throughout Britain Tory MP Enoch Powell warns of 'rivers of blood' if immigration is not ended Race Relations Act passed Voting age lowered to 18	Watford TIE set up [Many playwrights working from a left-wing perspective during this period, including Wesker, Arden, Hare, Edgar and Bond]

(Continued)

1969	Government attempts to implement *In Place of Strife* to curtail Trade Union power. Union opposition leads to withdrawal of proposals	Publication of *Black Papers* attacking progressive teaching approaches
	Internet created	TIE begins in Bolton, Edinburgh, Greenwich
1970	Equal Pay Act passed following the action by female workers at Ford's	Open University set up enabling distance learning at degree level
	Edward Heath (Tory) becomes prime minister	Freire's *Pedagogy of the Oppressed* published in the UK
		Clwyd sets up a DIE team in north Wales
1971	Unofficial strikes outlawed	Vygotsky's theory of the 'Zone of Proximal Development' finding popularity with TIE theorists
1972	Miner's Strike begins	School leaving age raised to 16
	'Bloody Sunday' in Belfast when British Army opens fire on civilians. Inquiry not set up until 1998 and reported in 2010	Perspectives TIE set up
		Belgrade TIE tours *The Price of Coal* encouraging deeper analysis of issues surrounding the strike
		Illich publishes *Deschooling Society*
		Rare Earth toured by Belgrade TIE and becomes a classic of the TIE canon
1973	Miners' Strike leads to power shortages and imposition of a three-day week	Breconshire Theatre Company (later Theatr Powys) set up
	Britain joins EEC	Cockpit TIE set up
1974	Labour wins election and Wilson return to Premiership. Miners' Strike settled	
	Oil crisis	

(*Continued*)

1975	Sex Discrimination Act passed	Most Local Authorities moving
	Vietnam War ends	to a system of Comprehensive Education
1976	Callaghan takes over from Wilson as prime minister who retires on health grounds	Standing Conference of Young People's Theatre set up as an organization to disseminate and develop TIE methodologies
	He invites a 'Great Debate' on Education	Also devoted a conference to discussion of company structures and working practices
	Financial Crisis leads to Britain having to borrow money from IMF	
		Theatr Gwent set up
		National Theatre opened
1977		M6 TIE set up. Now about ninety companies working in TIE and YPT
1978 ·	'Winter of Discontent' – major strikes across public services	
1979	Scotland and Wales reject devolution	Tory government removes requirement for schools to adopt Comprehensive education
	Thatcher (Tory) becomes prime minister	Boal's *Theatre of the Oppressed* published in English
	Unemployment reaches 13.3% by 1981	Pit Prop TIE, Tyne Wear TIE and Spectacle Theatre set up
1980	Property ownership encouraged by 'right to buy' scheme which sold off public housing to occupiers at much reduced rates	Education Act requires governing bodies to include parents. Assisted places scheme would help some children attend private schools
1981	Breakaway Labour MPs ('the Gang of Four') set up the Social Democratic Party. Merged with Liberals in 1988	Government requires LEAs to frame school policies in line with government's recommended content
	In Belfast, the Republican Bobby Sands dies as a result of his hunger strike	

(*Continued*)

Riots take place in major cities
in UK

Beginning of HIV/AIDs
'epidemic'

1982	Union 'closed shop' arrangements outlawed Malvinas/Falklands War boosts flagging support for Thatcher Channel 4, Britain's second commercial TV station begins	Technical and Vocational education Initiative set up administered by Department of Employment and excluding LEAs
1983	Thatcher re-elected with large majority	Duke's Playhouse sets up Lancaster TIE ILEA bans Cockpit's *The Pitcher Plant* which explored sexual aspects of human relations
1984	Miners' Strike was energetically put down by Thatcher's government (1985). Wholesale closure of mining industry followed British Telecoms privatized. This is followed by privatization of Gas, Aerospace, Rolls Royce and Airports	'O' level and GCE examinations combined in a system of GCSEs. Arts Council publishes *The Glory of the Garden* signalling a shift of funding to major 'centres of excellence' and away from other theatre forms
1985	6% of population receiving 25% of National Income. The poorest 20% are worse off than in 1979 Unemployment reaches 3.2 million First mobile phones available	Cardiff-based Action PIE loses funding for what appeared to be political reasons Theatre Company Blah Blah Blah set up
1986	Local Government Act abolishes metropolitan authorities and curtails the powers of other local authorities	Arts Councils adopt a market-led approach to funding and encourage private patronage

(Continued)

		Education Acts requires schools to have a range of policies on curriculum, sex education and governance. Corporal punishment outlawed in state schools
1987	Thatcher re-elected 'Black Monday' and Stock Market crash	ERA forces schools to reconsider the way in which they teach
1988	Education Reform Act (ERA)	Changes in funding arrangements leads to many TIE companies closing or adapting to deliver the new Curriculum. Drama excluded from subject status Clause 28 of the Local Government Act banned the 'promotion' of homosexuality by schools
1989	Market forces introduced into NHS through system of delegated budgets Interest Base Rates reach 15% End of Cold War. Berlin Wall comes down	Four hundred delegates attend the NATD Conference to hear Heathcote and Bond respond to the attacks on drama and TIE implicit in ERA
1990	Imposition of a 'Poll Tax' to replace domestic rates leads to riots and undermines Thatcher's hold on power. She is forced to resign and John Major (Tory) becomes prime minister Gulf War begins following Iraq's invasion of Kuwait Internal market set up in NHS	National Curriculum begins in schools. Subjects now to be delivered in four 'Key Stages' meeting a system of 'Learning Objectives' ASSITEJ acknowledges participatory theatre Introduction of 'top up loans' for students in Higher Education
1995	World Wide Web created	Standard Assessment Tests (SATs) introduced in UK schools

(*Continued*)

1992	John Major re-elected in surprise result	SCYPT offers a 'Curriculum for Living' as an alternative to the vision of education implied by the National Curriculum
	Britain forced to withdraw from ERM	
	Maastricht agreement – Single European Act – passed with a majority of three	International Drama/Theatre and Education Association (IDEA) set up to share and develop drama in schools as a learning medium
		School League Tables introduced
		[During the 1990s many TIE companies cease working whilst others adapt to the new education system. There is a growth of Theatre in Health Education, Theatre for Development, Prison Theatre and Heritage Theatre using TIE derived methods.]
1993	10% of population own 48% of nation's wealth	TheatreVan TIE closes
1994	Railways privatized	
	Mandela elected president of South Africa	
1995		Bond writes first play for Big Brum TIE. The beginning of a continuing association
		Lancaster TIE closes
		Department for Education becomes the Department for Education and Employment
1996		Belgrade TIE closes
		International Centre for Theatre in Education set up by remnants of SCYPT

(Continued)

1997	Tony Blair (New Labour) becomes prime minister after landslide victory Scotland and Wales vote for devolution Channel Five starts broadcasting	Last SCYPT Conference Publication of Excellence in Schools report which continued Tory policy of allowing secondary schools to select students on grounds of 'specialization'
1998	Good Friday Agreement marks the start of a long process of reconciliation after thirty years of 'troubles' in the north of Ireland	Student loans introduced to replace grants Last SCYPT Journal
1999		Corporal punishment banned in private schools
2000		Academy schools are resisted by many who see them as a means of privatizing education and creating unhealthy links with business
2001	Blair re-elected Al-Qaeda destroys World Trade Center in New York Britain joins in attacks on Afghanistan	Geoff Gillham dies NATD resigns from IDEA following a bitter dispute over the governance of the organization
2002	Euro introduced as single currency across EEC. UK opts out of joining	Education Act gives 85% of school's budget to headteacher, Provision for Public Private Partnerships involving business to invest in schools First academies opened
2003	Invasion of Iraq by coalition forces	
2004		SATs scrapped in Wales Student fees increased to £3000 p.a. Universities to be allowed to charge variable top-up fees

(Continued)

2005	Blair elected for a third term as prime minister	
	Terrorist attack on tube system in London	
2006	Britain finally pays off loans from Marshall Plan of 1948	Education and Inspections Act allowed schools to form links with external partners, appoint governors and employ their own staff
	Facebook open to all over 13	
2007	Direct rule in Northern Ireland ends	Wales devolved government sets up an Arts Strategy Board that decides to divert arts funding to companies offering international or economic regeneration
	Blair resigns and Gordon Brown takes over as Premier	
		National tests to be made shorter, but League Tables and National Targets would remain
		Report finds that children caused pervasive anxiety by SATs At the end of his tenure, Blair has extended covert selection, expanded privatization, diminished local influence and increased role of business and faith groups
2008	International Global Financial Crisis begins, leading to recession across Europe and other advanced economies	MacMaster report for UK government acknowledges importance of theatre in personal development and creativity within tight frameworks of control
2009	Obama elected President of US	Proposed to make sex education from age 5 compulsory (though parents could remove their children)
		Both main political parties agree that academies are the way forward for education

(Continued)

2010	Following an inconclusive election the Tories and Liberal Democrats forma coalition under David Cameron. Age of austerity and cuts in public spending are announced	A quarter of primary schools boycott the SATs tests
		New government proposes financial cuts, more academy schools and abandonment of building programmes. The ability of teachers' and parents' legal right to oppose, and the Local authorities' power to veto academies, removed
		Support for children from poorer families to attend post-16 education scrapped
2011	Osama bin Laden killed Gaddafi killed Iraq War declared over	Theatr Powys, Theatr Gwent and Spectacle, the last companies producing authentic TIE work in Wales, have their Arts Council funding removed
		Education Act requires new schools to be academies and gives power to the Minister to close schools and re-open them as academies
		Dorothy Heathcote dies
2012	Facebook reaches one billion users	Arts Council sets up system of funding for 'National Portfolio Organizations' to help long-term financial planning by companies. System soon becomes criticized for the way in which selection of companies is made with suggestions of aesthetic elitism and political interference

(*Continued*)

		Government removes requirement for teachers in academies to be qualified and proposes 'training on the job'
2013	Mandela dies	Reforms to GCSEs proposed to encourage academic rigour including in arts and humanities
2014	The rightwing United Kingdom Independence Party wins its first seats in Parliament campaigning on British withdrawal from Europe and opposition to immigration 85% of world has internet access	
2015	Terrorist attack on *Charlie Hebdo* satirical magazine in Paris Research paper from Oxfam predicts that world's richest 1% will own more than the other 99% by 2016 In May the Conservative Party wins the general election promising a programme of continuing austerity and a reduction of the National Debt	Stuart Bennett dies

BIBLIOGRAPHY

Allen, G., Allen, I. & Dalrymple, L. (1999), 'Ideology, Practice and Evaluation: Developing Effectiveness of Theatre in Education' in Somers, J. (ed.), *Research in Drama Education,* Vol. 4, No. 1, Oxford, Carfax International Publishers.

Arts Council of Great Britain (1992), *Guidance on Drama Education,* London, ACGB.

Arts Council Of Great Britain (1994), *The Glory of the Garden,* London, ACGB.

Alington, A.F. (1961), *Drama and Education,* Oxford, Blackwell.

Baldwin, B. (1988), 'Freire: Education and Politics' in *SCYPT, No.17,* London, SCYPT.

Bazeley, M., Gray, T., Pompeo, M. & Williams, G. (2001), 'An International Conference on Theatre for Social Development: "People in Movement", 24th–29th August 2000' in *NATD Journal,* Vol. 17, No. 1, London, NATD.

Beard, R.M. (1969), *An Outline of Piaget's Developmental Psychology,* London, Routledge and Kegan Paul.

Belgrade Theatre in Education Archives (1965–), held at the Herbert Museum, Coventry.

Belgrade Theatre Coventry (2010), *Theatre in Education at the Belgrade: Building on Our Heritage,* Coventry, University of Warwick.

Bennett S. (ed.) (2005), *Theatre for Children and Young People,* Twickenham, Aurora Metro Publications.

Best, D. (1992), *The Rationality of Feeling,* London, Falmer Press.

Bethlenfalvy, A. (2008), 'Stop "ere" Reflections on a Hungarian Production of Bone-Cage' in *The Journal for Drama in Education,* Vol. 24, No. 2, London, NATD.

Billington, M. (2007), *State of the Nation,* London, Faber and Faber.

Boal, A. (1979) (trans. Jackson, A.), *Theatre of the Oppressed,* London, Pluto Press.

Boal, A. (1993) (trans. Jackson, A.), *Games of Actors and Non Actors,* London, Routledge.

Boal, A. (1995) (trans. Jackson, A.), *The Rainbow of Desire,* London, Routledge.

Bolton, G. (1979), *Towards a Theory of Drama in Education*, London, Longman.

Bolton, G. (1998), *Acting in Classroom Drama*, Portland, Calendar Islands Publishers.

Bond, E. (1989), Keynote speech to NATD conference, printed in *The Fight for Drama, the Fight for Education*, London, NATD.

Bond, E. (2014), 'The Angry Roads Writer's Notes' in *Teachers' Resource Notes*, Birmingham, Big Brum.

Bruner, J. (1972), *The Relevance of Education*, London, George Allen & Unwin.

Bruner, J. (1992), *Towards a Theory of Instruction*, Cambridge, MA, Harvard University Press. (Originally published 1966.)

Bruner, J. (1996), *The Culture of Education*, Cambridge, MA, Harvard University Press.

Bruley, S. (1999), *Women in Britain Since 1900*, Basingstoke, Macmillan.

Byron, K. (1987), 'Drama at the Crossroads (Part Two)' in *2D*, Vol. 7, No. 1, Leicester, 2D.

Calouste Gulbenkian Foundation (Revised Edition 1989), *The Arts in Schools*, London, Calouste Gulbenkian Foundation.

Cattanach, A. (1996), *Drama for Children with Special Needs*, London, A&C Black.

Chamberlain, J. (2015), 'Learning Through Drama' in *Drama*, Vol. 21, No. 1, London, National Drama.

Chesner, A. (1995), *Dramatherapy for People with Learning Disabilities*, London, Jessica Kingsley.

Chinyowa, K. (2008), 'By Whom and for Whom? An Aesthetic Appraisal of Selected African Popular Theatre Workshops' in *Studies in Theatre and Performance*, Vol. 28, No. 1, Bristol, Intellect.

Confederation of British Industry (2014), *The Creative Nation*, www.cbi.org.uk/media/2535682/cbi_creative_industries_strategy__final_.pdf [accessed 2 February 2014].

Cook, H. C. (1915), *The Play Way*, London, Heinemann.

Cooke, B. & Kothari, U. (2001), *Participation: The New Tyranny*, London, Zed Books Ltd.

Coult, T. (1980), 'Inside the Company' in *SCYPT Journal 5*, London, SCYPT.

Cox, B. (1991), *Cox on Cox*, London, Hodder & Stoughton.

Cox, B. & Dyson, A. E. (eds) (1969), 'The Fight for Education: A Black Paper' in *London Critical Quarterly*, London, London Critical Quarterly.

Craig, S. (ed.) (1980), *Dreams and Deconstructions: Alternative Theatre in Britain*, Ambergate, Amber Lane Press.

Daniels, H. (2004), 'Vygotsky and Education: Some Preliminary Remarks' in *The Journal for Drama in Education*, Vol. 21, No. 1, London, NATD.

Davis, D. (1988), 'The Education Reform Bill Tory Class Legislation' in *Theatre and Education Journal*, Reprinted (2008) in *The Journal for Drama in Education*, Vol. 24, No. 2, London, NATD.

Davis, D. (1998), 'J'Accuse' in *Broadsheet*, Vol. 14, No, 2, London, NATD.

Department of Education and Science (1965), *Circular 10/65*, London, DES.

Department of Education and Science (1965), *Drama: Education Survey 2*, London, HMSO.

Department of Education and Science (1967), *Drama: Education Survey 2*, London, HMSO.

Department of Education and Science (1989), *Drama 5–16*, London, HMSO.

Department of Education and Skills (2004), *Homophobia, Sexual Orientation and Schools: A Review and Implications for Action*, http://webarchive.nationalarchives.gov.uk/20130401151715/http://www.education.gov.uk/publications/eOrderingDownload/RB594MIG1188.pdf [accessed 11 February 2014].

Dewey, J. (1938), *Experience and Education*, New York, Collier-Macmillan edition 1965.

Dice – Drama Improves Lisbon Key Competences in Education (2008), *The DICE has been cast*, DICE consortium http://www.dramanetwork.eu/educational_drama.html [accessed 11 February 2015].

Dodd, N. & Hickson, W. (eds) (1971), *Drama and Theatre in Education*, London, Heinemann.

Dyer, K. (1988), 'Paradox and Panic' in *SCYPT New Voices 17*, London, SCYPT.

Eek, N., Shaw, A.M. & Krzys, K. (2008), *Discovering a New Audience for Theatre*, Santa Fe, Sunstone Press.

Eek, N., Shaw, A.M. & Krzys, K. (2011), *Expanding the New Audience for Theatre*, Santa Fe, Sunstone Press.

Emunah, R. (1994), *Acting for Real – Drama, Therapy, Process, Technique and Performance*, New York, Brunner/Mazel.

Finlay-Johnson, H. (1911), *The Dramatic Method of Teaching*, London, Nisbet.

Freire, P. (1970), 'Cultural Action For Freedom' in Riordan, R. C. & Smethurst, W. (issue eds), *Harvard Educational Review and Center for the Study of Development and Social Change*, Cambridge, MA, Harvard.

Freire, P. (1972a) (trans. Ramos, M.), *Pedagogy of the Oppressed*, Harmondsworth, Penguin.

Freire, P. (1972b), 'Education: Domestication or Liberation?' in *Prospects*, Vol. II, No. 2, Paris, UNESCO.

Freire, P. (1985) (trans. Macedo, D.), *The Politics of Education: Culture, Power and Liberation*, London, MacMillan.

Freire, P. (2000) (trans. Ramos, M.), *Pedagogy of the Oppressed*, New York, Continuum.

Froebel, F. (1887), *On the Education of Man*, Clifton, NJ, Augustus M. Kelley Publishers (1974).

Gallagher, K. & Booth, D. (2003), *How Theatre Educates*, Toronto, University of Toronto Press.

Gardner, H. (1993), *Multiple Intelligences*, New York, Basic Books/ Perseus.

Giannouli, B. & Pammenter, D. (2009), 'Our Journey on the Road of Enquiry and Development' in *mPpact Manifest*, www.theatroedu.gr/ Portals/38/main/images/stories/files/Books/mPPACT/mPPACT%20 olo%20s.pdf [accessed 26 February 2015].

Gillham, G. (1993), 'International Drama and Education Association' in *SCYPT Journal, Vol. 25*, Lancaster, SCYPT.

Gillham, G. (1999), 'Notes on a Curriculum for Living' in *Broadsheet*, Vol. 15, No. 1, London, NATD.

Gillham, G. (2001), 'The Specific Value of TIE and DIE to Peace-Building' in *The Journal for Drama in Education*, Vol. 17, No. 1, Birmingham, NATD.

Gillham, G. (2011) (ed. Davis, D.), *Six Plays for Theatre in Education and Youth Theatre*, Trentham, Stoke on Trent.

Giroux, H.A. (1997), *Pedagogy and the Politics of Hope: Theory, Culture, and Schooling*, Oxford, Westview.

Giroux, H.A. (2000), *Stealing Innocence, Corporate Culture's War on Children*, New York, Palgrave.

Grady, T. & O'Sullivan, C. (eds) (1998), '*A Head Taller': Developing a Humanising Curriculum Through Drama*, Birmingham, NATD.

Gramsci, A. (1975) (ed. Lynne Lawner), *Letters from Prison*, London, Jonathan Cape.

Greer, S. (2011), 'Staging Legitimacy: Theorising Identity Claims in Anti-Homophobia Theatre-in-Education' in *RIDE: The Journal of Applied Theatre and Performance*, Vol. 16, No. 1, London, Routledge.

Haddon, A. (2014), 'Messerschmitt 'v' Spitfire – A Love Story' in *Drama*, Vol. 20, No. 2, London, National Drama.

Head, D. (ed.) (1974), *Free Way to Learning*, Harmondsworth, Penguin.

Heathcote, D. (1971), 'Drama and Education: Subject or System?' in Dodd, N. & Hickson, W. (eds), *Drama and Theatre in Education*, London, Heinemann.

Heathcote, D. (1972), 'Drama as Challenge' in Hodgson, J. (ed.), *The Uses of Drama*, London, Methuen.

Heathcote, D. (1975), 'Drama as Education' in McCaslin, N. (ed.), *Children and Drama*, New York, David McKay.

Heathcote, D. (1976), 'Drama as a Process for Change, reprinted in Drain, R. (1995), *Twentieth Century Theatre*, London, Routledge.

Heathcote, D. (1980a), 'From the Particular to the Universal' in Robinson, K. (ed.), *Exploring Theatre and Education*, London, Heinemann.

Heathcote, D. (1980b), 'Material for Meaning in Drama' in *London Drama*, Vol. 6, No. 2, London.

Heathcote, D. (1982), *Signs (and Portents) – the Use of Role for Actors*. *SCYPT Journal*, No. 9, London, SCYPT.

Heathcote, D. (1984), *Collected Writings on Education and Drama*, Evanston, IL: Northwestern University Press.

Heathcote, D. (1984), 'Moving into the Drama – an interview with Geoff Gillham', *SCYPT Journal*, No. 13, London.

Heathcote, D. (2000), 'Contexts for Active Learning' in *Drama Research*, Vol. 1, London, Heinemann.

Heathcote, D. (2012), 'The Fight for Drama – The Fight for Education' in *The Journal for Drama in Education*, Vol. 28, No. 1, London, NATD.

Heathcote, D. & Bolton, G. (1995), *Drama for Learning*, Portsmouth, New Hampshire, Heinemann.

Heathcote, D. & Bolton, G. (2010), *Drama for Learning*. 2nd ed. Portsmouth: Heinemann.

Her Majesty's Inspectorate (1989), *A Survey of Theatre in Education in Wales*, Cardiff, Welsh Office.

Holmes, P. & Karp, M. (eds) (1991), *Psychodrama: Inspiration and Technique*, London, Routledge.

Holt, J. (1964), *How Children Fail*, London, Penguin (1969).

Illich, I. (1973), *Deschooling Society*, Harmondsworth, Penguin.

Innes, C. (1992), *Modern British Drama*, Cambridge, Cambridge University Press.

Itzin, C. (1980), *Stages in the Revolution: Political Theatre Since 1968*, London, Methuen.

Jackson, A. (1993), *Learning Through Theatre*, 2nd Edition, Oxford, Routledge.

Jackson, A. (2007), *Theatre, Education and the Making of Meanings*, Manchester, MUP.

Jackson, A. (2011), *Performing Heritage*, Manchester, MUP.

Jackson, A. & Vine, C. (eds) (2013), *Learning Through Theatre*, 3rd Edition, Oxford, Routledge.

Jennings, S. (ed.) (1987), *Dramatherapy: Theory and Practice for Teachers and Clinicians*, Beckenham, Crook Helm.

Jennings, S. (1997), *Dramatherapy: Theory and Practice for Teachers and Clinicians*, Beckenham, Crooke Helm.

Jennings, S. (1998), *Introduction to Dramatherapy*, London, Jessica Kingsley.

Johnson, L. & O'neill C. (1984), *Dorothy Heathcote: Collected Writings*, London, Hutchison.

Jones, K. (2003), *Education in Britain 1944 to the Present*, Cambridge, Blackwell.

Kay-Shuttleworth, J. (reprinted 1973), 'Recent Measures for the Promotion of Education in England' in *Four Periods of Public Education*, Brighton, Harvester Press.

Klaic, D. (2012), *Resetting the Stage*, Bristol, Intellect.

Landy, R.J. & Montgomery, D.T. (2012), *Theatre for Change: Education, Social Action and Therapy*, New York, Palgrave MacMillan.

Langdon, E.M. (1948), *An Introduction to Dramatic Work with Children*, in Education Series (eds. Andrews, J. and Trilling, O.) London, Dennis Dobson.

Lawton, D. (1980), *The Politics of the School Curriculum*, London, Routledge and Kegan Paul.

Lawton, D. (1992), *Education and Politics in the 1990s*, London, Falmer Press.

Lazarus, J. (2012), *Signs of Change*, Bristol, Intellect.

Leeds Playhouse Theatre in Education Company (1984), *Raj*, Oxford, Amber Lane Press.

Lowenfold, M. (1935), *Play in Childhood*, Bath, Victor Gollancz.

McEntegart, T. (1981) 'Play and Theatre: A Summary of Vygotsky's Theories' in *SCYPT Journal,* No. 7, February 1981, London, SCYPT.

Mckean, A. (2006), 'Playing for Time in 'The Dolls' House': Issues of Community and Collaboration in the Devising of Theatre in a Women's Prison' in *Research in Drama Education Journal*, Vol. 11, No. 3, London, Routledge.

McMaster, B. (2008), *Supporting Excellence in the Arts: From Measurement to Judgement*, London, Department for Culture, Media and Sport.

Ministry of Education (1895), *Report of the Commission on Secondary Education*, London, HMSO.

Ministry of Education (1949), *The Story of a School*, London, HSMO.

Ministry of Education (1963), *Half Our Future* (The Newsom Report), London, HMSO.

Montessori, M. (1909), *The Montessori Method*, Cambridge, MA, Robert Bently Inc. (1967).

Murphy, E. (1975), *Sweetie Pie*, London, Eyre Methuen.

Neelands, J. (2004), 'The Idea of Idea Is a People's Theatre' in *Drama,* Vol. 12, No. 1, Glasgow, National Drama.

NATD (2012), *Dorothy Heathcote Special Issue*, London, NATD.

NATD (2015), *Journal 31.1*, London, NATD.

Nicholson, H. (2009), *Theatre and Education*, New York, Palgrave Macmillan.

O'Neill, C. (ed.) (2015), *Dorothy Heathcote on Education and Drama: Essential Writings*, Oxon, Routledge.

O'Farrell, L. (1999), 'A Response from the President of IDEA to 'J'Accuse' in *Broadsheet*, Vol. 15, No. 1, London, NATD.

OFSTED (1998), *The Arts Inspected*, Oxford, Heinemann.

O'Sullivan, C. (1999), 'IDEA: Report from 1998 Kenyan Conference' in *Broadsheet*, Vol. 15, No. 1, London, NATD.

O'Toole, J. (1976), *Theatre in Education: New Objectives for Theatre, New Techniques in Education*, London, Hodder & Stoughton.

O'Toole, J. (1992), *The Process of Drama*, London, Routledge.

O'Toole, J. (2009), 'Writing *Everyday Theatre*: Applied Theatre or Just TIE Rides Again?' in *Research in Drama Education*, Vol. 14, No. 4, London, Routledge.

Pestalozzi, J. H. (1801), *How Gertrude Teaches Her Children*, http://archive.org/stream/howgertrudeteach00pestuoft/howgertrudeteach00pestuoft_djvu.txt [accessed 11 February 2015].

Postman, N. & Weingartner, C. (1969), *Teaching As a Subversive Activity*, Harmondsworth, Penguin.

Prendergast, M. & Saxton, J. (2009), *Applied Theatre*, Bristol, Intellect.

Prendergast, M. & Saxton, J. (2013), *Applied Drama*, Bristol, Intellect.

Prentki, T. & Pammenter, D. (2014), 'Living Beyond Our Means, Meaning Beyond Our Lives: Theatre as Education for Change' in *Applied Theatre Research*, Vol. 2, No. 1, Bristol, Intellect.

Redington, C. (1983), *Can Theatre Teach?*, Oxford, Pergamon Press.

Robinson, K. (ed.) (1980), *Exploring Theatre and Education*, London, Heinemann.

Rousseau, J.J. (1762) (trans. Foxley, B. 1977), *Emile*, London, Everyman, Dent.

Samuel, R., MacColl, E. & Cosgrove, S. (1985), *Theatres of the Left 1880–1935*, London, Routledge & Kegan Paul.

Schweitzer, P. (1980), *Theatre in Education: Five Infant Programmes*, London, Eyre Methuen.

SCYPT Journal (1977), *No. 1*, London, SCYPT.

SCYPT Journal (1980), *No. 5*, London, SCYPT.

SCYPT Journal (1983), *No. 11*, London, SCYPT.

SCYPT Journal (1984), *No. 13*, London, SCYPT.

SCYPT Journal (New Voices, Conference Briefing Issue) (1989), London, SCYPT.

SCYPT Journal (1990), *No. 20*, London, SCYPT.

SCYPT (1992), *Manifesto*, London, SCYPT.

SCYPT Journal (1994), *No. 28*, London, SCYPT.

SCYPT Journal (1994), *No. 30*, London, SCYPT.

SCYPT (1995), *The Ground on Which We Stand: SCYPT Documents 1992–1995*, Lancaster, SCYPT.

Simon, B. (1974), *The Two Nations and the Educational Structure, 1780–1870*, London, Lawrence & Wishart.

Slade, P. (1954), *Child Drama*, London, Hodder and Stoughton.
Slade, P. (undated), *Freedom in Education?*, Birmingham, Educational Drama Association.
Somers, J. (2008), 'Interactive Theatre: Drama as a Social Intervention' in *Music and Arts in Action*, Vol. 1, No. 1, Exeter, University of Exeter.
Taylor, A.-M. (ed.) (1997), *Staging Wales*, Cardiff, University of Wales Press.
The Times (20 November 2013), 'Schools Produce Exam Robots, says CBI chief', London.
Theatre Company Blah Blah Blah (2013), *The Raft of the Medusa Teaching Pack*, Leeds, Theatre Company Blah Blah Blah.
Theatre Company Blah Blah Blah (2014), *Messerschmitt vs Spitfire Teaching Pack*, Leeds, Theatre Company Blah Blah Blah.
Todd, S. (2014), *The People*, London, John Murray.
Vygotsky, L. (1962) (trans. Kozulin, A.), *Thought and Language*, Cambridge, MA, MIT (1986).
Wagner, B.-J. (1979), *Dorothy Heathcote: Drama as a Learning Medium*, London, Hutchinson.
Way, B. (1967), *Development Through Drama*, London, Longman.
Whitehead, A.N. (1932), *The Aims of Education*, London, Earnest Benn.
Wooster, R. (2007), *Contemporary Theatre in Education*, Bristol, Intellect.
Wooster, R. (2012), 'The Role of Arts Subsidy in Making Wales' in *Planet, The Welsh Internationalist*, No. 205, Aberystwyth, Planet.
Wyse, D. (2014), *Creativity and the Curriculum*, London, IOE Press.
Yeoman, I. (1994), 'SCYPT – A Perspective' in *SCYPT Journal*, Vol. 28, Lancaster, SCYPT.
Yeoman, I. (2010), 'Developing a Dialogue only Just Commenced' in *The Journal for Drama in Education*, Vol. 26, No. 1, London, NATD.

Interviews and personal communications

Corbett, A. & Hammick, V. 10 February 2014, via email.
Davis, S. 30 January 2015, via email.
Dobson, W. 8 October 2014, via telephone.
Hicks, C. 18 June 2014, via Skype.
Jackson, A. 24 June 2014, Disley.
Lement, W. 13 October 2014, via telephone.
McEntegart, T. 23 June 2014, Telford.
Mayo, S. 6 October 2014, via email.
McKean, A. 21 October 2014, via telephone.
Pammenter, D. 11 June 2014, via telephone.
Prior, J. 27 May 2014, Cardiff.

Swift, P. 29 October 2014, via telephone.
Swift, P. 31 October 2014 and 9 November 2014, via email.
Vine, C. 21 September 2014, via Skype.
Wheelock, H. 7 December 2014, Skype.
Yeoman, I. 28 May 2014, Llandrindod.

Websites

http://Wales.gov.uk/topics/cultureandsport/arts/strategyboard/meetings
rttie.tumblr.com/ [Round Table, Hungary]
www.kerekasztalszinhaz.hu/English [Round Table, Hungary]
www.kerekasztalszinhaz.hu/videok [Round Table, video material]
www.youtube.com/watch?v=Gx8r-gPa6tA [video extracts of *Everyday Theatre*]
www.appliedtheatre.co.nz/
www.TheatroEdu.gr
www.creativeartsteam.org
www.aliveandkickingtheatrecompany.co.uk
www.belgrade.co.uk
www.bigbrum.org.uk
www.blahs.co.uk
www.hkrep.com
www.leedstie.co.uk
www.mantleoftheexpert.com
www.natd.eu
www.nationaldrama.org.uk
www.qendrahp.com
www.theatreespresso.org
www.tipoftheiceberg.biz
www.creativeartsteam.org/programs
www.drawntostars.co.uk

INDEX